Indonesian
Notebook

Brian Russell Roberts and Keith Foulcher, editors

Duke University Press   Durham and London   2016

Indonesian Notebook

A Sourcebook on Richard Wright and the Bandung Conference

Designed by Courtney Leigh Baker
Typeset in Whitman Roman by Westchester Publishing Services

Library of Congress Cataloging-in-Publication Data
Indonesian notebook : a sourcebook on Richard Wright and the Bandung Conference /
Brian Russell Roberts and Keith Foulcher, editors.
pages cm
Includes bibliographical references and index.
ISBN 978-0-8223-6051-3 (hardcover : alk. paper)
ISBN 978-0-8223-6066-7 (pbk. : alk. paper)
ISBN 978-0-8223-7464-0 (e-book)
1. Afro-Asian politics—Congresses. 2. Asian-African Conference (1st : 1955 : Bandung,
Indonesia)—Influence. 3. Wright, Richard, 1908–1960—Travel—Indonesia. 4. Wright,
Richard, 1908–1960—Political and social views. I. Roberts, Brian Russell, editor.
II. Foulcher, Keith, editor.
DS33.3.I57 2016
341.24'7—dc23   2015031597

RICHARD WRIGHT. "Seniman dan Masaalahnja." 1955. Supplemented with Wright's lecture notes.
Translated and published as "The Artist and His Problems." Copyright © 2015 by the Estate of
Richard Wright. Reprinted by permission of John Hawkins & Associates, Inc., and the Estate of
Richard Wright. FIGURE 1.1. Set in the mountains between Jakarta and Bandung. Copyright ©
2015 by the Estate of Richard Wright. Reprinted by permission of John Hawkins & Associates, Inc.,
and the Estate of Richard Wright. FIGURE 1.2. Set in the mountains between Jakarta and Bandung.
Copyright © 2015 by the Estate of Richard Wright. Reprinted by permission of John Hawkins &
Associates, Inc., and the Estate of Richard Wright. FIGURE 9.3. Set on the back patio of Takdir's
villa. Copyright © 2015 by the Estate of Richard Wright. Reprinted by permission of John Hawkins
& Associates, Inc., and the Estate of Richard Wright. FIGURE 9.4. Wright's photograph, set on the
patio. Copyright © 2015 by the Estate of Richard Wright. Reprinted by permission of John Hawkins
& Associates, Inc., and the Estate of Richard Wright.

COVER ART: *Photograph detail, reversed.* Wright on the patio of Takdir's villa with members of
the Konfrontasi Study Club. Seated are (*right to left*): Richard Wright and Fedja and Siti Nuraini.
Photographer unknown. Courtesy of the Beinecke Rare Book and Manuscript Library, Yale
University.

For Siti Nuraini Jatim, who brought the story to life

CONTENTS

ACKNOWLEDGMENTS

This book had its beginnings as we both, independently and from two different fields, began finding Indonesian-language sources on Richard Wright's Indonesian travels. As Brian (American literature and American studies, in the United States) was tracking down Indonesian-language sources on Wright for the final chapter of his book *Artistic Ambassadors: Literary and International Representation of the New Negro Era*, Keith (Indonesian studies, in Australia) was preparing a chapter for the collection *Heirs to World Culture: Being Indonesian, 1950–1965*, researching the literary culture surrounding the 1950s Konfrontasi Study Club, one of the organizations that hosted Wright during his Indonesian travels during April and May 1955. We met by e-mail, when Brian wrote to Keith asking for research leads on Pramoedya Ananta Toer's admiration for Wright. Sharing research sources led to commenting on each other's work and eventually collaborating to edit and introduce an English translation of Beb Vuyk's Dutch-language essay "Weekeinde met Richard Wright" for PMLA in 2011. Within a few months of this publication, we began working to imagine the shape of a volume that would reproduce, in translated form, many more of the Indonesian- and Dutch-language sources we had been gathering during our research. We are grateful to our editor at Duke University Press Courtney Berger, who has been encouraging throughout what has been a long and exciting process. We have benefited from the feedback—enthusiastic and constructive—offered by our manuscript's two anonymous readers.

Several institutions offered opportunities for us formulate and refine our understanding of the story and its significance. Together or individually, we gave presentations on Wright's Indonesian archive in Australia, the United

States, and the Netherlands: for the centenary Wright symposium hosted by the University of Virginia's Carter G. Woodson Institute for African-American and African Studies, for the University of Utah's centenary Wright symposium, for Soyica Diggs Colbert's seminar at the Futures of American Studies Institute at Dartmouth College, for the Cultural Traffic: Indonesia and the World 1950–1965 workshop at KITLV in the Netherlands, for Yale University's Southeast Asia Studies Seminar Program, for the University of Sydney's Indonesian Studies Seminar Series, for Monash University's Centre of Southeast Asian Studies Seminar Series, and for the sixtieth anniversary seminar The Bandung Asia-Africa Conference and Its Afterlives, held at the University of Sydney. This book is richer for dialogue with generous colleagues that arose from these presentations, and we are particularly grateful to Deborah McDowell, Jennifer Lindsay, Maya Liem, Sarah Weiss, Vannessa Hearman, and Julian Millie for invitations to speak at some of these venues.

Three years of language-study funding, generously granted by John Rosenberg, BYU's former dean of the College of the Humanities, permitted Brian to learn enough Indonesian to join Keith, this book's lead translator, in the process of translation. Additional funding from BYU's College of Humanities, as well as from the David M. Kennedy Center for International Studies, permitted Brian to research in Jakarta and Bandung for the duration of May 2013. During this trip, John McGlynn of the Lontar Foundation in Jakarta was unstinting in his generosity, providing and arranging lodging, helping to coordinate and publicize talks, and helping to set up individual meetings with Wright's Indonesian interlocutors and their families and descendants. Before Brian arrived in Jakarta, Siti Nuraini, who met Wright in Indonesia in 1955 and whose photograph was taken by Wright and included in the British edition of *The Color Curtain*, kindly made time to meet and talk with Keith over lunch in Melbourne. Following her suggestion that she could also meet with Brian in Jakarta, her daughter Anya Robertson was gracious in opening her home for Brian's conversation with Nuraini as well as with the Indonesian poet and intellectual Toeti Heraty. This conversation was incredibly illuminating, and Anya was a keen, insightful participant in the discussion. John McGlynn opened his home for Brian's conversation with Barbara Brouwer, wife of the now-late Sitor Situmorang, and Gulon Situmorang, Sitor's son. John also opened his home for Brian's discussion with two of Sutan Takdir Alisjahbana's daughters, Mirta Kartohadiprodjo and Tamalia Alisjahbana, whose commentary and narratives regarding Wright's Indonesian photographs were immensely enlightening. And Tamalia's generosity knew no bounds as she took Brian and Norma Roberts to the Alisjahbana villa in the Puncak, where Wright gave his lecture for the Konfrontasi Study Club. Tamalia led a tour of the home and grounds, including Takdir's library, and went out of her way to arrange a meal that approximated the meal Wright would have eaten during the weekend outlined in Beb Vuyk's "A Weekend with Richard Wright." Ratmini Soedjatmoko, wife of the late Soedjatmoko, and Nana (Kamala Chandrakirana Soedjatmoko), his daughter, were generous in inviting Brian to look through their family's collection of Siasat. Ajip Rosidi was extremely gracious, cutting into his visit to the capital city for Akademi Jakarta to spend an hour and a half discussing Wright's visit and the literary milieu of 1950s Jakarta. Also in Jakarta, the project benefited from dialogue following Brian's lecture at @America, among English undergraduates from the University of Indonesia, Binus University, and others. It was an honor to have Siti Nuraini in attendance as well as several family members of Wright's Indonesian interlocutors. Before, during, and after this lecture, Brian particularly benefited from comments and conversations with Melani Budianta, Myra Brown, Upik (S. R. Parvati Sjahrir), and Nana. A few days later, the project benefited from a discussion of "A Weekend with Richard Wright," kindly arranged by Melani Budianta, with faculty and graduate students at the University of Indonesia. In Bandung, Atep Kurnia was generous in providing a copy of his undergraduate thesis on Wright as well as a copy of a brief article he had recently published on Wright. Also in Bandung, Frances Affandi graciously met Brian at the Museum Konferensi Asia-Afrika to discuss Bandung hotels and architecture. In 2015, as we were finalizing the manuscript, Wikan Satriati of Lontar went out of her way in sending last-minute materials from Jakarta to Surakarta.

While Brian was in Jakarta and Bandung, we also benefited from the generosity of many archivists and librarians at the Perpustakaan Nasional and Arsip Nasional, as well as from Ariany Isnamurti of the Pusat Dokumentasi Sastra H. B. Jassin and Desmond Satria of the Museum Konferensi Asia-Afrika. In addition to helping to locate sources, Ariany and Desmond also helped in other ways, with Ariany arranging a space at the H. B. Jassin Center for Brian to speak with Ajip Rosidi, and Desmond arranging a special tour of Gedung Dwi Warna, a building Wright would have spent much time in as a member of the press.

From our home bases in Provo and Sydney, we have benefited from the interlibrary loan services of our respective libraries, as well as from funding— provided by BYU's English Department and College of Humanities—to draw on archival materials held at Columbia University's Rare Book and Manuscript Library; University of Chicago Special Collections; Emory University's Manuscript, Archives, and Rare Book Library; the University of Texas at Austin's Harry Ransom Center; Yale University's Beinecke Rare Book and Manuscript Library; the New York Public Library; and the Presbyterian Historical Society's

National Archives of the PC(USA). We are indebted to archivists at each of these repositories for close attention to our research interests, whether given on-site or remotely.

This project would not have been possible without the willingness of writers, photographers, their families, and their representatives to help arrange and grant permissions. We are grateful to: Astuti Ananta Toer and the extended family of Pramoedya Ananta Toer, Joke de Willigen-Riekerk, Fernand Willigen, John Hawkins & Associates, Inc. and the Estate of Richard Wright, Iwan Lubis, Mira Syam, Anya Robertson, the Yayasan Asrul Sani, Goenawan Mohamad, Seno Joko Suyono, John McGlynn, Daniela Holt Voith, Siti Nuraini, and Usman Iskandar.

Along the way, we have benefited immensely from generous feedback, commentary, e-mail responses, and on-the-ground archival work by numerous colleagues and other interested parties. Foremost among those to whom we are indebted is Paul Tickell, who devoted some of his own research time at the Perpustakaan Nasional to locating a number of important sources for us in the newspaper *Indonesia Raya*, including the Indonesian text of Wright's lecture "The Artist and His Problems." Toru Kiuchi helped us locate Wright's English-language notes for this lecture. Numerous other friends and colleagues helped us follow up leads, establish contacts, and track down information of various kinds, all the while offering valuable moral support: Tony Day, Liesbeth Dolk, Barbara Hatley, David Hill, Margaret Kartomi, Maya Liem, Anton Lucas, Julian Millie, Jean Taylor, Tiffany Tsao, and Adrian Vickers all generously contributed in various ways. After helping us track down sources and procure permissions, Jenny Lindsay read and gave important feedback on the entire manuscript. Els Bogaerts and Nicolaas Unlandt provided useful commentary on Dutch translations. Bryce Alcock and Wenny Achdiat helped identify figures in Wright's Indonesian photographs. Jan S. Aritonang and staff of the Jakarta Theological College (STT) kindly replied to our e-mail enquiries concerning Wright's possible links with the College. A sincere thank-you to Koesalah Soebagyo Toer for help sorting out some of Pramoedya Ananta Toer's publication history. Brent Edwards and Harry Stecopoulos each shared early and formative conversations on Bandung with Brian and later offered important suggestions on locating archival sources. At different stages, Soyica Diggs Colbert and Paul Giles offered useful commentary on framing Wright's Indonesian archive. Jerry Ward has been generous in his interest and willingness to offer perspective along the way. Lorenz Lüthi and R. John Williams shared unpublished or in-progress writings, and Williams pointed us toward an alternative version of Wright's narrative of the "Sterno incident." At different points, Bob Vitalis, Amritjit Singh, and Nina Berman have offered enlightening commentary on "A Weekend with Richard Wright" that has contributed to our vision for the project. Chris Lee, Emron Esplin, and Jamin Rowan read and offered suggestions on this book's introduction, while Emron and Marlene Hansen Esplin both offered insight on approaches to translation. Aaron Eastley and Peter Leman furthered our thinking on the project via several conversations during the past five years. Early on, Kristin Matthews arranged for a useful Americanist Circle discussion of "A Weekend with Richard Wright," and Phil Snyder, chair of BYU's English Department, has been generous and enthusiastic in his response to Brian's decision to pursue Wright's Bandung legacy via research into Indonesian literature and culture.

From Brian: A big thank-you to my parents and siblings—Roland, Cathy, David, Emily, Whitney, and Michael—for sharing insights, shaping experiences, and showing patience throughout our two and a half years in Jakarta during the early 1990s. Also an enormous debt of gratitude goes to Norma, William, and Sierra—for bringing joy and meaning to life, and for enthusiastically relocating with me to Indonesia for a Fulbright fellowship at Universitas Sebelas Maret during 2015. For this book, my greatest thanks goes to Keith for agreeing to collaborate on the project (even though you "retired" in 2006!), bringing a career's worth of deep knowledge and wisdom to every stage of *Indonesian Notebook*.

From Keith: I want to thank my partner, Craig, for making no less than everything possible, and Tim, Gabby, April, and Scarlett for the great privilege and happiness of family life. I am also deeply grateful to colleagues in the Department of Indonesian Studies at the University of Sydney, especially Michele, Novi, and Vannessa, for giving me a post-retirement academic home, and particularly for participation in the department's Indonesian Studies Working Papers series, which led to my contact with Brian and a much richer and more rewarding retirement than I could ever have hoped for.

ABBREVIATIONS FOR ARCHIVAL SOURCES

CHC
Claire Holt Collection of Indonesian Dance and Related Arts, New York
Public Library for the Performing Arts / Jerome Robbins Dance Division

CSCA
Christian Literature on Southeast Asia in Yale Libraries, Yale University,
New Haven, CT

CWP
Constance Webb Papers, 1918–2005, Columbia University,
Rare Book and Manuscript Library, New York

IACFR
International Association for Cultural Freedom Records, University of
Chicago Special Collections, Chicago

MFP
Michel Fabre Papers, MSS 932, Manuscript, Archives, and
Rare Book Library, Emory University, Atlanta

MJP
Michael Josselson Papers, Harry Ransom Center,
University of Texas at Austin

PATC

Pramoedya Ananta Toer Collection, Pusat Dokumentasi Sastra
H. B. Jassin (H. B. Jassin Center for Literary Documentation),
Taman Ismail Marzuki, Jakarta

PCIC

PEN Club Indonesia Collection, Pusat Dokumentasi Sastra H. B. Jassin (H. B.
Jassin Center for Literary Documentation), Taman Ismail Marzuki, Jakarta

RWP

Richard Wright Papers, JWJ MSS 3, Beinecke Rare Book and Manuscript
Library, Yale University, New Haven, CT

SNC

Siti Nuraini Collection, Pusat Dokumentasi Sastra H. B. Jassin (H. B. Jassin
Center for Literary Documentation), Taman Ismail Marzuki, Jakarta

UPC

United Presbyterian Church in the USA Commission on Ecumenical
Mission and Relations; Secretaries' files: Mission to Indonesia, 1950–1970
(RG 135); Presbyterian Historical Society, National Archives of the PC(USA);
Philadelphia

BIBLIOGRAPHY OF PRIMARY SOURCES
TRANSLATED OR REPUBLISHED IN THIS BOOK

Part I

Embassy of Indonesia. Excerpts from *The Cultural Life of Indonesia: Religion, the Arts, Education*. Washington, DC: H. K. Press, 1951. 47–55.

Pramoedya Ananta Toer. "Definisi dan Keindahan dalam Kesusastraan" (The Definition of Literature and the Question of Beauty). [*Indonesia* Aug. 1952: 14–17.] *Menggelinding I*. Ed. Astuti Ananta Toer. Jakarta: Lentera Dipantara, 2004. 173–79.

S. M. Ardan. "Pramoedya Keluar Negeri" (Pramoedya Heads Overseas). *Dwiwarna* 6 June 1953: n.p. PATC.

"Nieuwe Uitgaven" (New Publications). *De Preangerbode: Algemeen Indisch Dagblad* 28 Sept. 1954: 3.

Beb Vuyk. "Stories in the Modern Manner." *Indonesia Raya* 9 Feb. 1955: 3.

Part II

Articles in "A Sheaf of Newspaper Articles: Richard Wright in Indonesia's Daily Press":

"Siapa Mengapa" (Who's Doing What). *Indonesia Raya* 13 Apr. 1955: 2.

"Tadjuk Rentjana: Satu Usul Perbaikan" (Editorial: A Suggestion for Improvement). *Indonesia Raya* 13 Apr. 1955: 3.

"Richard Wright is Hier" (Richard Wright is Here). *De Nieuwsgier* 13 Apr. 1955: 3.

Front page photo of Richard Wright. "Telah Tiba di Djakarta" (Now Arrived in Jakarta). *Indonesia Raya* 14 Apr. 1955: 1.

"Richard Wright & Bau Kakus Dikamar" (Richard Wright and the Smell of Toilets in the Room). *Pedoman* 14 Apr. 1955: 1.

"Dipinggir Djalan" (Curbside). *Indonesia Raya* 14 Apr. 1955: 3.

"'Jajasan Impresariat Indonesia' Bestaat een Jaar" (First Anniversary of the 'Indonesian Impresario Foundation'). *Java Bode* 15 Apr. 1955: 2.

"Kunstenaarsavond" (Artists' Evening). *De Nieuwsgier* 15 Apr. 1955: 2.

"Rondom de AA-Conferentie" (Around and About the AA-Conference). *Het Nieuwsblad voor Sumatra* 19 Apr. 1955: 2.

"Kota Bandung Selama Konp. A-A" (Bandung during the A-A Conference). *Indonesia Raya* 21 Apr. 1955: 1.

"Cultureel Nieuws" (Cultural News). *Het Nieuwsblad voor Sumatra* 22 Apr. 1955: 3.

"Impressies uit Bandung" (Impressions from Bandung). *Het Nieuwsblad voor Sumatra* 22 Apr. 1955: 1.

"Famous US Negro Author Disappointed." *Indonesian Observer* 23 Apr. 1955: 2.

"Siapa Mengapa" (Who's Doing What). *Indonesia Raya* 4 May 1955: 2.

Photo of Richard Wright. "Pengarang Negro" (Negro Writer). *Indonesia Raya* 21 May 1955: 5.

Other sources

[Mochtar Lubis]. [A List of Indonesian Writers and Artists]. RWP, box 31, folder 433.

Sudjatmoko and Asrul Sani, eds. "Pertjakapan dengan Richard Wright" (A Conversation with Richard Wright). *Siasat: Warta Sepekan* 15 May 1955: 22–23.

"Synopsis." *Konfrontasi* May–June 1955: 25–28.

Richard Wright. "Seniman dan Masaalahnja" (The Artist and His Problems). *Indonesia Raya* 21 May 1955: 5. Supplemented by untitled lecture notes, RWP, box 79, folder 892.

A[nas] M[a'ruf]. "Richard Wright di Indonesia" (Richard Wright in Indonesia). *Seni: Bulanan Kesenian* July 1955: 333.

Part III

Beb Vuyk. "Black Power." *Indonesia Raya* 1 June 1955: 3.

Beb Vuyk. "H. Creekmore Dg. Roman² Bantahan" (H. Creekmore and Protest Novels). *Indonesia Raya* 23 Nov. 1955: 3.

Asrul Sani. "Richard Wright: Seniman jang Djadi Intelektuil" (Richard Wright: The Artist Turned Intellectual). *Siasat* 25 Apr. 1956: 24–25.

Frits Kandou. "Kesan-kesan Richard Wright tentang Indonesia" (Richard
Wright's Impressions of Indonesia). *Sebaran B.M.K.N.: Diedarkan oleh
Badan Musjawarat Kebudajaan Nasional* 8 [c. 15 May 1956] and 9 [c.
31 May 1956]: 1–4 and 1–4.

Beb Vuyk. "Weekeinde met Richard Wright" (A Weekend with Richard
Wright). *Vrij Nederland* 19 Nov. 1960: 19; 26 Nov. 1960: 8.

Goenawan Mohamad. ["Politikus"] (Politicians). *Tempo* 24 Sept. 1977: 4.

Seno Joko Suyono. "Sebuah Hotel yang Dilupakan" (A Forgotten Hotel).
Tempo 1 May 2005: 88–90.

ON THE TRANSLATIONS

In translating documents from Indonesian and Dutch for inclusion in this collection, we have adopted the long-established practice in the English-speaking world of aiming for fluency and readability in the translated English text. Generally speaking, our sources are documentary in nature rather than literary, and for that reason we have considered it important to attempt to convey their literal meanings as historical documents in standard English prose, Americanized in spelling and style but nonetheless bearing the impress of American, Australian, and international English usages. In routing the translations through these traditions, we have endeavored to make the translations as accessible and enjoyable for an English reader as we believe the source texts are for readers of Indonesian and Dutch. In rare cases where strict adherence to the literal meaning of part of a text would have resulted in unavoidable awkwardness or obscurity in English, we have chosen to translate more freely, but in all these cases we have taken care to ensure that the intent of the source text—as we understand it—has been preserved in the English translation we have provided.

For consistency and ease of reading, we have adopted a number of stylistic conventions in our presentation of the English versions. Titles cited by the authors of the source texts are indicated with quotation marks in the case of shorter works and italics in the case of longer works. In approaching the source texts, we have sometimes encountered phrases that are not set off by quotation marks but that in our judgment are offered as quoted material. In those cases, for consistency of style and clarity, we have tended to add quotation marks, indicating the addition in a note. Also using notes, we have indicated the use of English in the source texts where it may be considered significant. Where typographical errors or misspellings occur in the source texts, these are corrected in the translations, particularly when they relate to names and book titles. When this action results in a significant departure from the source text, we advise the reader in a note.

In contrast to English and other European languages, expression in Indonesian is almost always gender-neutral. As a result, and also in accordance with our own preference, we have attempted to avoid gender-biased English wherever possible in the translations. In a minority of cases, where keeping gender bias out of the English translation results in clumsy or non-idiomatic expression, and where the use of a gendered pronoun is in keeping with the English of the period of the source text, we have allowed instances of gender-biased language to stand.

Beyond this prefatory outline of our general translation practices, we give further consideration to some of the theoretical questions posed by our approach to translation in the afterword.

ON SPELLING AND PERSONAL NAMES

For centuries, the languages of the Malay Peninsula and island Southeast Asia were written in Arabic- and Indian-derived scripts. However, with the advent of British and Dutch colonialism in the region, these languages also came to be written in Roman script. In the case of Malay, which was a major indigenous language of the British and Dutch colonial domains, two different spelling systems evolved. From British colonizers, the region now known as the modern state of Malaysia adopted English-based spelling conventions. Meanwhile, the region now known as the modern state of Indonesia adopted Dutch-based spelling conventions. This remained the case until 1972, when a common spelling system combining aspects of both former orthographies was adopted by Indonesia and Malaysia for their respective national languages.

Most of the Indonesian-language documents included in this collection date from the 1950s and hence follow Dutch orthography, primarily recognizable in the consonants *j*, *dj*, and *tj*, which approximate the English sounds represented by *y*, hard *j*, and *ch*, respectively. The colonial-era Dutch *oe* had by this time generally been replaced by the Indonesian *u*, though *oe* remained in common usage in the names of individuals.

In this book, names (of institutions, publications, and people) and occasional Indonesian-language quotations are generally reproduced in their original spelling. Hence, sources from before 1972 follow Dutch orthography, while post-1972 sources are closer to English, with the notable exception of *c* for the sound that approximates the English *ch*. For names of organizations, we have adopted the spelling in use during the period under discussion. Similarly, titles of publications are given in the spelling in use at the time of publication, except when we are using a later edition to discuss aspects of a particular text. When this is the case, the spelling of the title follows that of the later edition. Place-names are in post-1972 spelling, unless they occur in quotations.

The spelling of Indonesian personal names follows the spelling preferred by the individuals concerned, or the spelling generally found during the period under discussion. In some cases, variations found in the spelling of an individual's name result in different spellings in different sources, most notably in the name of Indonesia's first president, generally known as "Soekarno" but sometimes also as "Sukarno." In these cases, we use the preferred, or usual, spelling of the name in reference to the person, with an occasional variation when the person's name is spelled differently as the author of a particular publication.

Until very recently, when international usage became more influential, Indonesian personal names have not included a family name. In most cases, Indonesians are known formally by the first component of their name, which depending on context may be preceded by an honorific or kinship term. In this book we have adopted Indonesian naming practice, which means that individuals are normally referred to by the first component of their name (e.g., "Pramoedya," not "Toer," in the case of "Pramoedya Ananta Toer"). In the list of works cited and the index, names of authors are listed according to the form in which they are cited in the text, with international practice also acknowledged in the form of cross-references (e.g., "Toer, Pramoedya Ananta. See Pramoedya Ananta Toer"). We have only varied this practice in the case of names that include a European personal name as the first component (e.g. "Martin Aleida") or where the first component of the name is an inherited or honorary title (e.g. "Sutan Takdir Alisjahbana"). In the latter case, the title is normally elided in the text, but cross-references are provided in the list of works cited and the index.

INTRODUCTION. Richard Wright on the Bandung Conference,
Modern Indonesia on Richard Wright

In December 1954, while living as an expatriate in France, the famous American
novelist Richard Wright picked up an evening newspaper and gazed in awe
when he read that in April 1955 the government of Indonesia would host a
meeting of twenty-nine "free and independent" Asian and African countries
(Wright, *Color* 437). Gathering in the Indonesian city Bandung, as Wright
learned from the newspaper, representatives from these countries were to
discuss "the position of Asia and Africa and their people in the world of today
and the contribution they can make to the promotion of world peace and cooperation." The representatives planned "to consider problems of special interest to Asian and African peoples, for example, problems affecting national
sovereignty and of racialism and colonialism" (*Color* 439).

Although Wright had published the popularly and critically successful
novel *Native Son* in 1940, and although his 1945 autobiography *Black Boy* had
been a number one best seller for three months, he had left the United States
in 1946 to escape continuing and virulent race prejudice.[1] Now, in Paris, after
reading about the conference to be held in Bandung, Wright told his wife,
Ellen Poplar, that his life had "given [him] some keys" for understanding this
gathering of Asian and African representatives (*Color* 440). He explained,

I'm an American Negro; as such, I've had a burden of race consciousness. So have these people. I worked in my youth as a common laborer,
and I've a class consciousness. So have these people. I grew up in the

Methodist and Seventh Day Adventist churches . . . ; and these people are religious. I was a member of the Communist Party for twelve years and I know something of the politics and psychology of rebellion. These people have had as their daily existence such politics. These emotions are my instruments. They are emotions, but I'm conscious of them as emotions. I want to use these emotions to try to find out what these people think and feel and why.

As Wright recalled, Ellen replied, "If you feel that way, you have to go" (*Color* 440–41).

With these emotional keys in hand, Wright arranged to travel to Southeast Asia, where he visited Indonesia for over three weeks (12 April through 5 May 1955) and reported as a member of the press on the Bandung Conference, which convened from 18 through 24 April. Based on his three-week sojourn in Indonesia, Wright published his Indonesian and Asian-African travelogue, *The Color Curtain: A Report on the Bandung Conference*, in 1956. This travelogue ranks among the first substantial accounts of the Asian-African Conference.[2] And it has emerged as a touchstone in the conference's scholarly treatments, which have frequently looked toward the Bandung Conference's world-historical significance and traced the "Bandung Spirit" as evolving into the Nonaligned Movement (founded in 1961) and more generally inhabiting "the political formation of postcoloniality" (Young 11).[3] Indeed, recent scholarly work has observed that "Bandung produced something: a belief that two-thirds of the world's people had the right to return to their own burned cities, cherish them, and rebuild them in their own image" (Prashad, *Darker* 32–33). Moreover, the conference has come to crystallize the "idea of the Third World . . . as a unity of Asian, African, and Latin American peoples on the basis of a common experience of colonialism and racism" (Espiritu 175). As Dilip M. Menon observes, Bandung has attained present-day status as the "condensation of many aspirations: Afro-Asian solidarity, the idea of decoloniality, and the possibility of new alignments in the world following the collapse of the Soviet Union and the emergence of . . . a unipolar world" (Menon 241).

Mythologies of Bandung and *The Color Curtain*

In attaining this explanatory power in relation to postcoloniality's late twentieth- and early twenty-first-century cultural conditions, the Bandung Conference that Wright reported on has concomitantly taken on a mythic dimension, in the sense of myth outlined by Wright's Parisian contemporary, Roland Barthes. Appearing a year after Wright's *The Color Curtain* and finding frequent recuperation in the context of postcolonial studies,[4] Barthes's 1957 book *Mythologies* offers a classic discussion that frames myth as the project of "giving an historical intention a natural justification, . . . making contingency appear eternal" (142). In *Mythologies'* famous example, Barthes illustrates this process through the case of "a young Negro in a French [military] uniform" (115) who had appeared on the cover of a prominent French weekly magazine of the day. As Barthes observes, this image required putting "the biography of [this individual] Negro in parentheses" (116) in order to "naturalize" the logic and coherence of the French Empire (131). If on the one hand the "young Negro" appearing on the magazine cover functioned to naturalize European empire, then the Bandung Conference (on the other hand) has worked at cross-purposes with the French "Negro," emerging in some scholarly and popular narratives as an equally mythic image but standing resolutely against European and American empire, as a naturalization of postcolonial ideals and conditions during the late twentieth and early twenty-first centuries.

The Bandung Conference's mythic quality found commentary just eleven years after it convened in 1955. A decade after Wright published *The Color Curtain*, the India-based British journalist G. H. Jansen wrote in his book *Nonalignment and the Afro-Asian States* that "two conferences were held at Bandung in April 1955. One was the real conference, about which not very much is known. . . . The other was a quite different conference, a crystallisation of what people wanted to believe had happened which, as a myth, took on reality in . . . the Bandung Spirit" (182). Nearly a half century after Jansen's observations on the two conferences, scholars have increasingly observed—and sought correctives for the fact—that while we know very little about the Bandung Conference, the Bandung myth has continued to grow. Historian Lorenz Lüthi has framed the conference as a mythic stand-in for a much more complex—and as yet undocumented—history of the development of Asian-African solidarity and "cooperation among countries from the Global South" (1), and political scientist Robert Vitalis has critiqued a sometimes superficial narrative of Bandung as the "birthplace of not one but two global 'solidarities'"—"non-alignment" and "global racial consciousness" (261). Vitalis calls on scholars to undertake "the work that is required to learn what we don't know about" the relevant historical circumstances (271), arguing that scholars should take as their "primary analytical terrain" the conference's "competing national state-building projects and regional state-systemic logics" (271). Historiographically allied with Vitalis and Lüthi, historian Christopher J. Lee's introduction to the 2010 *Making a World after Empire: The Bandung Moment and Its Political Afterlives* seeks to move beyond Bandung's airy importance to "theory-driven conventions of postcolonial studies" and rather to promote scholarship that, "armed with evidence, begin[s] to think more concretely and extensively about how to sharpen our reconception of postcolonial history" (32). In the epilogue to *Making a World after Empire*, Antoinette Burton praises Lee's collection for going a long way toward rejecting "the romance of racialism that haunts many accounts of Bandung . . . in favor of going to [the] ground, through a purposeful return to the complex and uneven geographies of the postcolonial cold war world" ("Sodalities" 352–53). With its aspirations toward "refus[ing] all of Bandung's pieties and romances" (358), *Making a World after Empire* pushes Bandung scholarship away from theoretical treatments of a mythic Bandung and toward a heightened valorization of engagement with historical archives.[5] Such a tack will indeed be crucial for scholars of postcolonialism, the Third World, and nonalignment, given the way intellectuals in many arenas have frequently taken the Bandung Conference's mythic meaning as more important than its archivally verifiable history, as has been vividly illustrated by a recent survey of the persistent repetition of the false commonplace that Gold Coast prime minister Kwame Nkrumah was among the important world leaders who attended the conference.[6]

Unlike Kwame Nkrumah's counterfactual appearance at the Bandung Conference, Richard Wright's conference attendance has been extensively documented in a primary historical text, namely, *The Color Curtain*. And yet Wright's attendance, like the Bandung Conference itself, has been mythic to varying degrees. Of course, as readers will well understand, we are not asserting a facile dichotomy between myth and history in which that which functions as myth is necessarily ahistorical while engagement with historical archives brooks no mythologizing component. Rather, we are asserting that Wright's conference attendance and his narrative in *The Color Curtain* have been taken up by numerous scholars as an ur-narrative in an array of cultural and disciplinary arenas. Along these lines, several transnationally oriented scholars of American and African American literary and cultural studies have framed *The Color Curtain* as evincing a commonality—or in some cases simply a desire to see commonality—between African American experiences with racism and decolonizing nations' experiences with colonialism and empire.[7] Similar to transnational American and African American studies, the field of postcolonial studies has also been invested in *The Color Curtain*. Bret Benjamin, for instance, points toward Wright's book as illustrating, "often more clearly than do the conference documents themselves," the Bandung participants' "bond forged from a common history of colonial exploitation, their shared status as *noncolonies*" (Benjamin 125). And even as he historicizes *The Color Curtain* by placing it in dialogue with the Bandung Conference memoir of Roeslan Abdulgani (the Indonesian secretary general of the conference), Dipesh Chakrabarty has framed some of Wright's positions in *The Color Curtain* as anticipatory of the "globalization as liberation" discourse in a world after empire ("Legacies" 61) and as a key element in considering "the question of the role that the humanities should play in a globalizing world" (64).[8] Meanwhile, the third edition of Bill Ashcroft, Gareth Griffiths, and Helen Tiffin's *Postcolonial Studies: The Key Concepts* (2013) has added an article on the Bandung Conference and has framed Wright's *Color Curtain* commentary on the new Asian and African governments as prescient of "the themes for much postcolonial writing in the years to come" (24). Yet even as postcolonial studies has sometimes taken *The Color Curtain* as prophetic of its major concerns, and even as transnational American and African American literary and cultural studies have taken Wright's Indonesian travel as an important moment of transnational exchange regarding racial questions, no area of study has asserted larger implications for Wright's Indonesian travels than has the emerging field of Afro-Asian studies. Consider the foreword to this field's landmark 2006 collection, *AfroAsian Encounters*, which has Vijay Prashad offering an opening paragraph asserting: "The book that Wright produced from his [Indonesian travels], *The Color Curtain*, inaugurates our tradition of AfroAsian studies" ("Foreword" xi).[9] Here *The Color Curtain* attains genesis status and hence mythic status in the most conventional sense of the term.

In advancing this book, we share the widely held view that Wright's Indonesian travels and his travelogue *The Color Curtain* ought to maintain a significant position in historical narratives and present understandings of transnationalism, postcolonialism, and Asian-African relations. However, like the historians and political scientists who are wary of the ways a mythic Bandung Conference has supplanted an archivally verifiable Bandung Conference, we are wary of the ways *The Color Curtain*, as the purveyor of a certain narrative of Wright's Indonesian sojourn, has come to supplant the largely unknown historical archive that surrounds Wright's travels. Indeed, we are concerned that *The Color Curtain*, as a single primary historical text, has sometimes come to function as a stand-in for broader primary historical research on Wright's attendance at the Bandung Conference and that, in the process, this travelogue has tended to be taken as documentary evidence for historical claims that it cannot verify. As a case in point, consider Robert J. C. Young's assertion that Wright's conference attendance and "presence helped to consolidate identifications between African-Americans and Third World nations" (11). In substantiating this assertion, Young in a note directs readers toward Wright's "analysis of the conference" in *The Color Curtain* (20, n2). With this note, then, Young assigns Wright's analysis in *The Color Curtain* the task of attesting to the ways Wright's attendance at the conference helped solidify global racial consciousness. Such a claim, if it were historically documented, would require evidence, including African American and third world testimonies about Wright's presence in Bandung as forging cross-cultural identifications. Instead, readers are directed to consider *The Color Curtain*. To be clear, we are not suggesting that Wright's presence at the conference did not play a certain role in the workings-out of a global racial consciousness. Rather, we are suggesting that such deployments of *The Color Curtain* are emblematic of a larger scholarly trend that sometimes takes *The Color Curtain* as a mythic stand-in for relevant or substantial historical evidence regarding the place of Wright's travels in transnational, postcolonial, and Afro-Asian histories and presents.

No doubt Harilaos Stecopoulos's comments on Wright's interactions with one of his Indonesian hosts, together with Bill V. Mullen's illuminating explorations of Wright's positions in relation to Bandung Conference delegates, have evinced important historicizing impulses vis-à-vis *The Color Curtain*.[10] And yet we would argue that the place of *The Color Curtain* in Bandung scholarship has remained, by and large, similar to what Chakrabarty has described as the place of European philosophy and terminology in the "postcolonial Calcutta" of his youth and student years (*Provincializing* ix). In this environment, according to Chakrabarty, European philosophies had a life that operated according to "Roland Barthes' idea that a myth works by making the historical seem 'natural'" (ix), attaining status as "a piece of truth" rather than as "something that was originally invented in the workshop of the Scottish Enlightenment" (xi). Like Chakrabarty in his work in demythologizing European thought's status as natural by rendering it parochial (and indeed provincialized) in its historical contingency and embeddedness (x), we are dedicated to a project of demythologizing *The Color Curtain* and Wright's Bandung Conference attendance, dislodging them from the realm of what Chakrabarty terms the "simply 'true'" (xi) and moving them toward a new critical and historical embeddedness in what Burton refers to as the Bandung moment's "crosshatchings, outcroppings, and tendrils" ("Sodalities" 353).

At first glance, marshaling historical documentation regarding the significance and ramifications of Wright's Indonesian travels and conference attendance may seem simple enough. After all, Wright's life and writings have been some of the most thoroughly documented among twentieth-century US writers. He has been the subject of at least nine significant biographies.[11] And his writings—published, unpublished, and translated—have been extensively catalogued in Charles T. Davis and Michel Fabre's 232-page *Richard Wright: A Primary Bibliography* (1982). Adding to this already substantial biographical and bibliographical documentation, Keneth Kinnamon in 1988 published *A Richard Wright Bibliography: Fifty Years of Criticism and Commentary*. As described by Kinnamon in the preface, this nearly one-thousand-page volume "is a bibliography of 13,117 annotated items published from 1933 to 1982 pertaining to Richard Wright" and is "the most comprehensive such list ever compiled for any American writer" (ix). The bibliography had "the original goal . . . to include every mention of Wright in print," and although "some practical compromises had to be made," Kinnamon's compendium does indeed present itself as coming "close to being comprehensive" (x).[12] But for as exceptionally and impressively thorough as Wright's bibliographers have been in cataloguing writings by and on Wright in the United States, Europe, and other regions, they have not been able to direct readers to the many Wright-related documents that were generated in Indonesia before, during, and after his travels for the Bandung Conference.[13] In partial consequence of this absence in the documented archive, Wright's biographers have relied very little on Indonesian sources in narrating his three weeks in Indonesia, instead opting to rely extensively on *The Color Curtain* and other non-Indonesian sources.[14]

Understandably, linguistic, communication, and disciplinary barriers have stymied Wright's many biographers and bibliographers in their efforts to document his Indonesian travels. However, with the transnational turn in the humanities and social sciences, and aided by the communications technologies and cross-disciplinary trends that have facilitated this turn, opportunities now exist to overcome these barriers. Accordingly, we are offering this book as a preliminary window into the historical grounding of Wright's Indonesian travels, which lasted only three weeks according to the calendar but have endured for several decades as a powerful and mythic narrative in cultural and scholarly arenas. Historicizing and in many cases complicating narratives of Wright's Indonesian travels, this book showcases numerous primary historical documents, nearly all of them translated into English for the first time. These documents range from daily press accounts of Wright's activities in Indonesia to Indonesian reviews of Wright's books and to articles based on interviews and conversations Wright took part in while visiting Indonesia. Also included is documentation of previously unknown talks Wright gave during his travels. In showcasing these documents and many others, *Indonesian Notebook* emerges as a modest and geographically specific continuation of Kinnamon's, Davis's, and Fabre's decades-long efforts to thoroughly document writing by and on Richard Wright. This anthology, then, becomes a crucial resource and starting place for any Wright biographer or scholar who is interested in representing or analyzing Wright's Indonesian travels or his representations of the Bandung Conference. It is also an important aid to the study of Wright's years of exile more generally, facilitating critical engagement with his 1957 book of lectures, *White Man, Listen!*, as well as with his still unpublished novel of the late 1950s, "Island of Hallucination," which references Indonesia repeatedly (75, 224, 422). More generally, *Indonesian Notebook*'s significance extends far beyond the realm of author studies. Challenging the mythic status of both the Bandung Conference and Wright's Indonesian travel writings, this book sets out to historicize and consequently reframe a major moment that has been pivotal in the disciplinary narratives of transnational American and African American studies, postcolonial studies, and Afro-Asian studies. Complementing and adding ground-level texture to Bandung's state-level histories, such as that rendered by Prashad in his compelling book *The Darker Nations* (31–50), *Indonesian Notebook* corresponds to Burton's recent assertion that "the time has come for new histories of 'Afro-Asian solidarity'" (*Brown* 1). Indeed, this book's intense and overarching investments in conveying translations of on-the-spot Indonesian source texts position it as a preliminary yet crucial answer to Dilip M. Menon's 2014 insistence that historical approaches to the Bandung Conference must "engage with entangled local histories that may not be accessible through literature in English alone" (244).

Beyond *The Color Curtain*

Intriguingly, in spite of *The Color Curtain*'s importance within an array of scholarly fields, Wright's conference travel and travelogue have received very little attention in Indonesian studies and Southeast Asian studies. Speculating on a logic for this absence is revealing with regard to how scholars might responsibly reassess *The Color Curtain* in light of *Indonesian Notebook*'s new documentation of Wright's travels in Indonesia. One is tempted to attribute this lack of attention to a scholarly iteration of a sentiment expressed by one of Wright's Indonesian interlocutors, as relayed in *The Color Curtain*. This young and well-known poet explained, "The Dutch, the Americans, and the English do not know us. . . . And our experience in meeting these Europeans has always turned out badly. When they leave Indonesia, they write false things about us. We are exotic children to them. Why, one white woman journalist went away and wrote an article saying that we grew banana trees in our homes! Can you imagine that?" (583). Indeed, ever since the late colonial era, observations of Indonesia by travelers or resident foreigners have often been characterized by a level of exoticizing and Orientalizing that frequently obscures and distorts as much as it reveals and explains about the Indonesian peoples' cultural practices and everyday realities. Both short- and long-term visitors have imparted views of Indonesian cultures that focus on their refinement and otherworldliness, but at the same time their irrationality and, at times, propensity for violence.[15] Quite similar to non-Indonesian representations of Indonesia in creative literature and the visual arts, seemingly nonfictional travel writing of this type can be seen as a series of reconstructions that owe as much to the observers' own cultural and ideological perspectives as to the people, places, and circumstances that are the subjects of their observations.

Although some might expect this substantial body of travel writing by foreign visitors to Indonesia to become fodder for numerous analyses informed by a regionally tailored understanding of Orientalism, the observations of travelers and visitors to Indonesia have so far not attracted the sustained attention of Indonesian studies scholars.[16] The reasons for this lacuna in the Indonesian studies literature are not entirely clear, but it can be said that the appeal of an Orientalist framework of analysis, which might provide a key to unlocking the significance of this body of travel writing, has been much more limited in Indonesian studies than in other regionally based fields of inquiry, especially South Asian studies. Indeed, very few scholars have attempted to extend the reach of Said's conception of Orientalism as "mainly . . . a British or French cultural enterprise" (4) to a Southeast Asian context.[17] In the absence of this or similar analytical frameworks, it appears that travel writing has been largely disregarded by scholars of Indonesia, easily dismissed as popular literature with little to offer a specialist audience. As such, it seems likely that Wright's observations on Indonesia have been seen as unremarkable, being merely the jottings of a first-time visitor who spent just three weeks in socially restricted surroundings in and around Jakarta and Bandung. Considered in this light, there is perhaps no reason for *The Color Curtain* to have been assigned the level of importance in Indonesian and Southeast Asian studies that it has received in other fields of inquiry.

Beyond the realm of scholarly inquiry, Indonesians have found reasons to suspect that Wright's writings lie within the tradition of inaccuracy and misrepresentation that they see in the way foreign visitors have tended to represent Indonesia to the world. Consider the reaction Wright received after publishing his article "Indonesian Notebook" (which later became part of *The Color Curtain*) in the August 1955 issue of the UK-based magazine *Encounter*. Appearing shortly after Wright returned from Southeast Asia, the essay generated a brief dialogue between Wright and his former host, the Indonesian novelist, newspaper editor, and PEN Club member Mochtar Lubis. *Encounter*'s March 1956 issue published the following letter from Mochtar:

> With great interest I read Mr. Richard Wright's "Indonesian Notebook"
> in *Encounter* No. 23. Mr. Wright wrote with great feeling and passion,

but I am afraid while he was here in Indonesia he had been looking through "coloured-glasses," and he had sought behind every attitude he met colour and racial feelings. The majority of the people with whom Mr. Wright had come into contact in Indonesia (one of the best-known novelists, and others) belong to the new generation in Indonesia, and are the least racial and colour conscious of the various groups in Indonesia. They are all amazed to read Mr. Wright's notebook in which Mr. Wright quotes them saying things which they never had said, or to which they did not put meaning as accepted by Mr. Wright.

I do not want to imply that there is no colour feeling in Indonesia, but I want to protest Mr. Wright's allegation that "this racial business" has become a way of life in Asia. This is just not true. While Mr. Wright's notebook makes interesting reading, I am afraid he failed to present a true and balanced picture of the intellectual situation in Indonesia today.

Colour or racial problems are just not our problems. ("Through")

Alongside Mochtar's protestations, *Encounter* published Wright's reply, which denied Mochtar's suggestion that he had looked at Indonesia through "coloured-glasses" and asserted that for the three weeks Wright stayed in Jakarta and Bandung, "all the talk [he] heard was of race and religion," with the speeches at the Bandung Conference "loaded with race and religion." Wright continued:

I would commend to Mr. Lubis's attention the full and definitive account of my Bandung report which will be published in the United States in March of this year under the title: *The Color Curtain*. There I discuss in detail the *nature* of the racial feeling I found not only in Indonesia, but in the Asian personality as a whole.

Think hard, my friend Lubis, and you will recall the discussions that took place in your car as we drove through the Java mountains. ("Mr. Wright")[18]

Had Mochtar taken Wright's advice to read *The Color Curtain*, he would have been still more bewildered by Wright's account of his Indonesian sojourn. In writing to *Encounter*, Mochtar was irritated at Wright's apparent misattribution of quotations to one of Indonesia's "best-known novelists," but in *The Color Curtain* Mochtar would have found a scene regarding this novelist that might have added to his irritation with Wright's account. As Wright tells it in *The Color Curtain*, before he leaves Europe for Indonesia, he prepares a questionnaire that he uses as the basis for some interviews he conducts with

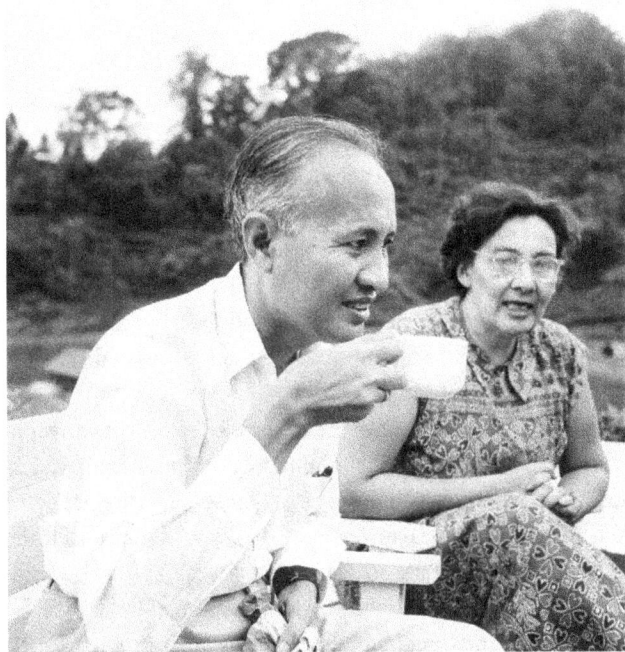

FIGURE I.1. Set in the mountains between Jakarta and Bandung, Wright's photograph portrays Sutan Takdir Alisjahbana (left) and Beb Vuyk (right). Reprinted by permission of John Hawkins & Associates, Inc., and the Estate of Richard Wright. Courtesy of the Beinecke Rare Book and Manuscript Library, Yale University.

Asian informants who are currently living in Europe. He undertakes these interviews to prepare himself for his upcoming travels.[19] Strikingly, one of these informants is described in so much detail that he can only be identified as the famous Indonesian linguist, novelist, and intellectual Sutan Takdir Alisjahbana (*Color* 465–72), and in fact the interview as narrated in *The Color Curtain* corresponds point-by-point to Wright's narrative of interviewing Takdir in his unpublished Indonesian travel journal ("Jakarta" 195–98, 202–6).[20] In the face of these similarities, however, the two accounts harbor a jolting difference: whereas the account in Wright's travel journal depicts the Takdir interview as taking place in Indonesia after the Bandung Conference, *The Color Curtain*'s narrative avers that Wright interviewed Takdir in Europe, thousands of miles from where Wright privately recorded the meeting as having taken place.[21]

Beyond offering Mochtar a misplaced scene depicting Wright's interview with Takdir occurring in Europe before the conference, *The Color Curtain* might have caused Mochtar much confusion with regard to Wright's counsel (as conveyed in *Encounter*) that Mochtar ought to "think hard" about the conversation he and Wright had while driving through the mountains between Jakarta and Bandung. Indeed, a reading of *The Color Curtain* would have given

Mochtar little reason to suspect that Wright himself could be counted on for a very basic narrative of the drive. *The Color Curtain*'s description of Wright and Mochtar's car ride offers the following scene: "The drive up the mountain slopes to Bandung lasted more than four hours and at no time were we out of sight of those brown, Javanese faces. . . . In many respects the Javanese countryside reminded me of Africa; . . . there were those same bare-breasted young women with somber-colored cloths—sarongs—rolled and tucked about their waists" (533). While granting that Wright may have viewed such a scene during his 1953 African travels (as documented in Wright's 1954 Gold Coast travelogue *Black Power*),[22] Mochtar and other Indonesian readers of the day would have been puzzled by an account featuring "bare-breasted" women walking casually along the roads of Muslim Java's countryside.

Pointing toward the nature of *The Color Curtain* as a retrospective reconstruction, such details have been easy enough for many non-Indonesian writers and scholars to gloss over and occasionally repeat.[23] Yet scholars and students seeking to approach Wright's Indonesian travels (or seeking to approach the Bandung Conference through Wright's account) must come to acknowledge and recalibrate their narratives in light of the provincialization of Indonesia and Southeast Asia that is written into incidents such as Wright's misremembering of the basic mores of modesty in Java, together with his decision to represent himself as having interviewed the famous Indonesian novelist Sutan Takdir Alisjahbana in Europe. To begin to appreciate the extent of this provincialization (which is at the heart of Mochtar's response to Wright's travel writing), imagine an Indonesian-authored mirror image of *The Color Curtain*. Hypothetically, this travelogue (set in 1955) might have an Indonesian author inaccurately reporting that he had crossed paths with and interviewed Ernest Hemingway in Jakarta, in preparation for a trip to Europe. After the interview, the hypothetical travelogue would represent its author's experiences in England. In London (as the travelogue would relay to its Indonesian readers), the women who work as bank tellers dress like Marilyn Monroe on the silver screen, specifically in order to attract the attention of male customers visiting the bank in order to withdraw money. For as fanciful as this hypothetical narrative would be on these points, the narrative might nonetheless pass as authoritative among certain 1950s Indonesian audiences who were unfamiliar with Hemingway's identity or travel itinerary, or who (as a result of viewing Hollywood movies) stereotyped American and European women as intentionally modest. Indeed, this hypothetical travelogue might emerge as a much-cited source among Indonesian scholars regarding cultural conditions in Euro-America during the 1950s. Meanwhile, if it were read among a Euro-American audience, a narrative of this type would seem an unlikely authority on North Atlantic attitudes or history.[24]

Yet in spite of the fact that an analogous representation of Indonesia takes place in *The Color Curtain*, Indonesian and Southeast Asian studies scholars (particularly those invested in tracing cultural traffic between Southeast Asia and the North Atlantic) have begun to consider the significance of Wright's Indonesian travels, now reading Wright's own account in conjunction with the historical texture offered in Indonesian accounts of Wright's visit.[25] Drawing on these Indonesian sources on Wright's Indonesian sojourn is possible because attending the weeklong Bandung Conference was far from Wright's only activity in Indonesia. During his three weeks in and around Jakarta and Bandung, he not only spoke with Bandung Conference attendees and Indonesian governmental figures but also interacted with a number of important arbiters of the Indonesian cultural and literary scene, associating closely with a highly visible subset of Indonesian modernists whose aesthetic philosophy had been designated a few years earlier as "universal humanism."[26] This current in modern Indonesian literary and cultural history had its origins in 1948, when a group of writers, artists, and intellectuals with an interest in the development of a modern Indonesian culture came together around a cultural column and supplement entitled *Gelanggang* (The Arena), which was printed in the weekly news journal *Siasat*.[27] In 1950, this group of like-minded individuals had issued a credo under the title "Surat Kepercayaan Gelanggang" (Gelanggang Testimony of Beliefs), which became the founding document of the Indonesian universal humanist ideology. It described Indonesian artists as the "rightful heirs to world culture," and it was essentially a statement of confidence about full and equal participation as Indonesian artists and intellectuals in international cultural trends and debates (Asrul, "Surat" 3).[28] The document's author was a prominent writer and cultural figure named Asrul Sani (Asrul, "Surat" 3), who in 1955 at the age of just twenty-four was an editor of the *Gelanggang* column. While in Jakarta, Wright granted *Gelanggang* an interview on his own work and his views on literature, which was published just after his departure under the title "A Conversation with Richard Wright." But this was only one aspect of Wright's contact with Asrul in April and May 1955. Through his Indonesian host, Mochtar Lubis, Wright was introduced to another universal humanist forum in which Asrul took an active part, the Studieclub Konfrontasi (Konfrontasi Study Club).[29] This study group was an extension of the cultural, political, and literary journal *Konfrontasi*, which had been founded in 1954 under the editorship of, among others, the well-known intellectual and cultural figure Sutan Takdir Alisjahbana, the "best-known" Indonesian novelist that *The Color Curtain* has Wright interviewing in Europe.

Takdir, who like Wright was born in 1908, was of a different generation from Asrul, Mochtar, and most of the other universal humanists Wright met and interacted with during his time in Indonesia. He had come into prominence as a pro-Western but Indonesian nationalist-oriented modernizer during the last years of Dutch colonial rule, and he had founded *Konfrontasi* as a post-independence successor to his famous 1930s cultural journal *Pujangga Baru* (New Poets). At the time of Wright's visit, Takdir was a highly respected senior figure in the world of the modern Indonesian arts, ideologically in sympathy with the outlooks of the universal humanists, though he himself was less of an aesthetic modernist than a cultural modernizer, impatient with the legacy of Indonesia's traditional cultures, which he saw as the main impediment to the development of a dynamic and forward-looking modern Indonesian culture. He was also a successful and wealthy businessman, and after making contact with Wright he invited the entire Konfrontasi Study Club to spend a weekend at his family bungalow in the mountains between Jakarta and Bandung in the company of this famous international visitor. On Sunday, 1 May 1955, Wright gave a lecture to the group on African American literature, and in the informal interactions that preceded and followed the lecture, he engaged in conversation with a representative sample of Indonesia's most prominent cultural figures of the time. Apart from Takdir, Mochtar, and Asrul, he associated with the older generation novelist and PEN Club leader Achdiat Karta Mihardja and the young and ambitious poet and short story writer Sitor Situmorang, who between 1952 and 1954 had been cultural attaché at the Indonesian Embassy in Paris.[30] Also among Wright's interlocutors were several other writers and artists belonging to the Konfrontasi Study Club, including its secretary, the Dutch-Indonesian writer and essayist Beb Vuyk, the essayist and member of the *Konfrontasi* editorial group Hazil Tanzil, and the young poet and translator Siti Nuraini. Back in Jakarta, and just two days before he left Indonesia, Wright continued circulating among many of these same contacts even as he also reached a wider Indonesian constituency through a lecture to a combined audience of members of PEN Club Indonesia and Indonesia's Council for Deliberations on National Culture (Badan Musjawarat Kebudajaan Nasional; BMKN) at the cultural center Balai Budaja. Wright's lecture on this occasion, on problems confronting Indonesian and Western writers, was later covered in Mochtar Lubis's newspaper *Indonesia Raya*.[31] Similar to his lecture at Takdir's mountain bungalow, Wright's lecture at the Balai Budaja receives no mention in either *The Color Curtain* or his unpublished travel journal, but it nevertheless represents an important though largely unknown window on the cultural traffic that Wright engaged in with his Indonesian counterparts.

At this time, the lectures sponsored by the BMKN and held in the Balai Budaja attracted a broad spectrum of the Indonesian cultural scene, and we can assume that on this occasion Wright and his views reached a wider range of

FIGURE I.2. Widening the frame of the photograph reproduced in figure I.1, another of Wright's photographs portrays (left to right): Achdiat Karta Mihardja, Sutan Takdir Alisjahbana, Beb Vuyk, Mochtar Lubis, Siti Nuraini, Fari (son of Achdiat and Tati Suprati Noor), and Tati Suprati Noor. Reprinted by permission of John Hawkins & Associates, Inc., and the Estate of Richard Wright. Courtesy of the Beinecke Rare Book and Manuscript Library, Yale University.

Indonesian cultural opinion than was the case with the more restricted circle of universal humanists affiliated with the Konfrontasi and Gelanggang groups. For instance, one member of the Balai Budaja audience was the seventeen-year-old Ajip Rosidi, who later recalled, "I first met Mochtar Lubis at the Balai Budaja around April 1955. At that point, the famous American writer Richard Wright was attending the Asian-African Conference in Bandung as a reporter, and before returning to his home country, he held a meeting with Indonesian writers" (*Mengenang* 133–34). After the lecture, as Ajip recalled, he shook Wright's hand and invited him to stay at his simple home, with its earthen floors and woven bamboo walls, because he believed Americans ought to get a feel for how ordinary Indonesians in Jakarta were living (Ajip, Interview). It is possible that Pramoedya Ananta Toer also attended this lecture. A member of the original Gelanggang group who by this time was distancing himself from the universal humanist camp, Pramoedya would later become a vociferous proponent of the opposing cultural ideology of Indonesian-style "socialist realism." Pramoedya was an admirer of Wright, and in an essay of 1953 he had held up the "bitter realism" of Wright's style as a model for the alternatives to "beauty" to which modern (Indonesian) writers should aspire.[32] As a figure central to generating content for the BMKN's news circular, he would have been well aware of the circular's publication of a 1956 review of the French translation of *The Color Curtain*, which provided Indonesian readers with Indonesian translations of large excerpts from Wright's travel writings.[33] Yet there is no known documentary or oral history record of Pramoedya interacting personally with Wright, either before or after the Balai Budaja lecture or during Wright's three-week sojourn more generally.

Pramoedya was an important writer and a prominent cultural figure in Jakarta during the 1950s, so this lack of documentation is surprising, and it serves as a reminder that Wright's interactions were culturally limited. To be sure, Wright spoke with a variety of cultural and governmental figures,[34] but his sustained and close association with Indonesia's universal humanists in and around Jakarta and Bandung undoubtedly made him less likely to forge close relationships (hence relationships more likely to be documented) with cultural figures whose stances did not resonate with universal humanism. Consequently, Wright's experiences and impressions remained substantially untouched—and undocumented—by a wider spectrum of Indonesian cultural thought and creative practice that included the more radical nationalist alternative being espoused by left-wing cultural activists (such as Bujung Saleh and A. S. Dharta), as well as by those writers associated with specifically Islamic-oriented Indonesian art and literature (such as Bahrum Rangkuti and Hamka) and the varieties of cultural practice under way in some of the capitals of Indonesia's outer provinces, such as Medan in North Sumatra and Makassar in South Sulawesi.[35]

The fact that Wright's impressions of Indonesian writers and intellectuals were formed largely through his interactions with those associated with the universal humanist outlook had to do in large part with the way his trip to Indonesia was funded and orchestrated. Although his source of funding remains undiscussed in *The Color Curtain* and in his travel diary, Wright's article "Indonesian Notebook" offers at least an oblique gesture. Of the airplane ride to Indonesia from Europe, he explains, "It had been arranged for me to pick up the plane in Madrid" (25). These and other arrangements were made on Wright's behalf by the Congress for Cultural Freedom (CCF). After deciding to attend the Bandung Conference, Wright began searching for funding and soon wrote to his literary agent that the CCF had told him that they wanted him to travel to Indonesia and "cover the conference for them."[36] During the 1950s, the CCF alleged that it was an independent organization dedicated to peace and intellectual freedom in opposition to Soviet-style totalitarianism,[37] but Wright believed it was a semiofficial organization with indirect support from the US State Department. By agreement with the CCF, he was "*officially . . . not covering*" the conference *for* the CCF but would in a putatively unaffiliated way write several articles on the conference to be published in the CCF's internationally distributed English-, French-, Spanish-, and German-language magazines.[38] The terms of the agreement also permitted Wright to publish these articles in book form.[39] Making arrangements for Wright's trip, CCF director Michael Josselson told Wright that an Indonesian journalist and PEN Club member, Mochtar Lubis, would meet him at the airport in Jakarta. Josselson wanted to do more than finance Wright's travels to the Bandung Conference. He wanted to orchestrate Wright's interactions with specific arbiters of Indonesian culture. The director wrote, "I am sure that Mr. Lubis will be delighted to be of assistance to you and on the other hand you will find him charming, interesting, and well informed. I have suggested to Mr. Lubis that while you are in Djakarta you may want to give a talk at the Pen Club there."[40] Since the late 1960s, it has been clear that Wright was correct in his belief that he was making these agreements with and through a semiofficial agency. What he did not know, however, was that the CCF was backed not by the State Department but by the CIA. Indeed, Josselson was both the CCF's director and a CIA agent.[41]

This intersection between Wright and the CCF has been acknowledged and minimized by biographers and scholars, with Wright normally represented in scholarly narratives as a freelance reporter able to speak and write freely, without interference from the CCF.[42] Even so, the Cold War United States was strategically invested in its black citizens speaking freely, or at least in an *image* of its black citizens speaking freely.[43] From this perspective, *The Color Curtain* and its surrounding Indonesian archive become relevant to an exploration of the contours of a specific approach that the United States took in attempting to intervene in the Bandung Conference and its representation to an international readership. Tellingly, the CCF published a handful of Wright's articles on Indonesia (which later became part of *The Color Curtain*) in its internationally distributed magazines, *Encounter* in English, *Preuves* in French, *Der Monat* in German, and *Cuadernos* in Spanish.[44] Furthermore, in paying for his travel and orchestrating his contacts, the CCF was inserting Wright into a community of Indonesian universal humanist writers who were specifically interested in cultural exchange with the rest of the world. As stated in the "Gelanggang Testimony of Beliefs," they not only considered themselves to be heirs to world culture but envisioned "Indonesian culture [as] determined by a multitude of stimuli coming from all corners of the world, hurled back to the world in our own voice" (Asrul, "Surat" 3).

This dedication to world culture prompted these Indonesian writers to seek out exposure to other cultures, and, intriguingly, they often engaged in cultural traffic with the rest of the world via the same organization that funded Wright's Indonesian travels. In 1954, for instance, Achdiat Karta Mihardja (who was later Wright's host with PEN Club Indonesia) reached out to poet and founding *Encounter* editor Stephen Spender, inviting him to make a side trip to Indonesia to meet with Indonesian writers during his upcoming travels to Australia.[45] The following year, just a few months before Wright's visit, his hosts Mochtar Lubis and Takdir Alisjahbana attended and made comments at the CCF's Conference on Cultural Freedom in Asia, held in Burma in February 1955.[46] A year after Wright's CCF-sponsored visit of 1955, Takdir and Mochtar again came together under the auspices of the CCF, now becoming interim heads of the CCF's Indonesian Committee, and holding a meeting in Jakarta at which the CCF representative for Asia, Prabhakar Padhye of India, spoke on the meaning of freedom in cultural life ("Panitya").[47] It was around this time that Takdir's journal, *Konfrontasi*, began publishing translated articles from the CCF magazine *Preuves* (Foulcher, "Bringing" 51). In 1963, Mochtar published his novel *Twilight in Djakarta*, with copyright assigned provisionally to the CCF before being returned to the author in 1968.[48] Also in the 1960s, Mochtar was in contact with Michael Josselson, discussing a new Indonesian magazine called *Horison* (modeled "somewhat along the lines of *Encounter*") and expressing hope that *Horison* would "have close relations with the Congress' publications—helping each other with editorial material, etc."[49] Taken in this context, *Indonesian Notebook* becomes a crucial tool not only for understanding the Bandung Conference as a touchstone moment within multiple arenas of study but also for accessing a moment when a major African American writer's travel for the conference emerged as a vehicle for furthering the CCF's CIA-funded work in cultural diplomacy. Wright's trip offered Indonesia's universal humanists an experience with world culture that they could (to draw language from the Gelanggang Testimony) subsequently rearticulate, "hurled back to the world in [their] own voice." Hence, the unwieldy vicissitudes of transnational cultural exchange among literary and cultural modernists intersect with what Jason Parker has described as the United States' uneven efforts at shaping the Asian-African Conference's geopolitical outcomes.[50]

Offering a window on the complex event of Wright's travels to Indonesia, this collection takes the first component of its title from the title of Wright's 1955 *Encounter* essay, "Indonesian Notebook," which, as we have previously mentioned, Wright published shortly after returning from Indonesia. During the half century since Mochtar rejected "Indonesian Notebook" and Wright counseled him to give serious consideration to the forthcoming *The Color Curtain*, Wright's book-length Indonesian travelogue has indeed emerged as the univocal account of his encounter with questions of race during his Indonesian travels. But our collection, complementing and sometimes countering *The Color Curtain*'s cryptic and often highly constructed mediation of the ways Wright's travels for the Bandung Conference prompted exchanges with Indonesian intellectuals, offers an alternative notebook on Indonesia, problematizing Wright's implication that Mochtar and his Indonesian colleagues had simply refrained from thinking "hard" enough. Rather, *Indonesian Notebook* presents a view of several Indonesian intellectuals thinking in sustained and deep ways about Wright specifically and the West more generally. It offers documents that will help scholars reconceive Wright's visit not as a unidirectional incident but rather as an event requiring narration from multiple and sometimes competing perspectives.

Accounting for these multiple perspectives—together with their cultural contexts and their legacies—will help scholars begin to adequately assess the significance of Wright's Bandung Conference attendance not only for transnational, postcolonial, and Afro-Asian studies but also for a global intellectual history of modernity. Here, recent calls for broader and deeper tracings of modernity's cultural traffic become key. Indeed, in this book, Indonesian studies scholar Jennifer Lindsay's call for investigating "Indonesia's cultural traffic abroad" ("Heirs" 7) meets African American studies scholar Kennell Jackson's emphasis on "systematic discussion of black cultural traffic" (13), under the umbrella of modernism/modernity scholar Susan Stanford Friedman's framing of the project of documenting "planetary cultural traffic" (483) as a means of piecing together a "planetary epistemology of modernity" (477). To borrow from Friedman, *Indonesian Notebook*'s translations—linguistic and cultural— permit a tracing of the "enmeshments of the global and local" (490), a crucial delineation of the ways global Asian-African consciousness and US cultural diplomacy precipitated a set of otherwise unlikely interpersonal relationships whose mutual misrecognitions have profound implications for how the Bandung Conference is taken up as a watershed event in narratives of global history.

In offering these multiple and competing perspectives, *Indonesian Notebook* is divided into three parts. Part I showcases documents illustrating intersections between Wright and modern Indonesian culture that preceded the 1955 face-to-face dialogue between the famous author and representatives of mid-twentieth-century Indonesian modernism. Part II offers primary historical sources that reveal Wright's interactions with the individuals, cultural organizations, and larger cultural milieux that helped mediate his access to the Bandung Conference and Indonesian society. Part III presents a selection of sources illustrating Wright's Indonesian reception since the Bandung Conference. Each of these parts is concerned with three major arenas of subject matter: Richard Wright, modern Indonesia, and the Bandung Conference. Even as some documents may be more relevant to Wright than to modern Indonesia, or more relevant to modern Indonesia than to the Bandung Conference, or more relevant to the Bandung Conference than to Wright, each document is in some way relevant to understanding all three categories. Certainly, these categories are interdependent, even if they have for too long been studied in ways that have been less than ideally integrated. Bringing them together in one volume, contextualized with substantive introductory essays and notes that draw on a multitude of other sources, including Brian Roberts's 2013 interviews with some of Wright's interlocutors and their descendants, presents readers with some of the complex cultural dynamics that must be acknowledged and taken into account when attempting to evaluate the significance of Wright's travel to mid-twentieth-century Indonesia for the Asian-African Conference.

Part I, "Transnational Crosscurrents," offers a view of modern Indonesia in dialogue with European and American culture generally and, occasionally, with Richard Wright in particular. The first document contained in this part is an excerpt from a booklet published in 1951 by the Indonesian Embassy in Washington, DC. This booklet, titled *Cultural Life in Indonesia: Religion, the Arts, Education*, features a "Language and Literature" section offering a 1950s-era narrative of Indonesian literary history that mentions Wright—among others—as a source of inspiration for the emerging writer Pramoedya Ananta Toer. Next are two other documents related to Pramoedya's interest in Wright: a 1953 essay by Pramoedya on the topic of beauty in literature, which takes Wright's autobiography *Black Boy* as one of its sources of inspiration, and a newspaper article of the same year that mentions Wright as a favorite author of Pramoedya and marks Pramoedya's departure for the Netherlands, funded by a scholarship from the Dutch Foundation for Cultural Cooperation. Certainly, these three initial documents are significant because they mention

FIGURE I.3. Brian Roberts with Gulon Situmorang, May 2013, discussing his father Sitor Situmorang's interactions with Richard Wright during a May 1955 meeting of the Konfrontasi Study Club. Used with permission of John McGlynn.

Pramoedya's admiration for Wright, but they are perhaps more important because of the way they offer readers a picture of the modern Indonesian literary scene that Wright would enter during his visit in 1955.

Following the Pramoedya-related items of 1951–1953, part I offers two documents that were published during the months leading up to Wright's visit. These are two book reviews drawn from newspapers; the first is a review of Wright's 1953 novel *The Outsider*, and the second is a review, by Beb Vuyk, of the 1953 *Partisan Review* anthology *Stories in the Modern Manner*. In reviewing this anthology of short fiction, Vuyk frames the *Partisan Review* as the largest of the "little magazines" and weaves Wright's emergence as a writer into the narrative of the *Partisan Review*'s emergence as a periodical.

Part II, "An Asian-African Encounter," offers press documents and other news items related to many of Wright's interactions with Indonesian intellectuals and the larger public. Among these interactions were a series of public and semipublic lectures that are not mentioned in either *The Color Curtain* or Wright's travel journal. In Wright's own record of his Indonesian travels, they appear only in a brief handwritten note, which is held in the Richard Wright Papers at Yale University's Beinecke Library. Here we see a cursory nod to his speaking activities. Wright notes that he found himself giving talks on "Negro literature and industrialization" to at least five groups, which he described as a gathering of divinity students, a cultural organization, an art league, a writers' group, and the PEN Club. In the same note, Wright mentions that Indonesia's daily press, using both English and the Indonesian language, reported fairly extensively on his remarks ("Retreat"). The record of Wright's lecturing activities may always remain incomplete, but the material published in this book affords readers documentary evidence related to four of Wright's lectures.

Two days after arriving in Jakarta, Wright attended a gathering in support of Indonesian artists, hosted by the city's mayor at his private residence. At some point during the evening, Wright spoke to the group at large, and some of his words during this speech, together with broader tableaux of the event, were recorded in two newspaper articles (included in chapter 6). After the Bandung Conference, Wright traveled to Takdir's mountain villa to give a lecture to the Konfrontasi Study Club, which was almost certainly the writers' group to which Wright refers in the handwritten note. Evidently, Wright provided the study club's leadership with a written copy of his lecture (titled "American Negro Writing"), because shortly thereafter, the editors of *Konfrontasi* published the lecture's full English-language text in the magazine's May–June 1955 issue, together with an editorial introduction and a loose Indonesian-language synopsis. Wright's *Konfrontasi* lecture is highly significant because it is the first known English-language publication of his *White Man, Listen!* lecture titled "The Literature of the Negro in the United States." However, what is perhaps more significant is the lecture's synopsis as it appeared in *Konfrontasi*, which relayed to a wider audience the study club's understandings (and sometimes misunderstandings) of Wright's lecture at Takdir's villa. The following day in Jakarta, Wright lectured at the Balai Budaja for a combined meeting of PEN Club Indonesia and the BMKN (the latter most likely being the cultural organization Wright mentions in his handwritten note). This lecture appeared in Indonesian translation in Mochtar Lubis's newspaper *Indonesia Raya*, together with a photograph of Wright, picturing him immediately prior to a lecture he gave at another point during his visit to an audience of university students.

Whereas three of Wright's talks can be dated (14 April for the art organization, 1 May for Konfrontasi, and 2 May for the BMKN/PEN Club), *Indonesia Raya*'s undated photograph of Wright's introduction to the university students is the only known documentary evidence of his lecture for a student group. This may or may not have been the lecture that Wright noted he gave to a group of divinity students, an event that almost certainly would have been orchestrated by Jakarta-based American Presbyterian missionary Winburn T.

Thomas, with whom Wright stayed for a week and a half after the Bandung Conference and who was connected to Jakarta Theological College's Bachelor of Divinity program (Thomas, "Reminiscences" 151).[51] The two had met while rooming together in Bandung, and in a letter to a colleague dated 21 April 1955, Thomas wrote from the conference that he had "spent hours in conversation" with Wright, and that Wright "awoke me last night to make a confession. 'In my book on Africa,' he said, 'I painted the missionary in a very bad light. He was a person who came to help but stood apart. He sought to draw near the Africans but his white prejudices and sense of inferiority got in his way. I now see that it is possible for the missionary to identify himself with his people, to lift their burdens, to make their life his life. I will hope to redeem myself in some later writing.'"[52] It may be that Wright's speech before the Indonesian divinity students addressed similar themes.

In addition to documenting a handful of Wright's lectures or talks while in Indonesia, part II offers a look at Wright's more day-to-day activities, together with the cultural milieux in which these activities took place, as mediated through the daily press as well as culturally oriented news outlets. Chapter 6 offers glimpses of Wright's hotel room on his arrival in Jakarta, his meetings with Indonesian politicians, his appearances on the street during the Bandung Conference, his commentary on the role of African countries at the conference, and other issues. Also in part II we see an article based on Wright's interview for *Siasat*'s *Gelanggang* column, as well as an article reporting on his visit in the pages of the monthly arts magazine *Seni*.

Part III, "In the Wake of Wright's Indonesian Travels," spans the period from June 1955 through the Bandung Conference's fifty-year commemoration in 2005 and thus documents the wake of an event that has generated controversy, animosity, admiration, and inspiration among Indonesians for over half a century. From 1955 through 1960, the year of Wright's death, his visit and writings seem to have prompted more controversy than admiration among his former hosts. Interestingly, it appears that this is precisely the way the CCF wanted things to play out. As is mentioned in the minutes of a meeting for a CCF gathering of 23 May 1955, the editors of the CCF's Europe-based magazines visited Wright at his home in Paris shortly after his return from Indonesia. The CCF at the time was especially attuned to "the attractiveness of controversial articles, or articles made controversial by inviting discussion and counterattack," and Wright's lengthy report on "his impressions of the rise of Asian nationalism and especially a 'new and dangerous racism' with strong mystical-religious elements" seems to have played a part in the editors' feeling "that the Richard Wright treatment of Bandung and Indo[n]esia might provide the proper point of departure" (Lasky).

Indeed, even before the CCF could publish Wright's Indonesian travel writing, Beb Vuyk (an editor of *Konfrontasi* and a writer for Mochtar's *Indonesia Raya*) published a pair of book reviews dealing with Wright, including a contentious review of Wright's *Black Power*, a copy of which apparently fell into her hands as a result of Wright's visit. Shortly thereafter, Wright's "Indonesian Notebook" appeared in *Encounter*, which of course elicited Mochtar's letter, something that the CCF editors would have approved of as an internationally visible counterattack. Following the appearance of Wright's book-length Indonesian travel writings, the BMKN (which had cohosted Wright's lecture at the Balai Budaja) and Asrul Sani (who had edited and probably conducted Wright's interview for *Gelanggang*) both published commentary on Wright. The BMKN offered measured and implicit critique in its biweekly newsletter, while Asrul in *Gelanggang* discussed Wright's 1953 novel *The Outsider* and pointedly framed him as an artist who had betrayed his calling to become a mere purveyor of ideas. Finally, in November 1960, during the week and a half before Wright died, Beb Vuyk published a controversial two-part article in the Dutch weekly news magazine *Vrij Nederland*. Five and a half years after Wright's Indonesian travels, Vuyk now offered an extensive outline and sometimes biting commentary on the events of Wright's visit, as seen from the perspectives of those associated with the Konfrontasi and Gelanggang groups. When Wright's friend and Dutch translator Margrit de Sablonière told him about Vuyk's article, Wright was upset, and de Sablonière was poised to publish a counter-attack. However, Wright's death a few days later brought those plans to a halt.[53]

Since his death, Wright has continued to find discussion in Indonesian circles, but Indonesian recollections of firsthand experiences with Wright have been less frequent. He has sometimes been mentioned without any reference to his visit, with Indonesian writers and commentators either unaware of or disinclined to remark on his three weeks of close interaction with prominent representatives of the cultural and literary life of mid-twentieth-century Jakarta. For instance, in the 1970s the creative writer and professor Ayatrohaedi (brother of Ajip Rosidi, who attended Wright's Balai Budaja lecture) published a number of translations of African American and black diasporan poetry. In a commentary appended to a selection of this poetry, Ayatrohaedi stated that among Indonesians Wright was the best known of African American writers but did not mention Wright's visit to Indonesia. Later, in the 1980s, as Mochtar compared the social consciousness of his own writing to that of Wright, he also refrained from mentioning Wright's trip to Indonesia. When Wright's Indonesian travels have been taken up by Indonesians, these discussions have tended to rely on the narrative that Wright himself offers in *The Color Curtain*. In 1977, Goenawan Mohamad (a prominent Indonesian poet and journalist and founder of the influential Indonesian weekly *Tempo*) took the contours of Wright's life as a template for addressing Indonesian political conditions, at one moment looking to *The Color Curtain* as a report on "an event [Wright] may not have fully understood, but whose significance he attempted to evaluate properly."[54] In 2005, however, during the commemorations of the Bandung Conference's fiftieth anniversary, a twenty-first-century *Tempo* journalist found no cause for skepticism and drew uncritically on *The Color Curtain* as a window on the conference's history. In 2015, during the conference's sixtieth anniversary, *Tempo* again drew on Wright and *The Color Curtain* as authoritative historical sources for commentary on the conference.[55]

Toward a Polyvocal History of Asia-Africa

In narrating a personal exchange Wright had with another reporter during the Bandung Conference, Wright's travel journal depicts him speaking with an African American woman from Chicago, who approaches him at noon and desperately requests his help in finding some Sterno (a jellied alcohol product, burned directly from the can in which it is sold) so she may heat her straightening comb. In the journal, Wright promises to help but reflects on the racial shame felt by black women in the United States, who, even while they are among people of color in Asia, still believe that their hair will look better if it is straightened to look like the hair of white women ("Jakarta" 150). But this narrative as offered in Wright's journal differs substantially from the narrative he published in 1956. In *The Color Curtain*, Wright's story of the Sterno incident represents the black US reporter not as a Chicagoan but as "a Negro girl from Boston" (578). And *The Color Curtain* does not depict Wright speaking directly to her but depicts him talking with her roommate, a reporter who is described as "a tall white woman" from the United States (577). Here, he listens patiently to the white woman, who earlier has overheard her African American roommate on the telephone, "begging some Negro reporter to try to find a can of Sterno for her" (582). The white reporter explains to Wright that she had wondered earlier, as she saw the African American woman late at night bent over in a corner using a blue flame, if her roommate were "practicing voodoo, or something?" (579). In *The Color Curtain*, Wright uses this perhaps embellished incident to illustrate, again, racial shame: in Asia, "where everybody was dark, that poor American Negro woman was worried about the hair she was born with" (580). Wright explains to the white reporter the meaning behind her black roommate's straightened hair: "Every day that woman commits psychological suicide" (581). In contrast to Wright's two ominous narrations of the Sterno incident, African American reporter Ethel Payne (a Chicagoan who met Wright at the Bandung Conference) offered yet a different story of the Sterno can. In a 1987 interview, Payne remembered unintentionally crossing paths with Wright and then complaining to him that her Sterno supply had run out. According to Payne, Wright said, "Well, don't worry. If there's any Sterno in Bandung, I'll find it for you." Then, after Payne had gone to bed for the evening, she was awakened at "about 3:00 o'clock in the morning," with Wright making "this anguished cry outside": "Ethel! Ethel! Please answer me! Ethel! Are you all right?" (Payne 69). Wright couldn't find any Sterno so he brought "some pure alcohol" and the two of them cooperated, apparently that very night, to heat the straightening comb over the alcohol as it burned in a saucer. Rather than recalling this event as psychological suicide, Payne recalled with laughter: "But that was a hilarious moment, because he was trying so hard to help me out" (70).

Our point in juxtaposing these three versions of the Sterno incident is not to present Wright's travel journal, or the Payne interview, as a necessarily accurate or authentic rendering. To be sure, this book is committed to the verifiable materiality of certain facts: for example, Wright did not interview Takdir in Europe; he would not have seen bare-breasted women walking along the roads of Muslim Java; he indeed lectured multiple times in Indonesia, though his book and travel journal elide these events. But *Indonesian Notebook* is also committed to advancing multiple versions of events, with this multiplicity permitting many events (to take the Sterno incident as a metaphor) to find representation simultaneously as voodoo, psychological suicide, and a hilarious moment. Of necessity, this collection is not doctrinaire in its reprinting of primary historical sources; agnostically, it reprints or relays primary sources that contradict each other and do not necessarily offer authoritative versions of events. Rather, if it is doctrinaire on any point, it is in its commitment to the rich polyvocality of narratives regarding Wright's interactions with modern Indonesia and the Bandung Conference. Hence, this book emerges as an attempt at accurately representing the contested readings of the incidents associated with Wright and modern Indonesia's mutual misreadings, with these misrecognitions generating more interest than any monological history. At one point, Wright's elision of his lectures might be answered with *Konfrontasi*'s locally specific adaptations of his lecture in its synopsis. At another point, his representation of himself interviewing Takdir in Europe might find a corollary in a 2005 *Tempo* article's puzzling representation of one of Wright's daughters visiting a museum in Bandung. Answering Wright's curious memory of bare-breasted women on the drive to Bandung is an article by Beb Vuyk that mistakenly has Wright giving his Konfrontasi lecture *before* rather than *after* the Bandung Conference. We could continue listing such moments almost indefinitely.

If, as Amritjit Singh has accurately observed, *The Color Curtain*'s narrative and ethical grapplings are in pivotal ways "defined by [Wright's] interaction with the Indonesian people and landscape" (619), then *Indonesian Notebook* (narrated as it is from the perspectives of those Indonesian personalities and cultural landscapes with which Wright interacted) becomes a crucial complement to *The Color Curtain*, as another volume of constructed, conflicted, and sometimes puzzling narratives. This book offers translations, translations of translations, translations of calculated and good-faith mistranslations and misrepresentations, and, inevitably, our own mistranslations, whether linguistic or cultural. In this way, it is our attempt, to borrow from Chakrabarty, to trace "that which resists and escapes the best human effort at translation across cultural and other semiotic systems," in a world imagined not as flattened by Euro-American modernity but rather reimagined "as radically heterogeneous" (*Provincializing* 45–46). Indeed, this book builds on and intensifies the project showcased by Lee and his contributors in *Making a World after Empire*, that of interrogating the Bandung Conference "through a purposeful return to the complex and uneven geographies of the postcolonial cold war world" (Burton, "Sodalities" 352–53). In this world, representatives of twenty-nine Asian and African countries came together in 1955 to discuss their significant points of commonality in the face of their unwieldy heterogeneities, heterogeneities not only among the representatives themselves but also among their nationalizing constituencies. It was this heterogeneous convening of the Bandung Conference that brought Richard Wright into an unwieldy and until now little-known dialogue with an equally heterogeneous modern Indonesia. Much more than a case study of the quandaries and misrecognitions involved in global intellectual exchange, this book highlights various counternarratives that call out for a reassessment of Wright's narratives of modern Indonesia and the Bandung Conference as offered in *The Color Curtain*. And because of *The Color Curtain*'s mythic status within multiple arenas of inquiry, *Indonesian Notebook*'s complications and contestations in turn call out for reassessments of the Bandung Conference's place in histories and theories of postcoloniality, the global South, nonalignment, and US investments in transnational cultural exchange.

Notes

1. On *Black Boy* and *Native Son*, see Ward and Butler 271 and 42. On Wright's relocation to Paris, see his "I Choose Exile" 4–6.

2. For other significant early accounts, see Romulo; Rowan 381–414; and Kahin.

3. On the Bandung Conference's "spirit" and role in the development of the Nonaligned Movement, see Ampiah 214–58.

4. On Barthes's fundamental contributions to anticolonial resistance and postcolonial studies, see Sandoval; and Hargreaves. For a view of Barthes's deployment in these arenas, see Chakrabarty, *Provincializing* ix–x; and Collits 109–11.

5. For allied scholarship that also seeks a deeper historical grounding for the Bandung Conference and its place in Asian-African and postcolonial history, see Mackie; McDougall and Finnane; and Tan and Acharya.

6. For this survey, see Vitalis 266.

7. See for instance Hakutani 69; Ahmad 179; and Stecopoulos 148.

8. For Chakrabarty's treatment of Roeslan Abdulgani's memoir, see Chakrabarty, "Legacies" 49–53.

9. For other work in Afro-Asian studies that frames *The Color Curtain* (and Wright's Indonesian travels) as a major event, see Mullen 59–71.

10. See Stecopoulos 149 and Mullen 59–67. We also admire Virginia Whatley Smith's "Richard Wright's Passage to Indonesia," with its archival work that uncovered preliminary evidence of Wright's lectures in Indonesia (110).

11. See Bakish; Fabre, *Unfinished*; Gayle; Rickles; Rowley; Walker; Wallach; Webb; J. Williams.

12. The Indonesian lacuna in Kinnamon's bibliography reminds us that even this one-thousand-page bibliography remains less than comprehensive in relation to what Kinnamon calls the "global dimensions" of Wright's reputation (x).

13. Other work attesting to scholars' extraordinarily thorough efforts in documenting Wright's life includes Fabre, *Richard*; Ward and Butler; and Kiuchi and Hakutani.

14. Biographers and scholars have largely relied on *The Color Curtain* and Wright's unpublished Indonesian travel journal. The only Indonesian source that has regularly figured in discussions has been Mochtar Lubis's response to Wright's *Encounter* article "Indonesian Notebook" (Rowley 468–69; Fabre, *Unfinished* 425; Stecopoulos 149; and Kiuchi 196).

15. For some examples of writing about Indonesia and Indonesians by short-term visitors or resident foreigners, from different eras and demonstrating different levels of insight, see: from the 1950s Stryker; from the 1960s M. Williams; from the 1970s Lucas; from the 1980s Naipaul 277–373; from the 1990s Lewis; from the 2000s Gilbert 215–331; and from the 2010s Pisani.

16. An exception is Vickers, 77–130. Outside of Indonesian studies, see E. Jansen 106.

17. See Curaming, who in 2009 suggested that in Philippine and Indonesian studies, "the out-in-the-open exchanges [on Said's *Orientalism*] belatedly started and have yet to peak, if at all moving" (2). In a 2013 interview, one of the most internationally prominent and highly respected Indonesian studies scholars, Benedict Anderson, commented

that despite his admiration for Edward Said's courage, he was "not a big fan of Said's work on Orientalism," finding it "biased and too polemical" (Gonzalez 664).

18. For Wright on his conversation with Mochtar as they drove through the mountains, see *The Color Curtain*, 534–35.

19. On the questionnaire and interviews, see *Color* 445–88.

20. For just a few of the correspondences, see Wright's two narratives on Takdir's bookshelves, his family, and his opinion on the relation between the state and religion (*Color* 464–65, "Jakarta" 195); on Takdir's stance on feelings of racial inferiority appearing in literature, see *Color* 466; and "Jakarta" 197.

21. The earliest draft of *The Color Curtain* (typed, with Wright's handwritten corrections) offers a frank explanation of the interviews that Wright recounts in the book before narrating his travel to Indonesia: the interviews, Wright explains, are not included in the order in which they occurred ("Color" 22), and the first interview recounted (with a young Indonesian-born Dutch journalist) occurred in Jakarta (21). However, Wright's handwritten revisions reveal his decision to simplify the narrative: he strikes out the acknowledgment that he is not recounting the interviews in the order in which they occurred (22), and he strikes through the explanation that the first interview took place in Jakarta (21). With these strike-throughs, Wright alters the narrative so that in the published version of *The Color Curtain* he may claim to interview both the Dutch journalist and Takdir in Europe before leaving for Indonesia. In the published draft, the first draft's Dutch journalist in Jakarta becomes "an Asian-born European who had once lived in Asia" (*Color* 449). In the same move, Wright's published narrative transports Takdir to Europe (*Color* 449, 464–72).

22. In his Indonesian travel journal, Wright comments on Indonesia's ubiquitous human faces, but he does not describe any women during the drive ("Jakarta" 126). However, in *Black Power*, Wright includes the following scene, narrating a ride through the African countryside: "I stared down at a bare-breasted young girl who held a huge pan of oranges perched atop her head" (56–57).

23. For a repetition of Wright's *Color Curtain* account of bare-breasted Javanese women, see Rowley 465, and for repetition of Wright's claim to have interviewed the unnamed Takdir figure *before* arriving in Indonesia, see Hakutani 69; Smith 94; and Reilly 512.

24. In offering this provincialized view of Euro-America, we are inspired by Dipesh Chakrabarty's *Provincializing Europe*.

25. See for instance Day 166; Foulcher, "Bringing"; and Roberts and Foulcher. Outside of Indonesian studies, Roberts draws extensively on Indonesian sources (145–72).

26. The term "humanisme universil" (universal humanism) appears to have been first used in Indonesian in 1951, by the literary critic H. B. Jassin, in reference to the beliefs of a group of writers originally centered on the revolutionary modernist poet Chairil Anwar, who died in 1949 (Foulcher, "Bringing" 34, n4). Their outlooks were founded on notions of secularism and individualism, while their commitment to political equality opposed colonialism and looked to the realization of a common and universal humanity. This stance superficially resembles a survey question Wright prepared before traveling to Indonesia: "Do you feel that man needs a universal humanism that can bind men

together in a common unity?" (Wright, *Color* 448). Yet by 1955, Indonesian discussions of universal humanism had acquired specific connotations—associated with domestic cultural debates—that were distinct from the way Wright was using the term.

27. Throughout this book, the term "Gelanggang" sometimes appears in italics and sometimes appears in roman script. Appearances of the term in italics refer to the supplement *Gelanggang* as published in the magazine *Siasat*. Appearances of the term in standard roman script refer to the Gelanggang group, which was affiliated with *Siasat*'s column.

28. The "Surat Kepercayaan Gelanggang" first appeared in the magazine *Siasat* in 1950. Throughout this book, English translations from the Indonesian source text are our own. For a standard English-language translation, see Teeuw, *Modern* 127.

29. Throughout this book, the term "Konfrontasi" sometimes appears in italics and sometimes appears in roman script. Appearances of the term in italics refer to the journal *Konfrontasi*. Appearances of the term in standard roman script refer to the Konfrontasi Study Club and others affiliated either with the group or the journal.

30. In his official Indonesian PEN Club correspondence, Achdiat identified himself at various points (from 1953 through 1955) as the PEN Club chairman, president, and head of manuscripts/magazines. See Achdiat to Sdr. M. S. Ashar, 26 July 1953; Achdiat to Stephen Spender, 25 Aug. 1954; Achdiat to Stephen Spender, 22 Oct. 1954; and Achdiat to Sdr. (Wakil) Kepala, 2 Feb. 1955 (PCIC). On Sitor in Paris and its impression on his literary art, see Teeuw, *Modern* 180–82.

31. See Wright's "The Artist and His Problems" in part II.

32. See Toer's "The Definition of Literature and the Question of Beauty" in part I.

33. Given that Pramoedya wrote the content for over one-fourth of all the issues of this circular, he seems to have had an editorial role, but we are unable to say so definitively. For more on Pramoedya's connection to this newsletter, see Roberts 169 and 196, n43.

34. See narratives in Wright, "Retreat"; and "Who's Doing What" (4 May 1955), in "A Sheaf of Newspaper Articles," in part II.

35. On the divides between Indonesian universal humanists and left-wing cultural figures, see Foulcher, "Literature." On Indonesian cultural production beyond Jakarta and surrounding regions, see Hatley, "Creating"; and Plomp. On the Islamic-oriented writers at the time, see Salim HS; and Kratz.

36. Wright to Paul Reynolds, 4 Feb. 1955 (MFP, box 31, folder 2). This sentence and subsequent sentences in this paragraph draw their narrative and some specific language from Roberts 148–49.

37. See Congress for Cultural Freedom, "Manifesto."

38. Wright to Reynolds, 4 Feb. 1955.

39. Wright to Reynolds, 4 Feb. 1955.

40. Josselson to Wright, 23 Feb. 1955 (IACFR, series 2, box 304, folder 11).

41. On the CCF's exposure as a CIA front, see Coleman 219–34. On the CIA's involvement in the arts via the CCF, see Cowen 78–79. On CCF director Michael Josselson as a CIA agent, see Saunders 153–56; and Coleman 6.

42. Apparently based on a 4 February 1955 letter from Wright to his literary agent, Paul Reynolds, scholars have repeatedly represented Wright as triumphantly indepen-

dent of the CCF in producing his Indonesian writing: Webb 381; Fabre, *Unfinished* 417; and Rowley 459. The letter in question, however, suggests that the CCF gave Wright an official story to share with others and with the Indonesian Embassy in Paris: that he was not covering the conference for the CCF but rather attending as a freelance writer.

43. See Roberts 151–52, 158–59.

44. On these essays, see Davis and Fabre 89–90.

45. See Spender to Achdiat, 14 Sept. and 17 Sept. 1954 (PCIC).

46. For Takdir's and Mochtar's comments, see Passin 38–44 and 134–35.

47. For another discussion of the CCF in Indonesia during this time, see Hill, *Journalism* 73.

48. For this publication history, we draw on the copyright pages of Mochtar, *Twilight* (1963) and Mochtar, *Twilight* (2011).

49. Mochtar Lubis to Michael Josselson, 24 June 1966 (MJP, box 29, folder 4). Also noteworthy: Takdir Alisjahbana's 1961 *Indonesia in the Modern World* was published by the CCF, and his interest in the CCF continued into the late twentieth century, as indicated by a copy of the September 1990 issue of *Encounter* (with a cover article titled "Remembering the Congress for Cultural Freedom") in the personal library he kept in the mountain villa at which Wright gave his 1955 speech for the Konfrontasi Study Club. Thanks to Norma Roberts, who found this issue of *Encounter* in Takdir's personal library during a May 2013 visit to the villa with Brian Roberts and Tamalia Alisjahbana.

50. On the United States' efforts via the conference-attending proxy nations and governmental agencies, including the CIA, see Parker.

51. In his 1950s overview of Christian theological training in Indonesia, Winburn T. Thomas noted only the Jakarta Theological College (Sekolah Tinggi Teologi Jakarta) as granting the bachelor of divinity degree ("Reformed" 7), so it is likely that Wright's lecture was for students of this school. Thomas indicated that he was—or likely would shortly be—teaching courses for the Theological College (Thomas to Mateo Occena, 6 May 1955 [UPC, box 1, folder 11]).

52. Winburn T. Thomas to Charles T. Leber, 21 April 1955 (UPC, box 1, folder 11).

53. De Sablonière to Webb, 3 Nov. 1966 (CWP, box 5, folder 10). "Margrit de Sablonière" is the pseudonym of Dutch translator and author Margaretha Catharina Bicker Carten-Stigter (1905–1979).

54. See Goenawan's "Politicians" in Part III.

55. In April 2015, to commemorate the conference's sixtieth anniversary, *Tempo* published a special issue, with both an Indonesian and an English edition. Introducing the special issue is an article that draws extensively on Wright and *The Color Curtain* to describe some of the conference themes and aspects of the Indonesian response to the conference's staging ("Panggilan"; "Resonating"). Elsewhere in the issue, Wright appears again, in an article that relies on *The Color Curtain* and describes Wright's deep impressions of Indonesia ("Dari"; "Outsiders"). In the subsequent issue of *Tempo*, Goenawan Mohamad engages with *The Color Curtain* and Wright's other writings in an article on the Bandung Conference (Goenawan, "Bandung").

Part I Transnational Crosscurrents

1

The Indonesian Embassy's *Cultural Life of Indonesia* (Excerpts) (1951)

In 1951, the Indonesian Embassy in Washington, DC, published a booklet titled *The Cultural Life of Indonesia: Religion, the Arts, Education*. Published six years after Indonesia's declaration of independence and only two years after its recognition as a sovereign nation, the booklet is a revealing example of the way the Republic of Indonesia, through what was one of its most geostrategically important embassies, was narrating itself and its culture internationally. It includes accounts regarding Indonesian history and literature that provide a window into the mid-twentieth-century Indonesia—and in particular its literary scene—that Wright visited when he attended the Bandung Conference.

The booklet's foreword was written by Ali Sastroamidjojo, who in 1951 was Indonesia's ambassador to the United States and one of his country's most prominent nationalist politicians. A Javanese aristocrat educated in the Netherlands in the 1920s and a member of the Indonesian delegation at the Round Table Conference in The Hague that negotiated the terms of Indonesian independence in late 1949, Ali was a leading figure in President Soekarno's Indonesian National Party. In July 1953 he became Indonesia's eighth prime minister, presiding over the first of two multiparty cabinets that played

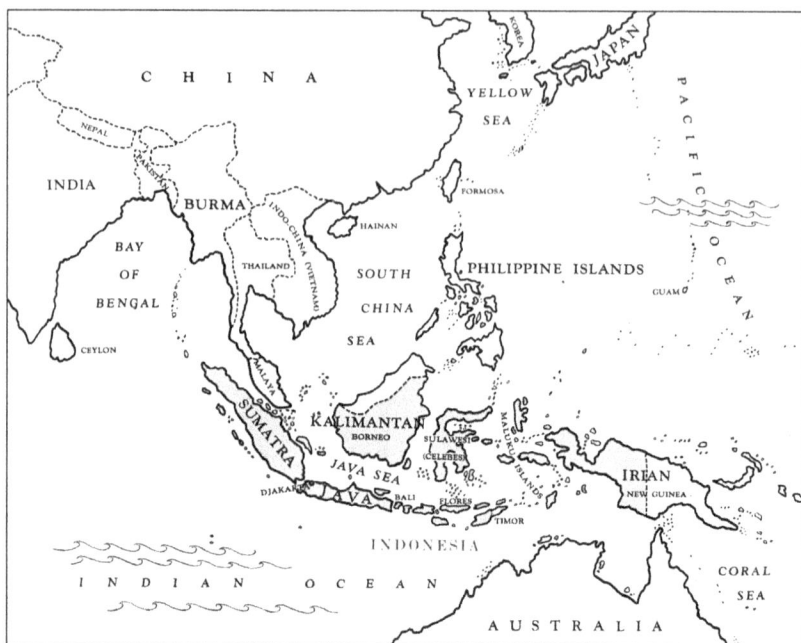

FIGURE 1.1. Map of Indonesia. From the Indonesian Embassy's booklet *The Cultural Life of Indonesia*.

a significant role in the country's experiment with parliamentary democracy between 1950 and 1957. Importantly, he was also the original proposer of the Bandung Conference, having suggested the convening of a high-level conference of the independent states of Asia and Africa to the then prime ministers of India, Pakistan, Ceylon, and Burma at a meeting in Colombo in April–May 1954 (Feith, *Decline* 387). In 1955, at the time of Wright's visit, Ali was prime minister of Indonesia as well as chair of the conference he had proposed only one year earlier. So when Wright met Ali while in Indonesia in 1955,[1] he was meeting someone who not only represented Indonesia on the world stage but was also a man whose career epitomized the rise of the Indonesian nation from a colonial state to a country at the forefront of nonaligned political philosophy in a world divided by the Cold War.

In its "Language and Literature" section, the Embassy's information booklet offers an account of the emergence of modern Indonesian literature that is heavily determined by the official narrative of Indonesian nationalism. In the decades since the publication of this booklet, scholarship on Indonesian literary history has come to see the origins of "modern" literary expression (i.e., modern expression via the indigenous languages of the Dutch East

Indies) in the hybridized works of early twentieth-century Sino-Malay and Indo-European writers, and has identified some of the earliest creative expression by indigenous Indonesians as emerging from within the Communist movement that was silenced by the Dutch in the 1920s.[2] In the Embassy's 1950s narrative, however, there is no suggestion of cultural hybridity or political radicalism in the conditions that gave birth to the transition out of older forms of literary expression in the language that came to be called Indonesian, or "Bahasa Indonesia." Instead, the history of modern Indonesian literature presented in *The Cultural Life of Indonesia* begins with the 1933 founding of the literary and cultural periodical *Poedjangga Baroe* (spelled *Pudjangga Baru* by the time of the booklet's printing, and *Pujangga Baru* after 1972). In this way, the booklet defines modern literature in Indonesian as a product of the moderate cultural nationalism that emerged among Dutch-educated and ethnically "pure" Indonesian nationalist youth from the late 1920s. This was a strand of modern literary expression made up of poetry and prose that grew out of a romantic nationalism combined with verse forms and narrative styles adapted from the examples of nineteenth- and early twentieth-century European literature that these young writers had come to know primarily through the colonial education system.

From this point, the Embassy's account moves directly to the work of a group of modernist authors who emerged in Dutch-occupied Jakarta during the years of national revolution. Impatient with the prewar generation's romanticism and provincialism, this new group of writers transformed the Indonesian language through a spare realism in prose and symbolist experiments in poetry. They also formulated the concept of "universal humanism" as an aesthetic and cultural credo. These writers formed the nucleus of the groups who interacted with Wright during his three weeks in and around Jakarta and Bandung.

It is particularly interesting to see in this account of Indonesian literary history the Indonesian Embassy narrating the in-progress emergence of Pramoedya Ananta Toer's career. Pramoedya was later to emerge as one of the most prominent voices in Indonesian literature and the country's best-known author outside Indonesia itself. At the time this booklet was written, he was loosely associated with the universal humanist circle, a twenty-six-year-old Javanese among writers and intellectuals who were mainly Sumatran in ethnic origin, and a contributor to the cultural and literary periodicals this group supported. However, Pramoedya later moved away from his early associations with the universal humanist outlooks and into close alignment with the more radical nationalist approach to the development of a modern Indonesian culture. In place of the universal humanists' focus on individual creative energy and its openness to influence from abroad (primarily western Europe), Pramoedya joined the call for a socially engaged art and literature consciously advancing the interests of ordinary people and the national struggle against neocolonialism and imperialism. While on one hand Pramoedya's openness to taking inspiration from Wright (as noted in the Embassy booklet) frames him as aligned with the universal humanists, this same openness to Wright's exceptionally socially conscious writings also may point toward the beginnings, even in 1951, of Pramoedya's later move toward closer identification with the anticolonial and nationalist struggle.

The Cultural Life of Indonesia (Excerpts)
by the Indonesian Embassy in Washington, DC
SOURCE LANGUAGE: ENGLISH

The motto, "One nation, one people, and one language," adopted by the nationalist movement at the Youth Congress of 1928 is a striking illustration of the close relationship of the cultural and the political development of Indonesia. The promotion of a single Indonesian language undoubtedly had political significance as a means of developing unity of purpose among all Indonesians in the struggle for independence; it has even greater significance, however, as a symbol of the reawakened sense of cultural unity.

The new Indonesian language is based on the pure Malayan tongue.[3] The decision to use this language as a base for the new Indonesian language involved historical, political, and practical considerations. The early Indonesian languages included ten major dialects such as Javanese, Sundanese, Madurese, Minangkabau, Atjeh, Buginese, and Balinese with almost two hundred dialects used by smaller numbers of people. All of these languages belonged to a single linguistic group, the Malayo-Polynesian, which includes also the languages spoken in the Malay peninsula and throughout the islands of the Pacific as far east as Hawaii and Easter Island. All of these languages developed quite separately and through the centuries have become mutually incomprehensible. On the other hand, the Malayan language, which is flexible and adaptable, came to be used widely by foreign traders in the coastal cities throughout Indonesia; thus, it gradually became the *lingua franca* of Indonesia. Because of its use by foreigners this language became considerably corrupted and came to be known as Bazar-Malay, distinguishing it from the pure Malayan tongue.

Meantime, throughout the period of Dutch rule, the Indonesians continued to use their own regional languages and many Indonesians were familiar with several of these. This diversity of local languages presented no problem to the Dutch as no attempt was made to provide education for the masses of Indonesian people. Those few Indonesians who were able to take advantage of the limited opportunities for education were expected to learn the Dutch language, which was used in the schools.

When the nationalist leaders began to consider the problem of constructing a new common language for all Indonesians it was obviously impossible, on a nationalistic basis, to promote the use of the Dutch language. It was equally impossible to consider the use of Bazar-Malay because of its lack of prestige among the Indonesian people. It was also quite universally understood that it would be unwise, from the standpoint of national unity, to promote the use of Javanese as the common Indonesian language, although this was spoken by more than 30,000,000 people or more than half of the total population of Indonesia at that time. It was, therefore, decided to base the new language on pure Malay. . . .

Although the original languages are still used among people of the same linguistic area the new Indonesian language has been rapidly adopted throughout the islands of Indonesia. It is of particular importance in relation to the need for a greatly expanded educational program, both at the formal school level and in adult fundamental education. Extensive literacy campaigns have already been undertaken to teach adults to read and write, and the Indonesian language is used in all government publications as well as in motion pictures and other forms of entertainment. It is also now used exclusively in all schools after the first two years of primary education.

Many of the classics of European, American, and Asian literature, including such works as Shakespeare's *Hamlet*, Cervantes' *Don Quixote*, Steinbeck's *Of Mice and Men*, and Chinese philosophical works, have now been translated into Indonesian, thus lending literary prestige to the new language. Quite obviously, the development of a common Indonesian language has also been of tremendous significance in relation to the growth of a modern Indonesian literature.

In literature, as in the other fine arts, the 20th century was the beginning of a new epoch, marking the transition from the static and traditional to the modern concepts of life. The literary work of the early years of this century, however, represented primarily a break with the Indonesian past and reflected the increasing contact of intellectuals with the Western world. Some of the European and American authors who have exerted the greatest influence on Indonesian writers are: Pushkin, Dostoievsky, Tolstoy, Malraux, Hemingway, and Steinbeck. The popularity of these authors has perhaps been due to their moralistic tone which is a quality in harmony with the values important in Indonesian culture. . . .

The revolutionary movement in Indonesian literature can be dated from the founding in 1933 of a monthly cultural review, the *Pudjangga Baru* (The New Scholar).[4] As in art, this movement was an expression of the desire of the writers to stress the liberation of the individual and the full development of the personality; it was essentially an outgrowth of the whole revolutionary spirit spreading throughout Asia and an expression of the desire of the colonial people to achieve their independence from foreign rule. While it was stimulated by the development of the new Indonesian language, it in turn gave added impetus to the growth of the language.

The founder and editor of the *Pudjangga Baru* was Takdir Alisjahbana, who published his first novel in the Indonesian language in 1929, only one year after the Youth Congress had proposed the adoption of a common language for all Indonesia as one of the fundamental bases for national sovereignty. Takdir was deeply aware of the static nature of both the cultural and material aspects of Indonesian life in the early 20th century. He stressed the cultural, material, and economic advantages enjoyed by the Western nations whose dynamic growth he attributed to the concept of freedom. He therefore believed ardently that the artist must be free to express his own ideas, released from the restraints imposed by tradition, but at the same time he was himself a product of the Indonesian cultural tradition of community cooperation and social responsibility. Accordingly, he felt that the artist should exercise his intellectual freedom not on the principles of "art for art's sake" but, rather, in fulfilling his function as a member of society and leader of his community by applying modern concepts to the problems of contemporary life in Indonesia. The individual artist should, therefore, subordinate himself to the struggle for freedom and should be conscious of the ties binding him to the community. . . .

At the end of the period of Japanese occupation there appeared, under the leadership of Chairil Anwar, a new group of writers, often known as "the generation of '45." This group formed in 1946 an association called Gelanggang ("The Arena"), and their clear and hopeful vision was expressed in a Manifesto:

> We are the rightful heirs to the culture of the world, and this culture we will advance according to ways of our own. We were born of the mass of the people, and the meaning of "people" to us is a group of mixed variety out of which a sound new world can be born.
>
> Our Indonesian-ness is not only because our skins are brown, our hair black, our cheek-bones high, but much more because of what is expressed as the true emanation of our hearts and minds. We are not

going to give a definition of what constitutes Indonesian culture. When we speak of Indonesian culture, we are not thinking of polishing up the products of the old culture to make them glitter and in order that they may be praised, but we are thinking of a new cultural life which is sound. Indonesian culture is determined by all the voices sounding from all parts of the world, and spoken out with our own voice, in our own language, in our own forms . . .[5]

This is a new and ringing voice, expressive of the sense of purpose in Indonesian cultural life today. At the same time, the work of this new generation was overshadowed by the revolution and reflects the deep despair and the grief suffered by the Indonesian people. All of these profound emotions are expressed by Chairil Anwar in the poems published shortly before his death in 1949 in a collection entitled "Mêlée of Noise and Dust."

But these young poets also saw a ray of hope and possessed an undying faith in ultimate victory. Two of the poets who express this spirit most eloquently and poignantly are Rivai Apin and Asrul Sani. Both of these men were very much alive to the world around them but, at the same time, they looked beyond into the future and felt a strong bond of unity with all their compatriots of both past and future generations as well as of the present. . . .

The short story and novelette forms also have had a special appeal to young Indonesian writers. Among the most outstanding contemporary prose writers is Idrus, who also began to write during the Japanese occupation. While his works indicate a critical and somewhat cynical mind, they are written in a vigorous and realistic style.

Another young prose writer who has attracted attention in recent years is P. A. Toer. His short stories and novelettes describe his experiences as a news correspondent during the revolution and his imprisonment. In 1949 his novel *Pursuit* won the first prize in the competition of the Balai Pustaka, a printing and publishing establishment administered by the Ministry of Education; his works reflect especially the influence of Steinbeck, de St. Exupéry, and Richard Wright.

Perhaps one of the most significant and controversial Indonesian writers is A. K. Mihardja, who has endeavored to delineate in his book *The Atheist* the moral and intellectual struggle between religious concepts, mysticism, and historical-materialism.

Other writers who have made significant contributions to the modern literature of Indonesia are the playwrights Ismail Usmar and El Hakim, as well as H. B. Jassin, literary critic and arts editor of the weekly magazine *Mimbar Indonesia*.

The new literature of Indonesia is a rich and dynamic one, which in its diversity of concept and style, reflects the renewed vigor and spirit of intellectual and cultural life. While it owes much to Western literature, it reveals also many attitudes which have developed out of the rich cultural heritage of Indonesia, as well as from the intimate and vital experiences of the recent past.

Notes

1. See "Who's Doing What" (4 May 1955), from "A Sheaf of Newspaper Articles" in part II.

2. See McGlynn on more contemporary approaches to the study of Indonesian languages and literary history.

3. Rather than the Embassy booklet's term *Malayan* (which is properly a geographical and political term), the usual term for the language is *Malay*.

4. Although the translation of *Pudjangga Baru* given here is *The New Scholar*, the word *pu(d)jangga* is a Sanskrit-derived term for "man of letters," which was used in Javanese—not Malay—to refer to a court poet. Its use in the title of the 1930s Indonesian-language journal reflects the attempt during this period to overlay "traditional" terminology with new, "modern" connotations.

5. This quotation is an English-language translation of an excerpt from the document that is usually referred to as "Surat Kepercayaan Gelanggang" (Gelanggang Testimony of Beliefs). In the excerpt, the phrase "our cheek-bones high" is a translation of the Indonesian phrase "tulang pelipis kami yang menjorok ke depan" (Asrul, "Surat" 3). This phrase presents a challenge to the translator, because the literal meaning of "tulang pelipis kami" is "our temporal bones," referring to the part of the skull between the eye and the ear, while "yang menjorok ke depan" means "which project forward." Other translators have rendered it as "our protruding foreheads" (Teeuw, *Modern* 127) and "slanting cheek bones" (Johns 238). The sentence as a whole goes to the heart of the document, highlighting the physical attributes of "race" only to discount them as secondary to the affective manifestations of a common humanity.

2

Pramoedya Ananta Toer's "The Definition of Literature
and the Question of Beauty" (1952)

Identified in *The Cultural Life of Indonesia* as an emerging young writer of note,
Pramoedya Ananta Toer was also a prolific essayist, and from the late 1940s
he was an active participant in the debates on literature that were conducted
through cultural columns in newspapers, magazines, and a range of other cultural periodicals. One of these was the BMKN magazine, *Indonesia*, where in
August 1952 Pramoedya published "Definisi dan Keindahan dalam Kesusastraan" (The Definition of Literature and the Question of Beauty). Republished
the following year in Pramoedya's own bulletin, *Mimbar Penyiaran* DUTA,[1] this
essay reads as a fairly random collection of thoughts on literary aesthetics.
However, it is nonetheless illuminating because it shows Pramoedya attempting to articulate the realist impulse that underlies his early fiction. The harsh
realities of war and national revolution, and ordinary people's struggle for
survival in the early years of independence, demanded, in his mind, a shift
from both classical Western notions of the relationship between "art" and
"beauty" and the indigenous concept of literature (*kesusastraan*) as the creation of beauty through the written word (Heinschke 153). In place of both,
Pramoedya casts about for a realist aesthetic that might point the way toward

a postcolonial Indonesian literature grounded in the social conditions that are its principal source of subject matter.

Confirming the Indonesian Embassy's narrative of Pramoedya as taking inspiration from Richard Wright, "The Definition of Literature and the Question of Beauty" expresses Pramoedya's admiration for Wright and discusses how Wright might become a template for writers experimenting with new modes of realism. Of particular note is Pramoedya's designation of Wright's writings as embodying a "bitter realism" insisting that "facts . . . have to be swallowed raw." Interestingly, the quality Pramoedya identifies in Wright's writing aligns with Wright's own analysis of the process that led to his breakthrough 1940 novel *Native Son*, which features the protagonist Bigger Thomas reacting in violent ways to the grinding and absurd conditions of his life as a black man living in poverty in 1930s Chicago. In his famous essay "How Bigger Was Born," Wright explained how *Native Son* grew out of his earlier experience in publishing a 1938 short story collection:

> I had written a book of short stories which was published under the title of *Uncle Tom's Children*. When the reviews of that book began to appear, I realized that I had made an awfully naïve mistake. I found that I had written a book which even bankers' daughters could read and weep over and feel good about. I swore to myself that if I ever wrote another book, no one would weep over it; that it would be so hard and deep that they would have to face it without the consolation of tears. (xxvii)

Whether or not Pramoedya was familiar with this specific passage, the goals expressed here seem to resonate strongly in Pramoedya's emphatic statement regarding Wright's autobiographical *Black Boy*: "The much-vaunted concept of beauty has no place in Wright's prose. None!"

The inspiration Pramoedya draws from Wright in this essay is not an isolated example of an interest in African American culture appearing in his writing at this time. In his seventh book of fiction, the 1951 novelette *Bukan Pasar Malam* (Life's Not a Night Bazaar), he made specific reference to the encapsulation of human suffering in the tradition of the Negro spiritual and its resonance with the personal experience the novelette recounts. A first person narrative, *Bukan Pasar Malam* tells the story of a son returning home from Jakarta to be with his dying father. The penultimate chapter frames the father's death in the larger historical context of Japan's World War II invasion of Indonesia, which freed the archipelago from Dutch control only to plunge it into a period of extreme suffering and destitution before the end of the war and the declaration of independence in 1945 (103–5). The final chapter portrays the narrator, after his father's funeral, returning to the family home, where he first hears his brother singing and then finds that unbidden "there came from my lips the sound of those Negro spirituals, the voice of an oppressed humanity, the voice of people longing for something they themselves didn't understand" (106). In this way, African American culture plays a major role in mediating the agony of what is perhaps the major pivot of Pramoedya's story, his perception of the conditions of life for ordinary Indonesians in the wake of a failed act of decolonization. Given Wright's 1955 sense of the ways he and his Indonesian interlocutors ought to feel united by analogous histories of race-based oppression and colonialism, Wright would probably have considered it appropriate that the narrator, as a postcolonial subject, should seize on the tradition of the Negro spiritual.[2]

Also of interest in relation to Indonesian cultural conditions in the run-up to Wright's visit is Pramoedya's discussion of the intersection of literary and visual arts, because it reflects the close association between the two in the Indonesian arts of this period. As Pramoedya mentions, the painter and author Trisno Sumardjo was equally prominent in both these fields of artistic expression, and visual artists regularly contributed both sketches and written commentary to literary forums like *Gelanggang/Siasat* in the early postwar period. Notably, two of the artists Pramoedya mentions in this connection— Trisno Sumardjo and Zaini—were later named as two of eight literary and artistic figures Mochtar Lubis suggested to Wright as possible contacts during his visit to Indonesia.[3]

The Definition of Literature and the Question of Beauty
by Pramoedya Ananta Toer

SOURCE LANGUAGE: INDONESIAN

It is difficult to impose a specific definition of literature on others, especially when they are already active in the field. The development of one's mental capacity and the discoveries that come with thinking will exert significant influence on one's approach to concepts and ideas. In classical terms, one can say that literature is an epitome of human creativity in prose or poetry, which gives expression to *beauty*. But once a person has moved on from the classroom, he or she will have doubts about the understanding of beauty imparted through this kind of instruction. Is it only beauty that literature expresses? This can't possibly be the case.

There are so many matters of concern in human life, not just beauty. And what is beauty? The term itself is full of ambiguities. No one can be persuaded that something is beautiful merely through argument, because it is a matter of personal experience. To put it at its most extreme, beauty is the expression of human subjectivity. There is indeed a middle way that represents the standard recognition of beauty. But everyone has the right to go beyond that standard norm. If someone is equipped to do so, he or she has the right to leap right over it. However, trying to do so without being fully equipped for it is a dangerous undertaking. It may result in complications and confusion in one's subsequent development.

To reiterate, beauty is not all that is important in human life. The definition of beauty in literature mentioned above is clearly a reflection of the glory days of the romantic era. In its present-day development, literature has a function and range that takes it beyond the mere expression of beauty. Justice, humanity, ethics, and even national consciousness, are all now commonly a part of literature, expressed with a full conviction that goes beyond anything that might be called the beautiful. Literature is no longer a hymn to beauty. Indeed, it is common to hear people say that those values are themselves a part of the expression of beauty. And if that is the case, how else would those concepts be defined in human language?

People say that the beauty they are referring to is the harmony that emerges from creative work. But this too is not accurate, because beauty is not harmony and harmony is not beauty. Harmony is something that is essential to all forms of creativity in this world of ours, whether it is the work of humans or of nature itself.

In reality, there is only one choice in literature: beauty, or literature itself. If the choice is for beauty, a person drifts about, without making a connection to anything. He or she becomes a victim of the senses, trapped in misconstrued labor, because things that are beautiful are negative, lifeless things, unless they are channeled into specific goals and forms. In literature, beauty is just raw material, no different from a writer's other raw materials. It has no right to force literature to conform to its demands. Given the huge variety of social formations today, a single concept of beauty no longer commands the pride of place it once enjoyed. It is no longer the essential vitamin that it was when rulers built their beautiful palaces on the misery and dead bodies of their people. It is just another everyday component of life like rice and water, and earth and sky, along with all the creatures within them.

The worship of beauty is no different from any other form of worship. It is a form of escapism, because people have lost the ability to recognize its function and use.

Literature should be accepted as it is, freed from imposed definitions. A greater familiarity with it will eventually yield its own definitions, in accordance with the terms one discovers in the course of reaching that degree of familiarity. And the definitions one acquires through that process will serve as guidelines for its subsequent development.

When we speak of literature, it would be best to keep the theme of beauty to one side. Defining literature as the creation of beauty imposes limitations on something that is alive and in motion. Literature is not a dead thing. It lives in the spiritual nature of its readers. And as it evolves, the concept of beauty recedes into the background. Bitter realism doesn't present the reader with beauty, but with facts that have to be swallowed raw. In Richard Wright's *Black Boy*, the reader sees how fear takes hold, with no reference to beauty whatsoever. The book sends a shiver down the spine of the reader as he or she becomes aware of the danger of genocide. The much-vaunted concept of beauty has no place in Wright's prose. None! And that type of realism, when it is linked to naturalism, psychologism, surrealism, and other recent labels, forms a strong chain that imprisons the earlier definitions mentioned above.

In reality, beauty in literature is something in the eye of the reader.

Indeed, the Indonesian term for "literature," "kesusastraan," is derived from Sanskrit, its base word made up of "su," meaning "more" (in the sense of more beautiful, good, useful) and "sastra" meaning script, book, or law. And it is understandable that people should continue to adhere to the idea that literature is what results from the creation of beauty in written form, or through the use of words. But it should not be forgotten that terms always change their meaning in line with their usage at a particular time and place, or by a particular person or group of people. Take for example the Indonesian term "pujangga," the word once used exclusively for "writer." Originally it implied an exalted status and described a person who was wise about all matters, had mastery over the arts, especially philosophy, and was of a noble and forgiving character. Now it is just one of several everyday terms for "writer." And words that once used to mean "foot," or something connected with the feet, have now become titles, or marks of highly dignified status, like "duli," "sampean," "cokorde," "paduka," "gamparan," and so on.[4] Since literature is something dynamic and growing, it has its own history of development, and is capable of diverging from concepts that were once imposed on it. This is something that doesn't happen just in the literary arena, but in all fields.

It is undeniably true that literature is a branch of the arts. In fact it is closely connected with other art forms. Sometimes the connection is so close that an artist can express the same concepts in a number of different art forms at the same time. Jean Cocteau, for example, apart from being a well-known writer, is also a dramatist, a painter, and a fashion designer. Rosihan Anwar is a writer, but also an actor. Trisno Sumardjo is a writer as well as painter, as are

Zaini, Sudjojono, and others. And art, as it is now understood, does not only signify the beautiful, but also the product of sensitivity.

The artist is not only a person of sensitivity, able to perceive matters of justice, humanitarianism, humiliation, and other concerns that the majority of people, having a less-developed sensitivity, are less able to perceive. It is clear that art does not exclusively refer to what is beautiful, and this is why literature, as just a small branch of art, is similarly informed.

Purism—that current in literature that can be seen as half reportage or snapshot, making use of the character's own language with punctuated emphases, with action and settings and its own particular atmosphere—is a direct challenge to the criterion of beauty. (Purism can be seen as an outgrowth of realism, and it goes without saying that a literary product of this type is difficult to translate well. In other words it is a localized variety of literature.)

And beauty in literature has different meanings for each individual writer. In his essay on James, Graham Greene says that the ultimate beauty in his stories is to be found in pity: "The poetry is in the pity."[5]

And Steinbeck, in *Tortilla Flat*, says that the beauty of a story lies in its unfinished state, leaving readers to complete it according to their own individual imaginings. Many people believe that the beauty of a story lies in those parts of it that contain touching new discoveries and insights about something. (What is "touching" is of course a very subjective matter.) Many beliefs concerning aesthetic qualities in literature do not in fact derive from theories generated by the intellect, or from the technical skills of a writer planned in advance. Beauty is something that is strongly empirical, in the sense that it can only be known from its existence. Wide familiarity with literature is the direct means by which someone is brought into contact with recognizable forms of beauty. Guide books can only impart the theory, leaving it still hard for a reader to appreciate the beauty of Chairil Anwar's poetry, for example. It is clear that this ability to appreciate one particular poet rests on a wide familiarity with poetry in general. This is not the only way to come to some appreciation, but it is certainly one of the most effective ways.

Let me reiterate that the definition of literature is best left to other people. Let the teachers and dictionaries devise their own definitions. The freedom to define something for oneself is perhaps a way of avoiding rigidity, opening up a dynamic freedom of movement. Nevertheless, the ability to perceive the difference between literature and nonliterature is something everyone should possess. Without it, the freedom to make definitions is indeed dangerous. The ability to discriminate enables us to be certain whether a book is a form of entertainment or a product of literature that enriches the spiritual life of its readers.

Notes

Pramoedya Ananta Toer. "Definisi dan Keindahan dalam Kesusastraan." 1952, 2004. Translated and published as "The Definition of Literature and the Question of Beauty" with the permission of Astuti Ananta Toer and the extended family of Pramoedya Ananta Toer.

1. *Mimbar Penyiaran DUTA* was a "Literary and Features Agency" set up and managed by Pramoedya himself in 1952. It was intended as a kind of clearinghouse, receiving articles on the arts, culture, and literature for distribution to the printed media in Jakarta and beyond (Koesalah xiii).

2. Pramoedya himself was known to be in the habit of singing "Swing Low, Sweet Chariot" (Aleida 90).

3. See Lubis's "A List of Indonesian Writers and Artists" in part II.

4. These terms, drawn from a variety of regional Indonesian languages, are honorifics or part of the accepted forms of address for royalty and other indigenous nobility. Their use as honorifics derives from the notion that the speaker only dares address the feet of a highly respected person.

5. Here Pramoedya draws from Greene's essay "Henry James: The Private Universe," which quotes Wilfred Owen's phrase "The poetry is in the pity" (29).

3

S. M. Ardan's "Pramoedya Heads Overseas" (1953)

This news article by journalist and short story writer S. M. Ardan was originally published on 6 June 1953 in *Dwiwarna*, a daily newspaper in the Central Javanese city of Solo. Republished in an incomplete form on 20 July 1953 in the Jakarta periodical *Duta Suasana*, it was written on the occasion of Pramoedya Ananta Toer's May 1953 departure for the Netherlands under the auspices of the Dutch Foundation for Cultural Cooperation (STICUSA).[1] Established in February 1948, STICUSA aimed to promote cultural exchange between the Netherlands and its current, contested, and former colonial territories (Dolk). Among the programs STICUSA sponsored was a series of residencies in the Netherlands that enabled a number of young Indonesian writers and artists—among them Pramoedya Ananta Toer—to gain firsthand experience of Dutch cultural and social life in the early years of Indonesian independence. In Pramoedya's case, however, the goodwill toward the former colonial power that these residencies were designed to foster was not forthcoming. Pramoedya stayed only six months in the Netherlands, and on his return to Indonesia accused STICUSA of harboring neocolonialist ambitions through the import of Western culture into Indonesia (Dolk 71–72, Liu 123). His reaction to Dutch life was in many ways ambiguous (Foulcher, "On" 14–16), but the negative aspects of his response to this firsthand view of the West are usually seen as marking the beginning of the shift in his cultural and literary outlooks that by the early 1960s led him to espouse a practice of art and literature that drew influence from the Chinese socialist realism of the period (Liu 139–42).

Evidently drawing on an interview with Pramoedya that took place before his departure, Ardan's article mentions Pramoedya's imprisonment by Dutch military authorities during the period of national revolution and discusses the way this period of imprisonment was intertwined with his writing career. Resentment toward the Dutch as a result of Pramoedya's nationalist convictions and experience of imprisonment no doubt contributed to the failure of his 1953 STICUSA-sponsored residency. Yet in the early writings that Ardan mentions here, it is the suffering of the Indonesian people under Japanese occupation during World War II that is as much a focus of Pramoedya's attention as the later war of independence against the Dutch. Like most Indonesians of his generation, Pramoedya had witnessed the starvation, torture, and slave labor that increasingly came to characterize Indonesia's experience of Japanese rule between 1942 and 1945, and like other writers of the period, he recorded in his creative writing some of the suffering and enduring bitterness these experiences occasioned.[2]

In Ardan's discussions and descriptions of the interview, readers see a view of an early-career Pramoedya, already reading widely and internationally, with Richard Wright named as one of his favorite authors. Intriguingly, the news article also reports on the beginnings of Pramoedya's conflicts with Takdir Alisjahbana and, perhaps by proxy, with the larger group of universal humanists who came into the orbit of Takdir's journal *Konfrontasi*. Knowledge of this early schism between Pramoedya and Takdir may provide a partial explanation for why Pramoedya, who was widely known to hold Wright as a favorite author, seems to have remained outside Wright's *Konfrontasi*-dominated circle of literary and cultural acquaintances in Indonesia.

Pramoedya Heads Overseas
by S. M. Ardan
SOURCE LANGUAGE: INDONESIAN

In May this year, the eldest child of a big family who was born in Blora on 6 February 1925, left for a period of study in the Netherlands. He was traveling on a scholarship from STICUSA, the Dutch-Indonesian Foundation for Cultural Exchange, which has sent many Indonesian artists to the Netherlands on a regular basis.

Pramoedya Ananta Toer is our most productive writer, both in terms of the work he produced during his imprisonment and what he has written since. His time in prison was a very important defining moment for Pramoedya. Because it was in prison that his talent emerged and developed, finally reaching its peak. Many people said that it was because of his imprisonment that Pramoedya became so productive, leading Rusman Sutiasumarga to wish that he had been imprisoned so that he might have been productive too. But Pram's productivity rested on an enormous imaginative capability; it wasn't just the result of imprisonment. He proved this with his continued productivity once he was released. However it must be said that the work he has produced in an environment of freedom is not of the same level as the work he produced while he was in prison.

Nevertheless, if we wish to understand Pramoedya's worldview, the experience of prison is very significant. In prison, he mixed with true revolutionaries and true bandits. He got to know humankind with its genuine and deeply hidden desires and passions, ideals, and hopes. It is all revealed in his writing, especially in the novel *Mereka Jang Dilumpuhkan* [The Paralyzed Ones]. It is here that he reveals, unpeels, and exposes the very center, the ultimate contours of the human heart.

Here, and also in *Keluarga Gerilja* [A Guerrilla Family], he tells of humankind with all its conceit and weaknesses, the human being who grows wild out of a sense of duty, from the pressures of life, from the force of his convictions. But in the end, humankind is no more and no less than human, and the time comes when his true humanity is revealed.

The things Pramoedya despises are killing, destruction, rape. These are things that awaken feelings of disgust in human beings generally, but Pram despises them without regard to the person committing the crime. He abhors the guilty party whether he happens to be a member of the Dutch administration attempting to reoccupy Indonesia, the Communist leader Musso, a member of the Indonesian National Army, or whatever. He doesn't care. He despises all of them! This attitude is reflected in his stories, especially in his book *Dia Jang Menjerah* [She Who Surrendered].[3]

Dia Jang Menjerah brought him into conflict with Sutan Takdir Alisjahbana. There was a series of polemics between them in *Merdeka* magazine. The problem was that Takdir issued the work in book form as well as a special edition of *Pudjangga Baru*, whereas Pram had only given his approval for publication in the journal.[4] The matter is still unresolved, because Pram does not feel his grasp of copyright law is sufficient to bring charges against Takdir, even though there are many people who support him and are prepared to stand with him. He says he has made a study of (Dutch-language) copyright law, in order to face up to Takdir. But till now, nothing more has been reported. It is regrettable indeed that in a sovereign and independent Indonesia, copyright is still unclear. And there the matter of Pram-Takdir rests. If this situation persists, writers, whose living conditions are already strained, will find themselves having the life squeezed out of them by publishers. In the end, they will wither and die. This is another cause for regret that Balai Pustaka is going under.[5]

This unfortunate course of events persists, and the matter has been, is, and continues to be a cause for concern. And where is the BMKN in all of this?

Where recognition as a writer is concerned, Pram himself proposes that writers everywhere should keep on writing. "Write as much as you can, and write what you want to write. Don't worry about quality in the first instance," he says. "If I had waited for recognition as a writer before believing I could write quality work, I wouldn't have written a single thing."[6]

In other words, Pram would say that a writer must take responsibility himself for his own fate. A work emerges out of a long period of sedimentation. A writer should not be too quick to find his own work satisfactory. He should keep on seriously evaluating it, keep on improving it.

"People who feel they have reached the heights are conceited. And people like this are soon destroyed," he says.

Pram despises writers who boast of their achievements. "'I write not to make money, but please give me advance payment anyway,'" Pram says with a sneer. "The fellow thinks he is a prophet. Prophets need to eat too."[7]

Look at the way Pram dealt with his "drought" as a creative writer. He kept on writing, turning out analyses and critiques for his publishing outlet *Duta*. This is another indication of the way writing is a necessity for him. He didn't become a writer because he was in jail. In the Japanese period he had already come up with two books that he had sent to a publisher, with no response. Whether it was because they didn't contain the spirit advocated by the Japanese, or whether because he was unknown at the time, is something he didn't explain.

"My family is a family possessed of sensitivity," Pram said when we were discussing his book *Bukan Pasar Malam*. His two younger brothers, Koesalah Soebagyo Toer and Soesilo Toer, are still in school, following in the footsteps of their oldest brother. In their short stories, their style, use of rhythm, and choice of words is reminiscent of that of Pram, something he says is because their family upbringing is the same. As both Soebagyo and Soesilo are still growing up, it isn't yet possible for us to determine whether they, or one of them, will be the equal of, or better than, their older brother. But this isn't important!

Apart from his original works and his subsequent analyses, Pramoedya has also translated John Steinbeck's *Of Mice and Men* and Tolstoy's *Return to Your Love.*[8] The American Negro writer, Richard Wright, is also a favorite of his.

Pramoedya has published many books: *Perburuan* [The Fugitive], *Keluarga Gerilja* [A Guerrilla Family], *Dia Jang Menjerah* [She Who Surrendered], *Mereka Jang Dilumpuhkan* [The Paralyzed Ones], *Di Tepi Kali Bekasi* [On the Banks of the Bekasi River], *Bukan Pasar Malam* [Life's Not a Night Bazaar], and the short story collections: *Subuh* [Dawn], *Pertjikan Revolusi* [Sparks of Revolution], *Tjerita dari Blora* [Stories from Blora], and most recently *Gulat di Djakarta* [Struggle in Jakarta]. Nevertheless, it can be said that there are still very few introductions to his work. Let us wish him bon voyage. Till we meet again. We await whatever he brings us from his travels.

Once again: Bon Voyage!!

Notes

1. See PATC for clippings of both articles.

2. See for example Pramoedya's story "Dia Yang Menyerah," 171–80.

3. Pramoedya's "Dia Yang Menyerah" is a work of fiction based on his own family's experiences of war and revolution. Because it appears in his story collection *Cerita dari Blora*, it may logically be considered a story. Yet Ardan discusses "Dia Yang Menyerah" as a book, which probably reflects the idea that the story's length, at fifty pages, positions it as a novella. Because Ardan discusses it as a book, we have italicized its title in the text of this essay.

4. Takdir's publishing house, Pustaka Rakjat, published the piece as *Dia Jang Menjerah* in 1950.

5. Balai Pustaka was established in the early twentieth century by the Dutch colonial administration as a publishing house for the provision of reading material in indigenous languages for the native population (Jedamski). After independence, it became an Indonesian government publishing house, which printed and distributed many significant works of Indonesian literature during the years of national revolution and early independence. By 1953, however, it was becoming one of the targets of cultural critics who declared that a "crisis" existed in Indonesian literature as a result of the loss of revolutionary élan (Teeuw, *Modern* 139–42). In 1957 Pramoedya joined Balai Pustaka's critics, publishing two articles in which he deplored the decline in Balai Pustaka's reputation since the end of the colonial period (Pramoedya, "Balai Pustaka Harum" and "Balai Pustaka Dialam").

6. The literal meaning of Pramoedya's quoted words here is unclear. We have offered a free translation based on our considered attempt to interpret this particular passage in the source text.

7. For clarity, we have added quotation marks to the spoken material in this paragraph and the paragraph preceding it. The single quotation marks within the double quotation marks indicate our understanding that Pramoedya is mockingly parroting the words of those who would situate themselves as "prophets" among literary figures.

8. *Return to Your Love* is our English translation of the title *Kembali Kepada Tjinta Kasihmu*, which is the Indonesian-language title of Pramoedya's translation of Tolstoy's 1859 novella *Family Happiness*. Pramoedya translated Tolstoy's novella into Indonesian from the Dutch translation, *Huwelijksgeluk*, and it was published by Balai Pustaka in 1950. See Teeuw, *Pramoedya* 381.

4

De Preangerbode's Review of *The Outsider* (1954)

The following review of Wright's 1953 novel *The Outsider* appeared in Dutch in the Bandung-based Dutch-language newspaper *De Preangerbode*, described in its masthead as a "General Indies Daily." The unsigned article was published on 28 September 1954 in the newspaper's "New Publications" section. One of several colonial-era Dutch-language newspapers that continued publication in the early years of Indonesian independence, *De Preangerbode* was founded in 1896 under the editorship of the Dutch playwright Jan Fabricius (1871–1964). In the early twentieth century, it developed a reputation for its liberal and ethical inclinations.[1]

Even though most of Wright's Indonesian interlocutors spoke Dutch, they were committed Indonesian nationalists who were vitally concerned with the development and propagation of the Indonesian language, as an embodiment of the new Indonesian nation. By the mid-1950s there was a well-developed and diverse Indonesian-language press, where the political and cultural issues of the day were reported and debated, and Wright's interlocutors were prominent producers and consumers of this new media culture. Indeed, as we mentioned in this book's introduction, Wright's host in Jakarta, Mochtar Lubis, was editor-in-chief of the prominent newspaper *Indonesia Raya*.

In spite of their nationalist commitments to the Indonesian language, Wright's hosts read widely in Dutch and other European languages, and it is highly likely that the Dutch translation of Wright's most recent novel was well known to them by the time of his visit. In 1956 Asrul Sani wrote of being able to purchase the novel in Jakarta as a mass-market paperback, apparently the New American Library's Signet Giant edition,[2] but as *De Preangerbode*'s review indicates, by September 1954 the novel was already available in Indonesia in Dutch translation, and some of Wright's hosts may well have first encountered the novel in its Dutch version. In this regard, it is worth noting that in October 1955 a Jakarta bookseller was offering the Dutch translation by mail order as one of its most frequently requested titles (Goede). Given this level of interest in the novel, this review of *De Buitenstaander* (The Outsider) may well have found readers among those Indonesians who regarded Wright as a significant representative of modern world literature and who invited him into their midst in the days after his attendance at the Asian-African Conference.

Review of *The Outsider*
from De Preangerbode

SOURCE LANGUAGE: DUTCH

Richard Wright, the American Negro writer who achieved world renown for his *Niggerboy*,[3] has written a new book, *The Outsider*, now available in a sound Dutch translation by Margrit de Sablonière entitled *De Buitenstaander*, and published by A. W. Sijthoff & Co. in Leiden.

The impression this new work made on us can be summarized in one word: chilling.

It deals with the last months in the life of the American Negro Cross, a human being without hope, without love, without hate, without fear. The book confronts us with a great number of questions about modern man, its central theme being the embodiment of the collective behavior of the whole of mankind in the individual Cross. That is why Cross kills without hating, why he expresses affection without love in his heart, and why he lives without being truly alive. In between events that follow one another at a frenzied pace—a series of horrors—Wright philosophizes about mankind and his world. To that end, he allows Cross to enter into contact with the Communist Party of the United States, an area where Wright, as a reformed Communist, finds himself in the same company as thinkers like Koestler and Gide. He browbeats his readers with fascinating disquisitions on man and industrialization, man and his racial problems, man and his fear, and man and his *"Untruth."*

"Primitive man, naked and afraid, found that only one thing could really quiet his terrors: that is, Untruth. He stuffed his head full of myths, and if he had not, he might well have died from fear itself [. . .] The ancient nations today we call great are the ones who left behind them those towering monuments of fear in the forms of their so-called cultures."[4]

Wright allows his desperado Cross to come out with this example in a debate with a Communist.

The fact that the nightmare in which we live is not yet—God be thanked—accepted as a normal condition, and that, on the contrary, our inner selves rise up against us, is conveyed to us by Wright on the protagonist's deathbed, when Cross says, "It (the killing) was horrible, because in my heart I felt I was innocent."[5]

Notes

1. The term "ethical" here refers to the newspaper's support for changes introduced in Dutch colonial policy at the beginning of the twentieth century that were based on "professions of concern for the welfare of Indonesians." These changes were collectively known as the "Ethical policy" (Ricklefs 193).

2. See Asrul's "Richard Wright: The Artist Turned Intellectual" in part III.

3. The epithet *Niggerboy* appears in the Dutch original. The 1953 Dutch translation of Wright's *Black Boy* carries the title *Negerjongen*.

4. For this translation from the book review's Dutch, we draw on Wright, *Outsider* 478–79. The brackets, which are ours, indicate where the review elides material from the quote in Wright's original English. In Wright's original, the final sentence of this quotation is placed within a parenthesis and ends with an exclamation point.

5. The Dutch-language quotation from *The Outsider* (here back-translated into English) originally appeared in Wright's *The Outsider* as follows: "It . . . It was . . . horrible . . . ," followed later by "Because in my heart . . . I'm . . . I felt . . . I'm *innocent* . . ." (586).

5

Beb Vuyk's "Stories in the Modern Manner" (1955)

Two months before Richard Wright's arrival in Indonesia, the Dutch-Indonesian writer Beb Vuyk published an article titled "Stories in the Modern Manner" in Mochtar Lubis's Jakarta-based daily newspaper *Indonesia Raya* (9 February 1955). Vuyk was born in Rotterdam in 1905, the daughter of a Dutch-Indonesian shipbuilder; her paternal grandmother was from the Indonesian island of Madura, near the port city of Surabaya in East Java. As a child in the Netherlands, Vuyk was mocked because of her "Indo," or mixed Indonesian and European, appearance. Having decided at a young age to become a writer and travel to Indonesia, she left the Netherlands in 1929 and spent some years in the isolated eastern reaches of the Indonesian archipelago. After Japan's invasion of the Dutch East Indies during World War II, she spent three years in Japanese concentration camps. When Indonesia emerged as a sovereign state in 1949, following a four-year struggle to defend its 1945 declaration of independence, Vuyk took the courageous step of assuming Indonesian citizenship (Beekman 468–70).[1]

Within a few years of doing so, Vuyk emerged as a significant figure among Indonesian cultural and literary modernists. By 1955, she was one of three editors of the magazine *Konfrontasi* and a prominent member of the magazine's study club. She was also a regular contributor to *Indonesia Raya*'s weekly cultural-literary news column, *Kebudajaan-Kesusasteraan*, in which her article "Stories in the Modern Manner" appeared.

Although it situates itself as a review of the 1953 collection *Stories in the Modern Manner: A Collection of Stories from the Partisan Review*, Vuyk's article is mainly concerned with offering Indonesian readers a view of the left-democratic (and CIA-funded) *Partisan Review*'s place in the larger European-American constellation of literary journals and "little magazines."[2] Vuyk's narrative draws on, quotes from, and expands on certain points made in the 1946 essay "In Retrospect: Ten Years of *Partisan Review*" by *Partisan Review* editors William Phillips and Philip Rahv, which discusses *Partisan Review*'s history in general and offers commentary on its relation to the genre and tradition of the little magazine (684–85). According to Vuyk's narrative, little magazines emerged in the United States a few years before World War I and continued into the 1950s with magazines like *Partisan Review*. In Vuyk's view, the London-based CCF publication *Encounter* is something of a cousin to *Partisan Review*.

Vuyk's narrative of the emergence and contributions of little magazines to American and European cultures is significant in the context of modern Indonesia, which, especially after the revolution, saw a proliferation of publishing venues producing little magazines. Such Indonesian publications of the day included not only *Konfrontasi* and *Gelanggang* but also *Zenith*, *Budaya*, *Indonesia: Madjalah Kebudajaan*, and many others, including, eventually, *Horison*, which as previously mentioned sought common cause with the CCF magazine *Encounter*. Assuming a political orientation that resonated strongly with the CCF's agenda, *Horison* emerged as the mouthpiece of Indonesia's anti-Communist and anti-Soekarno "Generation of 66" (Hill, "Two" 252–55; Teeuw, *Modern* 253–54).

At a certain point in her article, Vuyk discusses American literature's influence on German and Italian literature but maintains that these two European literary traditions "are not being Americanized, but rather, regenerated." It would be consistent with this view, and also consistent with the views expressed in the "Gelanggang Testimony of Beliefs" (Asrul, "Surat"), to suggest that even when postwar Indonesian literary culture engaged the world's literary and political cultures (including those in Asia, Europe, the Americas, Australia, and to a lesser extent Africa), the arbiters of Indonesian literary culture would have seen this engagement not as an abandoning of Indonesian culture in favor of other world cultures but as Indonesia's robust participation in what Vuyk, in her article, refers to as a modern process of "constant exchange and mutual influence across national borders in the field of art and literature."

Of course, one upcoming moment of mutual influence between Indonesia and Euro-America was Wright's April-May visit to Indonesia, which would be discussed in a handful of Indonesian little magazines. And yet, as we see in Vuyk's article, the conditions of mutual influence between Wright and modern Indonesia were already in place, present beneath the surface and sometimes already emerging. As Vuyk narrates in her article, Wright's literary work was a prominent part of the turbulent literary and social milieu from which *Partisan Review* emerged. In fact, in 1935, Wright published in *Partisan Review* a poem titled "Between the World and Me," from which he later quoted extensively in the 1957 version of his lecture for the Konfrontasi Study Club ("Literature" 760–62). Also notable is Vuyk's view of the CCF magazine *Encounter* (in which Wright would shortly publish his article "Indonesian Notebook") as a leading light among literary magazines of the 1950s. Furthermore, in referring to Richard Wright, André Gide, Stephen Spender, and Ignazio Silone, Vuyk's article discusses four of the six contributors to Richard Crossman's 1949 anti-Communist collection *The God That Failed*, which was published in Indonesian translation by the "Front Anti-Komunis" Indonesia, just two months before Wright's arrival in Indonesia (Hakim).

Stories in the Modern Manner
by Beb Vuyk
SOURCE LANGUAGE: INDONESIAN

Appearing in the Avon Series is *Stories in the Modern Manner*, and Bantam Giant has published Carson McCullers's *Seven*. Both these books are of much higher quality than the "pocketbook" usually associated with these publishers.

Stories in the Modern Manner is a collection of stories published in recent years in *Partisan Review*. The stories were selected by Philip Rahv and William Phillips, the magazine's editors, as modern stories of high literary value. *Partisan Review* is the largest of the so-called "Little Magazines." Originally, these magazines were dedicated to ensuring that American literature was free of the influence of regionalism and isolationism, presenting a point of view that went beyond American national borders. They made known the various trends in modern art in America itself, but they also introduced their readers to artists like Picasso, Rimbaud, Proust, and James Joyce, along with movements like Dadaism, Futurism, and Expressionism. Their circulation figures were small, but there were many little magazines, and their influence on the development of literature was significant. They appeared not long before World War I, and gradually changed their style, becoming less extreme and acquiring the character of guides to literature. This change was related to the emergence of universities as centers of literature, where many poets and writers found employment as professors. This focused their attention on the work of mentoring their peers and the issues confronting literature at that time. Many of these little magazines came to be publications of small universities, like *Sewanee Review* from the University of the South in Tennessee, and *Kenyon Review*, which began to be published in 1939 under the leadership of John Crowe Ransom, a well-known poet and critic and an influential professor of literature at Kenyon College.

Partisan Review began publication in the years of crisis, a time of enormous social deprivation, when writers like John Dos Passos, James Farrell, and Richard Wright began to publish their work. In the first issue, which appeared in February 1934, the publishers (Philip Rahv and William Phillips, the compilers of this collection) embraced Marxist philosophy, Soviet Russia, and revolutionary aesthetics. The magazine was the publication of the John Reed Club, an organization of prominent writers who were sympathetic to the communists. But a conflict soon arose on the editorial board, because however radical they might have been in the political field, William Phillips and Philip Rahv were unwilling to see art used as a tool of political propaganda.

"Nor could we go along with our comrades of the *New Masses* and other communist publications in their practice of ignoring the difference between good and bad writing in order to judge it primarily on grounds of political expediency, namely whether or not its political content coincided with the current specifications of the party line."[3]

This conflict of opinion, coming in the wake of the famous Moscow trials of 1936, brought about a split with the party. The editors of *Partisan Review* and many of their contributors suffered a sense of disillusionment, just like the European writers and artists who had sided with Moscow because of their political convictions. They were unable to surrender the intellectual freedom which set a premium on personal opinion. Gide in France, Plievier and his friends in Germany, Stephen Spender, Isherwood and Auden in Britain, Jef Last in the Netherlands, Ignazio Silone in Italy—these are just some examples.

Over the years, *Partisan Review* developed into a magazine with a broad cultural base, although it tended toward the left in political matters. The magazine's political radicalism is visible in opinion pieces, but other inclusions are selected entirely on the basis of their literary value.

Seven of the thirteen contributions to this book are by American writers: Jean Stafford, Saul Bellow, Charles Jackson, Lionel Trilling, Delmore Schwartz, Isaac Rosenfeld, and Max Wiseman. The others are by four French writers: André Gide, Marcel Aymé, Jean Genet, and Jean Cocteau; the Russian writer Isaac Babel from the post-revolutionary period, who was sidelined at the time of the Moscow trials; and finally the Italian writer Alberto Moravia, who is known in Indonesia for his novel *Woman of Rome*. *Partisan Review* has continued to publish works of literature from other countries. This is in the tradition of the earliest of the Little Magazines, which introduced trends in modern European literature into America, but it is also characteristic of literary magazines in Europe. The British magazines *Horizon* and *Penguin New Writing* made room for foreign literature from the beginning, and this tradition has been continued by *Encounter*. French magazines have shown the same concern. In *Les Temps Modernes*, Sartre has written extensively about American literature, which he much admires. The magazine also includes many translations from English.

I have discussed the very significant influence that American literature has had on modern German and Italian literature in previous book reviews. With the exception of countries behind the Iron Curtain, there is now constant exchange and mutual influence across national borders in the field of art and literature. Indeed, in reality this has always been the case, but it is now explicit practice in a number of magazines and a number of writers have contributed their energies to it. The results are not a uniform type of literature, but diversity of style and form, because domestic literatures are being influenced by foreign examples. As such, American influence is discernible on young German and Italian writers, but this doesn't mean German literature resembles modern Italian literature. German and Italian literatures are not being Americanized, but rather, regenerated.

For those drawn to the interesting phenomenon of mutual influence, this collection contains a lot of useful material. I leave Carson McCullers's book for another occasion.

Notes

Beb Vuyk. "Stories in the Modern Manner." 1955. Translated and published as "Stories in the Modern Manner" with the permission of Joke de Willigen-Riekerk.

1. For more on Vuyk's life and work, see Scova Righini. For a short biography see Kloek 1338–40.

2. On the *Partisan Review* and the CIA, see Saunders 132–37.

3. In Vuyk's original article, this quotation appears twice, first as an Indonesian translation and then as Phillips and Rahv's original English-language quotation, as it appears in their 1946 essay "In Retrospect: Ten Years of *Partisan Review*" (681). In Phillips and Rahv's original, the term *comrades* appears in quotation marks and the term *communist* is capitalized.

Part II   An Asian-African Encounter

6

A Sheaf of Newspaper Articles: Richard Wright in Indonesia's Daily Press (1955)

Originally proposed by the Indonesian prime minister Ali Sastroamidjojo, the Asian-African Conference was conceived and planned during two meetings—involving the prime ministers of India, Burma, Indonesia, Ceylon, and Pakistan—in the cities of Colombo (Ceylon) and Bogor (Indonesia) during 1954 (Ministry 11–13, 161). In the wake of these planning sessions, representatives from twenty-nine countries converged on the city of Bandung in 1955 for the 18–24 April conference.[1] At the conference's conclusion, these countries unanimously affirmed its Final Communique (6), which advocated for action and principled stances vis-à-vis economic cooperation, cultural cooperation, human rights and self-determination, problems of dependent peoples, territorial disputes, and world peace and cooperation based on human rights, territorial integrity, racial equality, non-interference, and self-defense (161–69). As Richard Wright described it in *The Color Curtain*, this was "a meeting of almost all of the human race living in the main geopolitical center of gravity of the earth" (438), and it was, unsurprisingly, a major international news event, with over four hundred reporters in attendance, hailing from Indonesia and all parts of the world.[2] Prominent among these reporters, Wright was often singled out, as in the 1980 memoir of the conference's secretary general, Indonesian diplomat Roeslan Abdulgani, who recalls the presence of "Richard Wright, the famous Negro writer" who later "wrote his famous book: *The Colour Curtain*" (65).

Wright's international stature was such that even as he joined his peers in taking notes and commenting on the conference, the press in Indonesia was taking notes and commenting on him. Indeed, from Wright's arrival on 12 April through his departure on 5 May, the daily press in Indonesia took a marked interest in his appearances, activities, and statements. The following fifteen newspaper items are drawn from Indonesian-, Dutch-, and English-language newspapers, with seven from *Indonesia Raya* (Indonesian language), three from *Het Nieuwsblad voor Sumatra* (Dutch language), two from *De Nieuwsgier* (Dutch language), one from *Pedoman* (Indonesian language), one from *Java Bode* (Dutch language), and one from *Indonesian Observer* (English language).[3]

Because *Indonesia Raya* editor Mochtar Lubis was Wright's host, Wright may be considered to have had a home newspaper in Mochtar's newspaper, which was aligned with the Partai Sosialis Indonesia (PSI, Indonesian Socialist Party). Carrying a front-page photograph of Wright on his arrival in the country, *Indonesia Raya* also took prominent umbrage with the Asian-African Conference's choice of accommodations for Wright during his first night in the country after flying into Jakarta. After settling into his accommodations at the Hotel Shutte Raaf, Wright wrote in his travel journal that the official welcoming committee had sent him to a hotel where he was assigned a dark, damp, and foul-smelling room with no electric lighting or proper ventilation ("Jakarta" 98). The very next day, on 13 April, *Indonesia Raya* took up the matter of Wright's accommodations, suggesting that this failure on the part of the conference organizing committee risked harming Indonesia's reputation among important visitors to the country. By 14 April, the PSI's official daily newspaper, *Pedoman*, was repeating *Indonesia Raya*'s indignant opinion that providing Asian-African Conference visitors "with a gloomy room next to the toilet amounts to nothing more than throwing cold water on guests to our country." At the same time, *Indonesia Raya* was now extending the implications of Wright's substandard hotel room, drawing attention to the Japanese journalist who had accompanied him to the hotel and suggesting that perhaps the Japanese journalist was intentionally placed in substandard accommodations with the goal of making "the point that Indonesia is still awaiting war reparations from Japan." The tale of Wright's accommodations reverberated as far as the neighboring Indonesian island of Sumatra, as, during the conference itself, *Het Nieuwsblad voor Sumatra* included a paragraph on the topic in its roundup of conference news (19 April).

FIGURE 6.1. Mochtar Lubis seated among journalists "who used the [Bandung] conference as a means of cementing their long-separated relationships and formed an Asian-
African Journalists Association." Film still and quotation excerpted from the ten-minute
news film "Konperensi Asia Afrika" (1955), produced by Indonesia's government-owned
film company, Perusahaan Film Negara. Konperensi Asia Afrika, reel 1, cassette 354.
Courtesy of Arsip Nasional Republik Indonesia.

Beyond illustrating the ways the small incident of Wright's accommodations could become a pretext for certain segments of the Indonesian media to
voice displeasure with conference organizers, the daily press offers details on
some of the social and cultural activities Wright engaged in before and after
the conference. As 15 April articles in *De Nieuwsgier* and *Java Bode* describe,
on the evening of 14 April Wright attended an art event that was organized by
the Jajasan Impresariat Indonesia (Indonesian Impresario Foundation) and
hosted at the home of Soediro, mayor of Jakarta from 1953 through 1960. In
his travel journal, Wright seems dismissive of the event, describing it as con-
servative and bourgeois to the same degree as art events in Chicago, Madrid,
and London ("Jakarta" 113). Seen in this light, readers will detect a degree of
antibourgeois pique on Wright's part in these two Dutch-language newspapers'
report that he spoke at the event with a greeting given on behalf of the "ordinary poor people" of North and South America. By the conclusion of Wright's
stay in Indonesia, as we learn from a 4 May article in *Indonesia Raya*, he had
met some of the most prominent Indonesian politicians of the day, and he had
spoken during the first days of May before a group of Indonesian writers at
the mountain villa of Takdir Alisjahbana and before the PEN Club and BMKN

at the Cultural Center in Jakarta. At another point, according to the caption beneath a 21 May 1955 *Indonesia Raya* illustration (published after Wright's departure), he addressed a group of university students. Though Wright did "not particularly relish public speaking" and confessed that it evoked in him "reluctance" and "malingering" (Wright, *White* 15), the social interactions that these Indonesian events permitted were indeed part of his goals for the trip. As he reportedly told *De Nieuwsgier* on his arrival in Indonesia, "I am staying in Indonesia until the beginning of May, and I hope to meet a great many people here. If my notes turn out to be worth it, I will be writing a book about my experiences."

Wright, of course, took notes not only on individuals he met but on the larger Asian-African Conference, and as Wright was taking notes in Indonesia, so too were the reporters for Indonesia-based newspapers taking notes on him. Reports of Wright at the conference itself range from those that give detailed attention to his opinions to others merely noting his presence as a minor element in the kaleidoscope of a much larger geopolitical event. *Indonesia Raya* noted (14 April) that Wright had arrived to cover the conference as a "correspondent for *Encounter* magazine," which was an accurate statement of his affiliation even if it departed from the official freelance designation that Wright and the CCF had agreed on. The *Indonesian Observer* and later the *Times of Indonesia* offered an article giving a focused look at Wright's frustration with Africa's place at the conference, and *Indonesia Raya* (21 April) and *Het Nieuwsblad voor Sumatra* (22 April) mentioned Wright briefly (in one article he is nonplussed by crowds of indiscriminate autograph-seekers, and in the other he is uniquely from Paris among "Negro journalists from America"). The newspapers made these observations even as their wide-ranging articles gave more attention to the changes Bandung underwent during conference preparations, street-side applause for specific conference delegates, security measures for the event, local cultural entertainment for attendees, the reluctance of the wives of Indonesian dignitaries to entertain the second wife of a visiting head of state who had entered into a polygamous marriage, the delegates' disagreements over President Soekarno's framing of the event as the "first intercontinental conference of coloured people," and alliances among delegates hailing from particular regions and political orientations.

Some of the newspaper articles, as they include Wright in a roundup of conference and other news, also discuss issues that afford readers greater insights into the way Wright (and particularly his commentary on the Japanese) was received among his Indonesian hosts. For a window on the tense ways the Japanese were being discussed in 1950s Indonesia, we have included

Het Nieuwsblad voor Sumatra's discussion of the complexities of the Japanese delegation's attendance at the conference in light of Japan's World War II–era ideology of a "Greater East Asian Co-prosperity Sphere" (19 April),[4] and the same newspaper's announcement of a reading of Dutch writer Willem Brandt's poetry of imprisonment in Japan's World War II concentration camps in Indonesia (22 April). Such discussions help explain why, during his sojourn in the new country, Wright's comments on color commonalities between Indonesians and the Japanese sounded a dissonant note in relation to Indonesia's World War II history with Japan.

The articles appear in chronological order here, offering a sense of how Wright's travels unfolded in relation to the unfolding Bandung Conference.

Who's Doing What
Initial publication: *Indonesia Raya*, Wednesday, 13 April 1955
SOURCE LANGUAGE: INDONESIAN

"Siapa Mengapa" (translated here as "Who's Doing What") was a regular column in *Indonesia Raya* at this time. Wright appeared in the column twice during his stay, on the day after his arrival and on the day before his departure.

- Dr. Opet, a linguist and professor of Southeast Asian languages, who according to Novotny is part of a cultural mission from Czechoslovakia, has compiled a sizable Indonesian-Czech dictionary.
- Candidates in the general election from the League of Supporters of Indonesian Independence (Moluccas region) are, for the House of Representatives: Soetarto, Z. A. Leuwol, A. H. Nasution and E. J. Magenda. For the Constituent Assembly: Soetarto, A. H. Nasution, A. Soekendro and Z. A. Leuwol.
- Mr. W. D. Bartlett, head of the technical aid section of the Colombo Plan in Canada, arrived in Indonesia on 9 April to hold discussions with the State Planning Bureau and other senior government agencies. Mr. Bartlett expects to be here for a week.
- Richard Wright, the American Negro writer, arrived yesterday in Jakarta to attend the AA conference as a freelance journalist.[5]

Editorial: A Suggestion for Improvement
Initial publication: *Indonesia Raya*, Wednesday, 13 April 1955
SOURCE LANGUAGE: INDONESIAN

As the invited participants start arriving for the Asia-Africa conference, and the journalists covering the conference need to be given accommodations, the shortcomings in the preparations for incoming visitors are becoming apparent. Without wishing to underestimate the hard work and activity of those who have been making preparations since the conference was first announced, we would like to draw attention especially to the matter of the hotels in which conference participants and journalists have had to lodge in Jakarta before being able to travel on to Bandung.

Yesterday, for example, a Japanese journalist and the famous writer Richard Wright were assigned a gloomy room next to the toilet and bathroom in the Hotel Shutte Raaf. The smell from the toilet went right into the room. As it happens, both these guests, the journalist and the writer, are people who are very sympathetic to Indonesia and the Asia-Africa conference. Welcoming them with a gloomy room next to the toilet amounts to nothing more than throwing cold water on guests to our country.

As individual experiences have a great effect on the way human beings view their surroundings, we suggest that those responsible for welcoming conference participants and journalists should pay attention to matters like this. Certainly, there must be a minimum standard for the hotel rooms we are able to provide for guests arriving in this country.

We hope that this suggestion for improvement will be noted, in the interest of the reputation of the government, and also the reputation of Indonesia itself.

Richard Wright is Here
Initial publication: *De Nieuwsgier*, Wednesday, 13 April 1955
SOURCE LANGUAGE: DUTCH

Arriving in Indonesia on the KLM flight from Tokyo yesterday afternoon was the well-known American writer, Richard Wright.[6] Wright is the author of *Black Boy* and other books, and was also a contributor to *The God That Failed*, a collection put together by ex-communists. He was welcomed on behalf of PEN Club Indonesia by Achdiat Karta Mihardja and Mr. Sutan Moh. Sjah.[7]

We were only able to speak to him very briefly, because there were many AA guests on the flight, including Salah ben Yousef from Tunisia, who visited Indonesia a few months ago, and members of the Pakistani and Burmese delegations.

Mr. Wright, who lives in Paris—"But I am an American!"—will also cover the AA Conference while he is here. "The political aspects don't particularly interest me. For me it is a question of human beings," he said. "I am staying in Indonesia until the beginning of May, and I hope to meet a great many people here. If my notes turn out to be worth it, I will be writing a book about my experiences. Of course, my notes will depend on the people I get to meet."

During the conversation, we were struck by the outstanding service that the (mostly young) officials of the Department of Foreign Affairs were providing to the AA guests. It relieved them of any anxiety about immigration and customs documents and immediately put them at their ease.

Front Page Photo of Richard Wright and Caption (see fig. 6.2)
Initial publication: *Indonesia Raya*, Thursday, 14 April 1955
SOURCE LANGUAGE: INDONESIAN

Now arrived in Jakarta, Richard Wright, Correspondent for *Encounter* magazine and one of America's famous writers. Among his books are *Native Son* and *Black Boy*. He will be visiting the A-A Conference.

Richard Wright and the Smell of Toilets in the Room (see fig. 6.3)
Initial publication: *Pedoman*, Thursday, 14 April 1955
SOURCE LANGUAGE: INDONESIAN

Give some attention to the adequacy of accommodations
for journalists covering the A-A conference

Jakarta.

Recently arrived in Jakarta is the American (Negro) writer Richard Wright, who is intending to travel on to Bandung to cover the A-A Conference as a freelance journalist. Together with a Japanese journalist, he was assigned a room in the Hotel Shutte Raaf. Their room was dark, next door to the toilet and bathroom, and the smell of the toilet came right into the room.

In its editorial, *Indonesia Raya* wrote, among other things: "As it happens, both these guests, the journalist and the writer, are people who are very sympathetic to Indonesia and the Asia-Africa conference. Welcoming them with a gloomy room next to the toilet amounts to nothing more than throwing cold water on guests to our country."

As individual experiences have a great effect on the way human beings view their surroundings, we suggest that those responsible for welcoming conference participants and journalists should pay attention to matters like this."

Richard Wright is the author of books like *Native Son* and *Black Boy*, and also a contributor to the book that removed the mask from the face of communism, *The God That Failed*.

FIGURE 6.2. Front page photo of Richard Wright and caption, *Indonesia Raya*, 14 April 1955. Courtesy of the Beinecke Rare Book and Manuscript Library, Yale University.

Telah tiba di Djakarta, Richard Wright, Koresponden madjalah Encounter, dan salah seorang pengarang Amerika jang terkenal. Buku2nja antara lain adalah „Native Son" dan „Black Boy". Dia akan mengundjungi konperensi A-A-

(Gambar Antara)

FIGURE 6.3. Source text for "Richard Wright and the Smell of Toilets in the Room," front page of *Pedoman*, 14 April 1955. Courtesy of the Beinecke Rare Book and Manuscript Library, Yale University.

Curbside

Initial publication: *Indonesia Raya*, Thursday, 14 April 1955

SOURCE LANGUAGE: INDONESIAN

"Dipinggir Djalan" ("By the Side of the Road" or "Curbside") was a regular column in *Indonesia Raya* offering informal commentary on the news of the day. These two items are extracted from the column for this date.

It's AA season. A friend of mine dropped in to complain that the people on the street are really under attack at the moment from AAs. First to hit them was the Ali-Arifin cabinet,[8] then they had the AA conference in Bandung to deal with. It's gotten so bad that a lot of people have had to go looking for Aspirin Aspro to sort out their headaches, and if the AA cabinet keeps carrying on like this, the people on the street are going to end up All Awry.

Just to make a point! A journalist from Japan intending to visit the AA conference was put in a gloomy little mouse hole next to the toilet in the Hotel Shutte Raaf. The word is that it was done deliberately to make the point that Indonesia is still awaiting war reparations from Japan.

First Anniversary of the "Indonesian Impresario Foundation"
Initial publication: *Java Bode*, Friday, 15 April 1955
SOURCE LANGUAGE: DUTCH

It was one year ago yesterday that the "Indonesian Impresario Foundation" came together for the first time in the home of Mayor Soediro with the aim of uniting Jakarta's artists and in so doing to promote art in Jakarta in general. The occasion was commemorated last night by another gathering at the mayor's house in Taman Suropati that attracted many people interested in the foundation's work, yet, for unknown reasons, few of the artists the evening was primarily intended for.

The chairperson of the foundation, Mrs. Siwabessy-Putiray,[9] opened the meeting, following which Mayor Soediro delivered a few words to those present. He pointed to the importance of cooperation between artists and expressed the hope that the foundation would extend its activities in this area. He also referred to the importance of the propagation of Indonesian culture overseas, where still so little is known about Indonesia, something he experienced himself on his journey through Asia.

Next to speak was a special guest, the American writer Richard Wright, who is presently in Indonesia as a freelance journalist covering the AA-Conference. The writer of *Black Boy*, *Native Son*, *The God That Failed*, and other internationally known books, conveyed the greetings of all the "ordinary poor people" in North and South America, as well as in Europe, that he had recently visited. He told the gathering how people in the US had been supportive of the Indonesian struggle for independence and were now observing further developments in Indonesia with interest. On the AA-Conference, he remarked that it was "long overdue," by which he meant that a meeting of free Asian countries like this should have taken place sooner.

Next, Mayor Soediro, who has always displayed great interest in the artistic life of Jakarta, was presented with an oil painting by the Indonesian watercolorist, Umar Basalamah, as a token of appreciation. The painter himself was prevented from attending through illness, so it fell to Mr. Sukowati as a member of the foundation to make the presentation.

Mrs. Soediro was not forgotten as hostess of the occasion, and was presented with a magnificent cake, decorated with a ship made of chocolate.

The evening concluded with the showing of several art films, along with the film about preparations for the AA-Conference, "Bandung Menanti" [Bandung Awaits].

Artists' Evening
Initial publication: *De Nieuwsgier*, Friday, 15 April 1955
SOURCE LANGUAGE: DUTCH

Last night, Mrs. Soediro and the mayor of Jakarta hosted a reception for the city's artists. The evening was organized by the Indonesian Impresario Foundation, whose chairperson is Mrs. Siwabessy-Putiray.

Apart from the Italian ambassador, Marquis P. La Terza and the American writer Richard Wright, who is covering the AA-Conference as a freelance journalist, several film stars and painters were in attendance.

Most of the other guests were aficionados of art and artists.

Richard Wright delivered a few words of greeting from the people of North and South America. To him the AA-Conference was a perfectly reasonable idea. He even considered it long overdue. He did not want to see any further instances of some races being used by others to fight against yet other races, as had happened in the Second World War.

He went on to say that the world was waiting for Indonesia, and what its culture promised to bring to the world. "The world will bid you welcome."

To mark the first anniversary of the Foundation's establishment, the painter Umar Basalamah, who recently exhibited his work in the Kolff gallery, presented a painting to the host, Mayor Soediro.

Around and About the AA-Conference
Initial publication: *Het Nieuwsblad voor Sumatra*, Tuesday,
19 April 1955
SOURCE LANGUAGE: DUTCH

These items are extracted from a more extensive source text for this article.

The Tokyo newspaper *Yomiuri* wrote on Saturday that it was "regrettable" that Takasaki, who during the war was president of the Manchurian Society for Heavy Industry and as such was a "standard bearer" of the colonial policy of the then Japanese government, should now be assuming the role of leader of the Japanese delegation to Bandung. *Yomiuri* declared that it was also "embarrassing" that the delegation included Masayuko Tani among its members, since during the war he had been head of the information bureau of the Ministry of Foreign Affairs, which had tried to implement the Japanese ideology of a "Greater East Asian Co-Prosperity Sphere."

"That these persons have been dispatched cannot be helped," the newspaper wrote, "and we must trust that they will do their utmost to explain the new Japan to the countries of Asia. It is our wish that when they speak they will look to Asia, and not to the US."

Without wishing to detract from the hard work of those responsible for making preparations for the AA-Conference, *Indonesia Raya* wishes to draw attention to the fact that various correspondents who have transited in Jakarta on their way to Bandung have been accommodated in third-class hotel rooms. A case in point is that of the well-known writer Richard Wright and a Japanese journalist, who found themselves in a small room next to the toilet in the Hotel Shutte Raaf. Being accommodated in a room like this must have been a bitter disillusionment for both these men, who are very sympathetic to Indonesia and the AA-Conference. The newspaper expressed the hope that cases like this will not surface again in future.

Bandung during the A-A Conference
by *Indonesia Raya* reporters
Initial publication: *Indonesia Raya*, Thursday, 21 April 1955
SOURCE LANGUAGE: INDONESIAN

Chou, Nehru, and Nasser Most Popular—Police Mobilized from All Over Indonesia—"Where Do You Come From, Sir?"—Even Reporters from Jakarta Attacked by Autograph Hunters— "Hartini" from Pakistan—Regarding Mrs. Ali from Indonesia and Mrs. Ali from Pakistan.[10]
Bandung, Thursday.

The Asian-African Conference has brought the people of Bandung a new level of activity and the sense of being part of a great festival. Although the ordinary people of this city, famous for its "peuyeum,"[11] do not know much about what the delegates from the countries of Asia and Africa are talking about—other than what they read in the newspapers—and the conference centers like the "Merdeka" building (formerly Concordia) and the "Dwiwarna" building (formerly Pensioenfonds) are closed to the public, there is a great level of interest in the conference among the city's people.

FROM MORNING TILL early evening, crowds of people gather in front of the "Merdeka" building in the center of Bandung to watch the members of the various delegations alight from their cars and enter the conference halls, or leave the building whenever a session concludes.

Chou En Lai, Nehru, and Nasser most popular

The people of Bandung cheer each head of delegation, but they reserve their most enthusiastic welcome for the head of the delegation from the People's Republic of China, Chou En Lai, the Indian Prime Minister, Nehru, and the Egyptian Prime Minister, Gamal Abdel Nasser.

The state security forces have difficulty restraining the crowd when the leaders of those countries pass by, which, famously, is also usually the case in his home country when Chou is welcomed by applause from the people of the PRC.

Representatives of the Gold Coast in their colorful national costumes also attract the attention of the crowds. The photographers mostly aim their cameras at Chou and Nehru when they exchange a few words of conversation before a session begins. It is very rare to see Chou smile, and his features are almost always those of someone on the verge of anger. This was also the case when he stepped up to the rostrum to deliver his speech, which he did in Chinese. An interpreter stood beside him to translate his speech. Maybe Chou was feeling somewhat incensed by the speech delivered by the head of the Iraqi delegation, Dr. Moh. Fadhil El Jamali, who criticized communism vociferously.

Police mobilized from all over Indonesia

To maintain the security of the delegations, members of the police force with the rank of commissioner or inspector have been brought in from all over Indonesia. Of course those who have been temporarily transferred to each delegation have a full command of English. Each delegation has been assigned a police commissioner or inspector as an "aide de camp," assisted by a number of regular police officers. They wear a badge on their chests with the name of the country whose delegation they have been assigned to. The task of maintaining the security of each of the delegations is understandably an onerous responsibility. It should not be surprising that anyone wanting to enter a restricted area is subjected to very strict inspection by the security forces. Fortunately, journalists are given some freedom of movement, unlike during the Bogor Conference, when the movement of both local and foreign journalists was severely restricted.[12] While the A-A conference is under way, responsibility for the security of the city of Bandung lies with a coordinating committee consisting of Lieutenant-Colonel Kosasih, Commissioner A. Dt. Palindih, Head of the Department of National Defense and Security in West Java, and Major Roesli.

"Where do you come from, Sir?"

At night, when members of the conference delegations or foreign journalists go walking on Jalan Braga [Braga Street], taking in the Bandung air and buying souvenirs or just "window shopping," they are assailed by groups of teenagers, most of them junior high school students of various sorts. These students compete with one another in pursuit of autographs from foreign visitors, leaving the visitors somewhat nonplussed. The famous Negro writer Richard Wright was one of those who was targeted by these autograph hunters.[13]

Some of the local journalists from Jakarta have also found themselves the object of these attacks, even after telling the students that they too were Indonesians, from Jakarta. "Where do you come from, Sir?" was one of the questions put to the *Pedoman* reporter Amir Daud, who, it would seem, looks like someone from South Korea. All Amir's efforts to avoid these "attackers" were in vain, and he was forced to write his signature in some of their notebooks. Drenched in sweat, he finally managed to escape them. Several other journalists met the same fate. The people of Bandung, all out and about because the shops on Jalan Braga are open at night to mark the A-A conference, just laugh at incidents like this.

Attractions during the conference

While the conference is in session, a number of restaurants are putting on nightly displays of a variety of dances, martial arts, *wayang golek* puppetry, and other art forms.[14]

Every night, people flood into restaurants like Naga Mas, Merdeka, Baltic, Snoephuis, and Bogerijen for these shows. Last night for example the Naga Mas held a "Batik Show,"[15] with many of Bandung's most prominent ladies appearing as models.

The proceeds from these shows go to charity.

"Hartini" from Pakistan

One evening there was an uproar among the crowds walking up and down Jalan Braga, when a rumor started to spread that "Hartini from Pakistan" was there. It appeared that Prime Minister Moh. Ali from Pakistan and his second wife, his former secretary, were browsing Jalan Braga, moving in and out of shops along the way. The police had a hard time dispersing the crowds that gathered around the shops visited by these distinguished guests.

It was reported that Mrs. Ali Sastroamidjojo kept her distance from this second wife of the Pakistani Prime Minister. When Prime Minister Ali Sastroamidjojo and PM Ali were ambassadors of Indonesia and Pakistan respectively to the United States some years ago, Mrs. Ali Sastroamidjojo knew the Pakistani PM's second wife as his secretary, someone who was not her equal.

Apparently, while Mrs. Moh. Ali was in Bandung, the wives of the Indonesian dignitaries did not go out of their way to entertain her. This may have been because Perwari and other Indonesian women's organizations found it difficult to deal with a woman who was the second wife of a head of state.[16]

Cultural News

Initial publication: *Het Nieuwsblad voor Sumatra*,
Friday, 22 April 1955

SOURCE LANGUAGE: DUTCH

The "Cultural News" column regularly listed a roundup of news items. These two items are extracted from the column for this date.

As part of the commemoration of the 10th anniversary of liberation in the Netherlands on 5 May next, ten poets have been invited to read a few of their poems from the period of the resistance or the concentration camps, in the Amsterdam Municipal Theater. An indication that this gesture also extends to Dutch people who suffered under the Japanese Occupation in Indonesia can be seen in the fact that among these poets is Willem Brandt, who will read a number of poems from his collection, *Binnen Japansch Prikkeldraad* [Behind Japanese Barbed Wire]. However, in view of the poet's absence abroad on 5 May, the task of reading his poems will be assumed by the well-known declaimer of poetry, the Honorable Mrs. Witsen-Elias, who will present a number of Willem Brandt's poems on that occasion, poems referring to the suffering of Dutch people in the Japanese camps during the last world war.

Richard Wright, the famous Negro writer who fled America and now lives in Paris, is at this moment in Bandung, where he is attending the AA-Conference as a journalist. His well-known books are: *Native Son*, *Uncle Tom's Children*, and *The Outsider*.

Impressions from Bandung
Initial publication: *Het Nieuwsblad voor Sumatra,*
Friday, 22 April 1955
SOURCE LANGUAGE: DUTCH

Our principal editor, who is also Indonesian correspondent for the Amsterdam daily *De Tijd*, is presently staying in Bandung in that capacity. In this article, he records his impressions for *Het Nieuwsblad voor Sumatra*.

Bandung, 20 April

Bandung is caught up in the atmosphere of the AA-Conference. Thousands of people fill the streets in an attempt to catch a glimpse of the conference participants. And no sooner do the guests leave their specially designated streets than they are besieged by young people asking for autographs.

The shopkeepers in Bandung are doing well out of it all. The trade in souvenirs is brisk, and many shops have not hesitated to raise their prices dramatically for the occasion. The price of foodstuffs in Bandung has also risen sharply.

Specially tidied up for the conference, Bandung gives off an air of prosperity. The streets are clean, the houses whitewashed, the beggars and prostitutes have been rounded up, and street lighting is much improved. For all that, however, even here the shops offer little to choose from, and in many shop windows you can find a sign reading "exhibition," to indicate that what is on display is not for sale.

The Concordia Society's building is unrecognizable.[17] It has been completely rebuilt, and the burnt-out section has been reconstructed. However, members of this Bandung club are wondering where they might begin to join in the conversation regarding the building's future. Their club has been developed, rebuilt, newly fitted out and even renamed the Gedung Merdeka. They are seriously wondering whether the building will be returned to them after the conference. Should this be the case, matters are still not straightforward, because then the costs of rebuilding will have to be repaid to the government, and that is beyond Concordia's means. It seems most likely that the government will purchase the Concordia building and the club will be assigned another building for its use.

The big hotels have also been tidied up. This has also been financed by the Indonesian government, through interest-free loans, but the hotels will have to repay these sums. It is probable that the current increase in prices (we might well say doubling of prices) will have to be maintained.

For AA-Conference guests there are evening performances of Indonesian dancing and so on in different restaurants.

Press interest in the AA-Conference is intense. There are no fewer than 400 journalists on hand to cover the conference. Virtually every newspaper in Indonesia is represented, each of the eight papers in Singapore has sent a reporter, and Indonesian and foreign press bureaus have dispatched strong squads of reporters and photographers. *Life* and *Time* both have their people here. You can find Negro journalists from America (but also the writer Richard Wright from Paris), journalists from the Netherlands, Belgium, France, India, Egypt etc. etc. And it is all being recorded on film as much as in photographs.

The Conference Itself

So much for the context. In relation to the conference itself there is both a lot to tell, and also very little. At the moment we are still at the stage of a cautious exchange of views, and for the most part this naturally takes place behind closed doors. It is rumored that differences of opinion between delegates were apparent right from the day the conference agenda had to be finalized. Finally there was agreement on five or six in themselves meaningless points (cultural cooperation, economic cooperation, cooperation in the interest of peace, human rights, and the rights of colonized peoples).[18]

In his opening address, President Soekarno tried to direct the conference mainly toward the struggle against colonialism, speaking also of the "first intercontinental conference of coloured people."[19] This was something that the Turkish delegation found not quite to their liking, since they do not regard themselves as colored. Indeed, the Turks also objected to the statement that this was a gathering of people who had cast off the colonial yoke, as they have never been colonized. Likewise the Japanese.

So from the very beginning of the conference there were differences of opinion. Prime Minister Ali Sastroamidjojo of Indonesia spoke about cooperation in the interest of peace, arguing that willingness to cooperate in the interest of peace should not hinge on first attaining military supremacy, a statement that Prime Minister Moh. Ali of Pakistan appeared to be very critical of. The leader of the Iraqi delegation did not hesitate to warn against the immediate danger of communism.

Yet despite these differences of opinion, no one can doubt that this conference will succeed in establishing a basis for closer cooperation between many, if not all, the countries represented here.

The friendship between Egypt's Nasser and India's Nehru is striking. They are continually in each other's company, engaged in animated discussion. When Nehru stepped up to the podium in the general session, Nasser listened to him with rapt attention, a consideration he certainly did not give to other delegates when they spoke. What we see here is, as it were, close cooperation being marked out in future dealings between Nehru's bloc (India, Indonesia, Burma, Ceylon) and that of Nasser (Egypt, Saudi Arabia, Yemen, Jordan, Lebanon). On the other hand, anti-communist countries such as Turkey, Iraq, Pakistan, and the Philippines, and perhaps also Japan, have found a common alliance in this forum.

The speculation could be taken further, but it is certain that both in the restricted sense as well as in the broader context, delegates to the conference have been engaged in an interesting exchange of views, which will be of great significance for future international relations.

Famous US Negro Author Disappointed
Initial publication: *Indonesian Observer*, Saturday, 23 April 1955
SOURCE LANGUAGE: ENGLISH

Bandung, Friday (Antara)
Richard Wright, the famous American Negro author who as an individual observer has come to Bandung for the African-Asian Conference, is disappointed. The reason he gave an Antara correspondent is that until now the representatives of Negro-Africa have neither brought up a single question nor produced a single constructive idea at this conference.[20]

He deplored this fact the more because Negro-Africa is full of problems which should be dealt with here. However he said, it may well be that in the forthcoming days, when consultations between the individual delegations have reached a further stage, one of the Negro statesmen of Africa will think it fit to bring forward more explicitly some of black Africa's problems in order that they may be discussed with the statesmen of the Near and Far East and the representatives of other parts of the African continent.

Richard Wright expressed it as his opinion that the American Negro never can attain leadership of the political and cultural movement of the African Negro-world. "We are Americans," he said, "and African leadership has to be assumed by the Africans themselves. They have already produced some remarkable leaders, who most certainly are going to take their place among the statesmen of the world. In cooperation with the other nations of Africa and Asia, they will have to fight their own battle against colonialism and racial discrimination."[21]

Who's Doing What

Initial publication: *Indonesia Raya*, Wednesday, 4 May 1955

SOURCE LANGUAGE: INDONESIAN

Richard Wright, the famous American Negro writer who visited Indonesia to attend the AA conference will return to Paris tomorrow (Thursday). While in Indonesia, he gave two lectures. Last Sunday in the home of Takdir Alisjahbana in Tugu, attended by Indonesian writers. And last Monday night at Balai Budaja, attended by invitees from BMKN and PEN Club Indonesia. He met with Natsir, Sjahrir, the Sultan of Yogyakarta, Prime Minister Ali Sastroamidjojo, Major General Simatupang, and Indonesian writers.[22] His impression of Indonesia? A country full of potential for the future!

Pengarang Negro Richard Wright (duduk dikursi), ketika dia diperkenalkan oleh Prof. Imam Slamat Santoso pada para mahasiswa jg mendengar tjeramahnja di Puntjak bulan April jang lalu. (foto I.R.)

FIGURE 6.4. Photo of Richard Wright and caption, from *Indonesia Raya*, 21 May 1955. Courtesy of the Library of Congress.

Photo of Richard Wright and Caption (see fig. 6.4)
Initial publication: *Indonesia Raya*, Saturday, 21 May 1955
SOURCE LANGUAGE: INDONESIAN

Negro writer Richard Wright (seated), when he was introduced by Prof. Imam Slamat Santoso to the university students who listened to his lecture at Puncak during this past April.[23]

Notes

1. These countries were: Afghanistan, Burma, Cambodia, Ceylon, China, Egypt, Ethiopia, Gold Coast, India, Indonesia, Iran, Iraq, Japan, Jordan, Laos, Lebanon, Liberia, Libya, Nepal, Pakistan, the Philippines, Saudi Arabia, Sudan, Syria, Thailand, Turkey, the Democratic Republic of Vietnam, the State of Vietnam, and Yemen (Ministry 227–37).

2. See "Impressions from Bandung," in this chapter.

3. *Indonesia Raya* began publication under the editorship of Mochtar Lubis on 27 December 1949 and closed on 2 January 1959 (Hill, *Journalism* 35, 59). Mrázek describes it as an "'independent' but pro-Sjahrir daily" (413). *Pedoman*, which was the official organ of Sjahrir's Indonesian Socialist Party, began publication in 1948 (164). *Indonesian Observer* was Indonesia's longest running English daily, founded by the pro-Soekarno journalist B. M. Diah and his wife, Herawati Diah, in 1955 to coincide with the Asian-African Conference. It continued publishing until June 2001 ("Surabaya"). The oldest of the Dutch-language newspapers mentioned is *Java Bode*, founded in Batavia in 1852 and published as a liberal-minded daily from 1869 through 1957. *De Nieuwsgier* began as a stenciled bulletin in 1945 and became a daily in newspaper form in 1948. While in Indonesia, Wright spoke with and took photographs of J. H. Ritman, editor of *De Nieuwsgier*, whom he described with a caption in the British edition of *The Colour Curtain* as "a 'good' Dutchman . . . he has selected Indonesia as his country. Married to a Eurasian, he is hopeful of the future." *Het Nieuwsblad voor Sumatra* was founded in 1948 in a merger of two long-established Sumatran newspapers from the colonial era, *Sumatra Post* and *Deli Courant*. Until the expulsion of Dutch nationals from Indonesia in 1957–1958, these Dutch-language newspapers circulated among members of the Dutch community who were permitted to remain in Indonesia and conduct business in the country under the terms of the 1949 Transfer of Sovereignty. However, they also had a readership among the Indonesian elite, who were educated in Dutch in the prewar period. Items concerning Wright may also have appeared elsewhere in the Indonesian press; the survey included here is not intended to be comprehensive. However, it is worth noting that we were unable to find any mention of Wright, either during or after his visit, in *Harian Rakjat*, the mass circulation daily newspaper of the Indonesian Communist Party.

4. On World War II Japan's notion of the "Greater East Asian Co-prosperity Sphere," see Van Sant, Mauch, and Sugita 93–94.

5. The term *freelance* appears in the source text.

6. Wright's flight to Jakarta was not routed through Tokyo but rather was KLM flight KL 829 from Rome to Jakarta, with stops along the way including Cairo, Egypt; Baghdad, Iraq; Karachi, Pakistan; and Calcutta, India (Kiuchi and Hakutani 325).

7. Our *Mr.* is the Dutch *mr*, a title indicating that the person holds the degree of *Meester in de Rechten*, or *Master of Laws*.

8. The "Ali-Arifin cabinet" refers to the coalition cabinet led by Prime Minister Ali Sastroamidjojo, which held power between July 1953 and July 1955. Most of its members, including Ali, were drawn from Soekarno's Indonesian National Party. *Indonesia Raya*, like *Pedoman* and the Indonesian Socialist Party as a whole, was a fierce critic of Soekarno and his government and saw the Asian-African Conference as an attempt to divert attention from the government's own domestic problems (Feith, *Decline* 393).

9. Reny Siwabessy-Putiray was a musician who published a series of arrangements of Indonesian folk songs and original songs for children in the period 1952–1973.

10. The phrase "Where Do You Come From, Sir?" appears in English in the source text.

11. *Peuyeum* is a snack of fermented cassava that typifies the cuisine of West Java and its provincial capital, Bandung. Thanks to Julian Millie for his input on the place of peuyeum in the culture of West Java.

12. The Bogor Conference was held in December 1954 in the Indonesian city of Bogor. It was a meeting among the prime ministers of Burma, Ceylon, India, Indonesia, and Pakistan and was dedicated to planning the Bandung Conference (Newsom 129).

13. For Wright on autograph seekers, see *Color* 537.

14. Wayang golek are wooden doll-like puppets typically associated with the Sundanese culture of West Java.

15. Batik is a wax-relief textile dying process that became highly developed in Java. The term *Batik Show* appears in the source text, in quotation marks.

16. Perwari (Persatuan Wanita Republik Indonesia; Union of the Women of the Indonesian Republic) was a secular organization founded in the immediate aftermath of the Indonesian declaration of independence in August 1945. The historian Susan Blackburn describes it as "one of the most important and enduring" of Indonesia's independent women's organizations (21). Its reluctance to entertain the "second wife" of a visiting head of state reflects the strength of opposition among Indonesian women at this time to the institution of polygamy, described by Blackburn as the issue that "has aroused the greatest depth of feeling among the largest number of Indonesian women" (111). In late 1954 and 1955 there were widespread protests when President Soekarno took Hartini Suwondo as a second wife. This is alluded to in the title of this section of the article. The marriage took place in June 1954 but was kept secret until Mochtar Lubis's *Indonesia Raya* exposed the news in September that year (Hill, *Journalism* 43).

17. This building was repurposed for use during the Bandung Conference: "Known as the Societeit Concordia, this club was the source of much resentment during colonial times because all 'natives' other than those serving European guests were banned from entering" (Barker 525).

18. Here, the *Nieuwsblad voor Sumatra* reporter apparently disparages the joint communique issued by the five participating prime ministers at the close of the 1954 Bogor Conference. During the opening session of the Bandung Conference, Ali Sastroamidjojo

quoted from the joint communique and explained that "it was precisely these purposes on which our invitation to attend [the Bandung] Conference was based, and it was these very purposes on which 29 Governments of Asia and Africa could agree." He continued: "Let these purposes therefore be our guidance in our discussions" (Ministry 32).

19. Soekarno's speech was given in English, and this quotation appears in English in the Dutch-language original of this newspaper article. For the original quotation, see Ministry 19.

20. This article was republished on Monday, 25 April 1955, in *Times of Indonesia*, an English-language newspaper of which Mochtar was the first editor-in-chief (Hill, *Journalism* 39). The second publication differs from the first in suggesting Wright's comments were given on Sunday, 24 April ("Negro").

21. For other accounts of Wright's disappointment with black Africa's participation in the conference, see Gordon 304; and Wright, "Jakarta" 128.

22. According to *The Color Curtain*, Mochtar Lubis introduced Wright to Mohammed Natsir (523–28). A West Sumatran politician who was a prominent leader of the modernist Islamic Masyumi party, Natsir was the first prime minister of the unitary Republic of Indonesia (September 1950–March 1951) (Ricklefs 295). Given that Mochtar's newspaper was close to Sjahrir and his party, Mochtar probably facilitated Wright's *Color Curtain* conversation with Sjahrir as well (515–18). Sjahrir, who had been prime minister during the war of independence against the Dutch, was leader of the Indonesian Socialist Party and one of the country's most prominent politicians. However, both he and his party became increasingly marginalized by political developments in Indonesia following independence (Mrázek 463–64). Wright described an hour-and-a-half conversation with Indonesian prime minister Ali Sastroamidjojo ("Jakarta" 201–2). The Sultan of Yogyakarta in Central Java during Wright's visit was Hamengkubuwono IX, who later became the second Indonesian vice-president, from 1973 through 1978. Wright is not known to have written of meeting Major General Simpatupang.

23. Slamet Iman Santoso (1907–2004) was popularly known as the "Father of Indonesian Psychology." He was appointed professor of psychology at the University of Indonesia in 1950 and in 1960 became inaugural dean of the university's Faculty of Psychology ("Slamet").

7

Mochtar Lubis's "A List of Indonesian Writers and Artists" (1955)

Shortly after Wright's arrival in Indonesia, it appears that his host, Mochtar Lubis, gave him a typed list of names and addresses for several potential contacts in the literary and art world of Jakarta. Among a number of annotations to the list in Mochtar's handwriting is the name "Pramudya Ananta Tur," followed by a description of Pramoedya as a novelist and the intriguing comment, "in my personal opinion in some way influenced by R. Wright." One can imagine Wright and Mochtar discussing the list together, with Mochtar adding further annotations specifying the generational gap that separated St. (Sutan) Takdir Alisjahbana and Asrul Sani, the two figures on the list whom Wright came to know most intimately during his Indonesian sojourn. As Mochtar's handwritten notes point out, Takdir belonged to the prewar generation of cultural nationalists who were associated with the journal *Pujangga Baru*, while Asrul was of the younger generation who came to prominence after the Declaration of Independence on 17 August 1945 and were later dubbed the "Generation of '45." Perhaps it was during this same discussion with Mochtar that Wright himself added a three-word, handwritten notation, remarking that Takdir was oriented toward the West.[1]

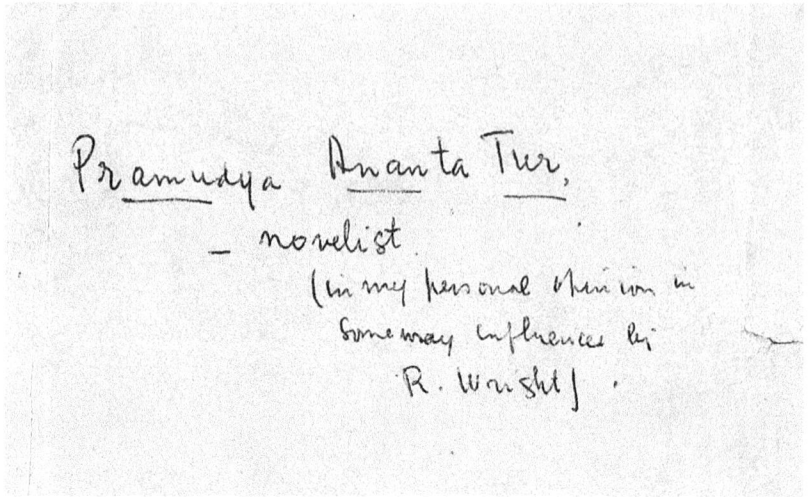

FIGURE 7.1. Mochtar Lubis's handwritten commentary on Pramoedya Ananta Toer and Richard Wright. Used with permission of Iwan Lubis. Courtesy of the Beinecke Rare Book and Manuscript Library, Yale University.

The list begins and ends with mention of the critic H. B. Jassin (1917–2000), the final typed annotation ("for addresses not indicated, ask H. B. Jassin") serving to indicate that Jassin's reputation as a meticulous documenter of the works and biographies of modern Indonesian writers was already well established at this time.[2] Jassin's reputation as a critic is somewhat undermined by the candid parenthetical comment "doubtful for many authors," and there is no record of Wright ever having encountered Jassin during his stay in Indonesia. Despite the prominent role Jassin played as an editor and contributor to other literary and cultural magazines at this time, he was not associated with *Konfrontasi* in any way, and in the absence of focused effort on Wright's part, the trajectory of his encounters with Indonesian literary and artistic circles worked against the possibility that the two men would ever meet.

More surprising, perhaps, is the fact that the Indonesian archive offers no indication that Wright encountered the writer Mochtar had marked out as influenced by Wright's own work: Pramoedya Ananta Toer. One can imagine that Wright's curiosity may have been piqued by Mochtar's comment, and it is to be expected that a visit to Indonesia by a writer Pramoedya clearly admired would have aroused considerable interest on Pramoedya's part. However, like Jassin, Pramoedya was not part of the Konfrontasi Study Club or a contributor to the magazine, and his absence among those known to have met and interacted with Wright in Indonesia is perhaps an indication of increasing ideological tensions among Indonesian writers at this time. By the mid-1950s, Pramoedya's earlier location "at the fringes of the Gelanggang group" (Heinschke 151–53) was already shifting toward a growing affinity with the approach to literary and cultural development being articulated at this time by writers and intellectuals associated with more nationalist and anti-neocolonialist positions. In addition, Pramoedya's growing distance from the Gelanggang authors was exacerbated by personal animosities stemming from critiques of his work that had left him feeling "enraged" and "misunderstood" (158). Some five years earlier, as mentioned elsewhere in this book, Pramoedya had also come into conflict with Takdir Alisjahbana, due to a dispute over Takdir's alleged misuse of Pramoedya's copyrighted material; as of 1953 Pramoedya was trying to take legal action against the Konfrontasi leader.[3] All this meant that in addition to ideological distancing, there were also personal barriers in the way of a possible exchange between Pramoedya and Wright, who would likely have been perceived as a guest of Mochtar Lubis and the Konfrontasi group. There is no indication in Mochtar's annotations that Pramoedya was perceived at this time as "Communist"—that would come later—but it is possible that the ideological and personal distance that currently existed between Mochtar and Pramoedya would have meant that Mochtar was unable—or perhaps disinclined—to facilitate a meeting between Wright and a fellow Indonesian writer who was not part of his circle, despite the obvious potential for a meeting of minds between them. Importantly, Mochtar's note on Pramoedya does not appear as part of the typewritten list but rather as an apparent afterthought, perhaps jotted down while Wright and his host were discussing the sheet of paper and the Indonesian literary scene more generally. Pramoedya's appearance on the list as something of an afterthought also may be indicative of Mochtar's hesitancy regarding Pramoedya's approachability and willingness to respond to an invitation perceived to come from the Gelanggang-Konfrontasi portion of the ideological spectrum.

However, if Wright knew of Pramoedya's proto-Communist leanings, and if he took the initiative to organize meetings independent of his host's involvement, it is possible that he might have sought Pramoedya out specifically. For although Wright had indeed contributed to the 1949 anti-Communist collection *The God That Failed* (published in Indonesian translation in February 1955), he nonetheless placed a high value on the intellectual development and world-historical understanding that he acquired through his years as member of the Communist Party and as a fellow-traveler (Wright, "Jakarta" 218). We can only speculate on what might have occurred if Wright and Pramoedya had engaged—or indeed did engage—in an exchange of ideas during Wright's stay in Jakarta. If such a meeting did take place, it is possible that Wright would have found a greater degree of common ground with Pramoedya than proved to be the case with his Indonesian interlocutors in general. After all, during this era Wright was a friend and close associate of the West Indian writer and activist Aimé Césaire, who was a committed member of the Communist Party, and Wright (though careful to disavow "Marxist Communism") believed "Marxist instrumentalities of thought" and "Marxist analysis of historic events" to offer the most fitting explanation for "what has happened in this world for the past five hundred years or more" (Wright, *Black Power* 10, 12).[4]

The painters on Mochtar's list, Basuki Resobowo, Usman Effendi, and Zaini, and the "author, painter, editor" (and, as appended in Mochtar's handwriting, "translator of Shakespeare") Trisno Sumardjo, did not attain a prominent place in Wright's orbit in Indonesia. Though Wright's travel journal mentions that he attended an art event and two dinners with Indonesian artists ("Jakarta" 113, 121, 190), none of the painters on Mochtar's list appears by name in these accounts or elsewhere in the written record of Wright's encounters in Indonesia. Nevertheless, all these artists—except Basuki Resobowo (1917–1999), who was following a path very similar to that of Pramoedya Ananta Toer at this time (Holt 327)—were associated with Gelanggang and its outlooks, so it is possible that some or all of them were part of the audiences Wright addressed, either in Jakarta or at Takdir's villa in Tugu. However, it was the second and third names on Mochtar's list, Sutan Takdir Alisjahbana and Asrul Sani, who were to figure most prominently among Wright's Indonesian contacts, as is attested by the documents and discussions included elsewhere in this book. Wright would spend a weekend at Takdir's mountain retreat in the company of Konfrontasi figures, including members of Asrul Sani's family, and he would later be interviewed for a feature item in Asrul's *Gelanggang*, the cultural affairs column of the weekly news magazine *Siasat*. Wright's handwritten annotation—marking up Takdir's Western orientation—suggests that Wright may have been struck by this detail in a discussion of the list of names with his host before any meetings were arranged. It later formed the central theme of his description of the quintessential westernized Asian intellectual in *The Color Curtain*. And although Wright did not identify Takdir by name in his text (*Color* 464–72), his photograph of Takdir and Beb Vuyk, included among the illustrations for the UK edition of the book, described Takdir as "more western than the west and a compassionate aristocrat." Clearly, his encounter with Takdir was to prove central to Wright's description of the various manifestations he had found of "the Asian mind" (487) during his visit to Jakarta and Bandung.

A List of Indonesian Writers and Artists
by Mochtar Lubis
SOURCE LANGUAGE: INDONESIAN AND ENGLISH

H. B. Jassin
  c/o "Mimbar Indonesia" (magazine)
       Djalan Tjikini 31
       Djakarta

  –critic (doubtful for many authors)
  –lecturer on modern Indonesian Literature at University
  –editor

St. Takdir Alisjahbana
  Djalan Sukabumi 36

  Group: "New Poets" 1930
  –author
  –linguist
  –editor & publisher
  –lecturer
  politics: socialist

Asrul Sani *generation group 45*
  c/o *"Siasat"* (magazine)
       Gunung Sahari Antjol 13

  –poet & essayist
  –editor
  politics: soc.

Trisno Sumardjo   *Pramudya Ananta Tur,*
  –author   *–novelist*
  –painter   *(In my personal opinion in*
  –editor   *some way influenced by*
  –translator of Shakespeare   *R. Wright)*

Basuki Resobowo

Usman Effendi

Zaini
  –painters

for addresses not indicated, ask H. B. Jassin

Notes

Mochtar Lubis, "A List of Indonesian Writers and Artists." Reproduced with the permission of Iwan Lubis. Italics indicate Mochtar's handwritten annotations to the typed list.

1. Thanks to David Hill for sending the handwriting samples that helped us identify the handwriting on the list as Mochtar's. The note on Takdir's Western orientation matches Wright's handwriting as preserved in RWP. Though not included in our representation of the list, this handwriting appears on the top portion of the original list, next to Takdir's name.

2. In 1976, Jassin's personal documentation collection became the H. B. Jassin Center for Literary Documentation, Jakarta.

3. See Ardan's "Pramoedya Heads Overseas" in part I.

4. On Wright and Césaire's relationship, see Ward and Butler 69–71.

8

Gelanggang's "A Conversation with Richard Wright" (1955)

After attending the Bandung Conference, Richard Wright returned to Jakarta, where he spent the remainder of his time in Indonesia as the houseguest of the Presbyterian minister and missionary Winburn T. Thomas (Thomas, "Reminiscences" 151). At some point during this period, Wright participated in a conversation or interview for the prominent cultural affairs publication *Gelanggang*. With its masthead announcing it as a "Cahier Seni dan Sastera" (Cahier for Art and Literature), *Gelanggang* was a column for news and debates related to the modern Indonesian arts in the news magazine *Siasat*, which was aligned with the Indonesian Socialist Party (PSI). It began publication in 1948 with editors Chairil Anwar, Rivai Apin, and Asrul Sani at the helm, and in 1949 it gave its name to the cultural manifesto discussed in this book's introduction, the Gelanggang Testimony of Beliefs. By the time of Wright's visit, Asrul Sani was continuing with the column, while his wife, the poet Siti Nuraini, was working as the group's secretary. Asrul's coeditor of *Gelanggang* at this time was Soedjatmoko, a prominent political and publishing figure who had represented Indonesia in the United Nations and had helped found

FIGURE 8.1. Illustration for *Gelanggang*'s "A Conversation with Richard Wright" (1955) and later for Asrul Sani's "Richard Wright: The Artist Turned Intellectual" (1956). *Siasat* gives credit for the photograph to "Muller" (no full name provided).

the newspaper *Pedoman*. In 1955, Soedjatmoko also served with the Indonesian delegation to the Bandung Conference.[1]

Both Asrul and Soedjatmoko are credited as editors of the otherwise unsigned 15 May 1955 *Gelanggang* article "Pertjakapan dengan Richard Wright" (A Conversation with Richard Wright).[2] The article exhibits several similarities to Asrul's 1956 *Gelanggang* article "Richard Wright: Seniman jang Djadi Intelektuil" (Richard Wright: The Artist Turned Intellectual), which is included in part III: both articles use the same photograph of Wright, both discuss the genre of the *document humain*, and both refer to Wright's interest in the Bible. These similarities suggest that the most likely author of the 1955 article is Asrul Sani, although it is possible that it was authored by another figure with whom Wright spoke individually. It might also be a write-up of remarks made by Wright in a Gelanggang forum with a larger audience. Such an event, if it transpired, would perhaps correspond to the lecture that Wright, in his handwritten notes, mentions having given after the Bandung Conference for an Indonesian art group.[3]

The "Conversation" opens as the interviewer provides readers with an indication of Wright's stance on the world-historical significance of Asia's and Africa's decolonization. Notably, Wright's opinion seems to be a response to one of his own questions, as it appeared on the questionnaire he developed in preparation for his attendance at the Asian-African Conference. With the ambition of "getting to know the Asian personality," Wright's questionnaire included the query "What was the single most important event of the twentieth century?" (Wright, Color 445, 447).[4] As if his interviewer had asked Wright to respond to this component of his own questionnaire, the "Conversation" begins by conveying Wright's opinion that the "rise of the peoples of Asia and Africa" is "one of the most important events" of the twentieth century.

After this opening, the conversation quickly begins tracing Wright's development as a writer. Here we see a comparison between Wright's oeuvre and the 1852 novel Uncle Tom's Cabin, written by the white American author Harriet Beecher Stowe. Stowe's popular and widely influential novel, with its emotionally charged condemnations of slavery, added fuel to antislavery sentiment in the run-up to the US Civil War. According to legend, when Stowe met President Abraham Lincoln, he exclaimed, "So this is the little lady who made this big war?" (Sizer 49). Gelanggang's comparison of Wright to Stowe—together with its vague reference to the opinion of "one essayist"—suggests that the author of the "Conversation" article was familiar with James Baldwin's 1949 essay "Everybody's Protest Novel," which famously and scathingly compares Wright's 1940 Native Son to Stowe's nineteenth-century novel: "Below the surface of [Native Son] there lies, as it seems to me, a continuation, a complement of that monstrous legend it was written to destroy. Bigger [Native Son's protagonist] is Uncle Tom's descendant, flesh of his flesh, so exactly opposite a portrait that, when the books are placed together, it seems that the contemporary Negro novelist and the dead New England woman are locked together in a deadly, timeless battle" (100). Discussing both Uncle Tom's Cabin and Native Son as protest novels, Baldwin concludes: "The failure of the protest novel lies in its rejection of life, the human being" (100). Whereas Baldwin's comparison between Stowe and Wright constitutes a sharp jab at Wright, Gelanggang's "Conversation" seems to misunderstand Baldwin, stating that Baldwin sees in the progression from Stowe to Wright "a cause for optimism about the progress of humanity."

Further discussing Wright's development as a writer, his Indonesian interlocutor asks about Wright's ideal readers and his stance on the function of literature. Wright's answers to these questions confirm that when he had this conversation with Gelanggang, he was in the process of thinking through and drafting the talk he was planning on giving for a PEN Club/BMKN event that was scheduled for 2 May at Jakarta's Cultural Affairs Center, Balai Budaja. In the *Gelanggang* conversation Wright is quoted as saying that "writers only have a 'public,' not an 'audience.' We try to reach everyone, we try to win them over, to call out to people, to touch the heart of anyone who will listen." Later in the conversation, on the topic of literature's function, he delineates his thinking further: "One function among others is the moral function. Then there's the possibility of taking part in some form of enjoyment. An active process of convincing the reader about the truth of something." Clearly, these statements indicate that Wright was working through the ideas he expressed in his 2 May lecture, shortly before his departure from Indonesia, especially as showcased in the sections of the talk titled "The writer and his audience" and "Morality and art."[5]

In further discussing Wright's development as a writer, the *Gelanggang* article turns toward the shift in subject matter that took place in Wright's writing when he published his 1953 novel *The Outsider*. According to *Gelanggang*, this shift involved moving away from preoccupations with racism and toward broader preoccupations pertaining to human existence, inspired by Wright's interest in existentialism. Whether through dialogue or narrative commentary, the conversation intersects several times with the question of existentialism. The *Gelanggang* author points out that Wright's apparent change in subject matter owes something to his associations with the writers Jean-Paul Sartre and Simone de Beauvoir. His new thematic interests are explained in the article by recourse to an allusion to Sartre's series of novels *Les Chemins de la Liberté*. The conversation's preoccupation with existentialism continues as Wright comments, toward the article's conclusion, that in his opinion Sartre—like the West in general—is so distracted by left-right politics that he has overlooked the importance of events in Asia. As an antidote for Western disregard, even among existentialist philosophers, Wright suggests that *Gelanggang* might invite Albert Camus to Indonesia with the hope that Camus would intelligently relay to the West something about the importance of Asia.

The *Gelanggang* conversation's focus on existentialist writers and philosophers, and its interest in Wright's 1953 novel, are readily understandable in terms of an existing Indonesian preoccupation with existentialism at this time. In his spirited description of the health of Indonesian literature at the end of 1954, H. B. Jassin had vigorously defended the interest Indonesian writers had shown in existentialist themes against accusations that existentialist philosophy "severed the relationship between human beings and God" and so robbed human life of its depth and meaning. He pointed to existentialism's origins in the thought of both Protestant and Roman Catholic philosophers and suggested that even the great Muslim poet Muhammad Iqbal was in essence "an existentialist in his way of thinking" (Jassin 3:23). Acknowledging that Sartre and Heidegger represented an atheistic strand of existentialist thought, Jassin nevertheless argued that whether theistic or atheistic, existentialism spoke to a spiritually rich notion of humanity and a responsible approach to human life and behavior (3:24).

Jassin's 1954 remarks reflected an interest in the humanist implications of existentialist thought that was consistent with the evolving Indonesian aesthetic philosophy of universal humanism. This interest extended into Indonesian understandings of absurdist thinking, as can be seen in the attention given to Albert Camus during this period as an embodiment of the humanist vocation of the writer's grappling with matters of religion, ethics, and the meaning of human life. In May 1953, the literary and cultural monthly *Zenith*, edited by Jassin with occasional help from the editors of *Gelanggang* (Teeuw, *Modern* 115), published an Indonesian translation of an essay by the Dutch critic Pierre H. Dubois under the title "Buah-tangan Albert Camus" (The Literary Works of Albert Camus). Considerable effort must have gone into the translation of this philosophically dense and linguistically complex argument concerning Camus's confrontation with the human condition as he found it in his own times and circumstances. Like other reports on contemporary developments in modern European literature and culture, it was published in *Zenith* for its perceived relevance to Indonesian concerns and discussions of the day.

In the following year—and exactly one year before Wright's arrival in Indonesia—another essay in the same magazine noted the Indonesian interest in Camus and suggested it was understandable, "because Camus is a representative of a particular kind of Europe, a Europe that places importance on human dignity and freedom" (Lemaire 117). Once again, the emphasis is on the humanist connection and its universal implications. In a discussion of Camus's *L'Homme revolté*, the writer here asserts that "in the 'no' of revolt, the human being says 'yes' to the world and his fellow human beings. Here we have the assertion of the humanist ideal" (122).

This theme was pursued the following month, with an Indonesian translation of Jean-Paul Sartre's 1946 lecture "La responsabilité de l'écrivain." Here, *Zenith*'s readers considered Sartre's assertion that language "brings the person face to face with his responsibilities" ("Responsibility" 169). Sartre observes, "We held every German who did not protest against the Nazi regime responsible for that regime, and should there exist among us, or in any other nation, any form of economic or racial oppression, we hold responsible all those who do not denounce it" (165). Giving flesh to this principle, the essay explains, "The oppression of Negroes is nothing, so long as no one says,

'Negroes are oppressed.' Until then, nobody realizes it, perhaps not even the Negroes themselves; but it only needs a word for the act to take on meaning" (169). The writer "must demand plainly and above all else . . . the liberation of all oppressed people, proletarians, Jews, Negroes, colonial subjects, occupied countries, and so on" (181). Given this acquaintance with the stances of one of the most prominent existentialist philosophers, some of Wright's Indonesian interlocutors may well have seen existentialist thought as the framework Wright was using to make analogies between African American and Asian-African populations. Of course, as Wright's friend C. L. R. James later recalled, Wright felt his experiences had acquainted him with existentialist thought before he ever encountered existentialist writings. Speaking with James, Wright once pointed to a collection of volumes on a bookshelf and stated, "Look here, . . . you see those books there? They are by Kierkegaard . . . I want to tell you something. Everything that he writes in those books, I knew before I had them." In retracing this recollection, James remarked, "What he was telling me was that he was a black man in the United States and that gave him an insight into what today is the universal opinion and attitude of the modern personality." James continued: "What there was in Dick's life, what there was in the experience of a black man in the United States in the 1930s that made him understand everything that Kierkegaard had written before he had read it . . . is something that I believe has to be studied" (196).

If Wright sensed that his experiences as a black man in the US South permitted his independent arrival at the existentialist thought of Søren Kierkegaard, then his Indonesian travel journal reveals that he also believed that Asians—in, as Wright alleged, their ability to see the world of things outside of time, and to see things without looking—had arrived independently at the phenomenological thought of Edmund Husserl. He felt so strongly about this that he wanted to reread Husserl in light of what he was learning from the Asians with whom he spoke as he prepared to travel to Indonesia ("Jakarta" 80).

A Conversation with Richard Wright
from *Gelanggang*, edited by Soedjatmoko and Asrul Sani
SOURCE LANGUAGE: INDONESIAN

"One of the most important events of this century has been the rise of the peoples of Asia and Africa." Such is the conviction of Richard Wright. And it was his interest in matters arising from this opinion that brought Wright to Bandung to visit the Asia-Africa conference.[6]

Richard Wright is an American Negro writer who has gained fame in the world of modern literature with his books *Uncle Tom's Children*, *Twelve Million Black Voices*, *Native Son*, and *Black Boy*, all of which take the lives and suffering of Negro people in America as their principal theme. They give voice to a ringing protest at the treatment of the Negro race by white people, to the extent that one essayist was moved to see in them a cause for optimism about the progress of humanity. This particular observer compared Wright's books with Harriet Beecher Stowe's *Uncle Tom's Cabin*, and concluded that the more aggressive tone of Wright's books was an indication not that the treatment of Negroes in Stowe's time was more moderate—quite the opposite in fact—but that humanity's sensitivity to injustice is now much more developed than in the past. Much has changed since Stowe's time, but the situation is still far from satisfactory. In Wright's words, "The situation is not as bright as white people often make it out to be, but neither is it as bad as the communist press would have us believe." And with a smile bearing no trace of hatred or bitterness, he continued, "It's a hopeless situation. I say 'hopeless' because what we are facing isn't a 'Negro problem' but a 'white problem.' This is a disease we can't cure, but the fear that whites harbor in relation to Negroes will be put to rest by the Negro people themselves. In terms of race relations as they are today, it makes no sense at all for us to come together and mount an organized program of resistance. That would see us wiped out completely. But this is just a temporary problem."

I asked Wright, "If the problem is temporary, what are the issues that Negro writing will address in the future?" "Universal human issues!" came the reply. Wright's own work has been the proof of this. In March 1953, he published *The Outsider*, a very different book from his previous works. If we bear in mind that Wright has lived for many years in Paris and has no intention of returning to America—he occupies an apartment in the rue Monsieur le Prince with his family—as well as the fact that he is close to Jean-Paul Sartre and Simone de Beauvoir (both of them are referred to as existentialist writers), then the change of style makes sense. It is still of interest, however, especially if we recognize that the feeling of "race" can be rationalized but never completely erased. Because in *The Outsider*, the issue is no longer the Negro who is not yet free of the oppression of the white race, but the Negro who has been able to rise above his situation as a member of that oppressed caste. Wright asks how this person, released from the old beliefs and superstitions that once filled his life, may become a liberated human being. Or, in the words of the title of a series of novels by Sartre, what are "the roads to freedom" (*Les Chemins de la liberté*)? The Negro of this book is no longer the Negro who passively accepts his suffering, but one who takes an active part in determining his own fate. The question is no longer that of racial discrimination.

Even though Richard Wright has described himself as an expert in poverty, there is not much trace of poverty and bitterness in the clear lines of his face. To look at him, to note his solid build and hear his uninhibited laughter, you would think he was a writer whose past was bathed in jasmine and rosewater. It's only his books that reveal the opposite was in fact the case. Still, it is possible that his joviality serves some purpose in his life, functioning as a kind of shield against the humiliations that have been inflicted on him, just as the Spanish try to overcome the bitterness of their lives through song. It is strange, but it is also true that many peoples who suffer outward oppression appear happier than those who oppress others, or those who have the power to overcome oppression through other means.

"I write because I want to make connections with other people. That's all. There's no bitterness in me when I write my books. I only want to tell stories."

"What sort of readers do you want to reach through your writings?"

He paused for a moment. "We writers only have a 'public,' not an 'audience.' We try to reach everyone, we try to win them over, to call out to people, to touch the heart of anyone who will listen."

"What is the function of literature in this?"

"Function? One function among others is the moral function. Then there's the possibility of taking part in some form of enjoyment. An active process of convincing the reader about the truth of something."

"Mr. Wright, in one of your interviews you remarked that among the writers you like are the nineteenth-century Russian novelists, as well as Flaubert and Kafka.[7] Is there a connection between your choice of these writers and the way you see the function of literature? Or to put it more clearly, what is it that you find in these writers?"

"What I find in the nineteenth-century Russian novelists is a kind of 'sense of life,' a wonderful capacity to embody the 'experience of life in their time' in a work of art. In Flaubert we find a supreme appreciation of beauty combined with a moral sensibility. He succeeds in combining the aesthetic and the moral. In Kafka, well. . . ." He paused a moment and thought, before going on. "The simplicity of his relationship with the reader, just as though he were a child. His fundamental basis is the Jewish question. And then we also find in him a judgment on what constitutes a healthy humanity."

"Do you see in him a kind of fatalism?"

"One of the strengths of the conscious human being is his understanding of the limits imposed on him. He may suffer pain, but the consciousness of risk, of what one is doing, is the most important thing."

Richard Wright was one of the contributors to *The God That Failed*, a collection of articles by writers who had once been members of the Communist Party, but who gave up their party membership out of a sense that its aims conflicted with their humanity. The "consciousness of risk" he spoke of seems to have been an important factor behind that decision. In *The Outsider* this matter again comes to the fore. In this book he writes that being a member of the Communist Party means "negating yourself, blotting out your personal life and listening only to the voice of the Party" (Molotov once said, "I have no will of my own. My will is that of the party."). Wright's comment on this was ". . . its victim would deny its reality perhaps more vociferously than those who controlled this system of power."[8]

I asked him what it was he wanted to bring out in *The Outsider*.

"A situation that gives rise to other situations," was the reply.

"What would you regard as the most important time in your life?"

"When I was weighing up whether to stay in Chicago or go to New York." Seeing my surprise, he laughed. "Yes, it's strange," he said. "What was so important about deciding whether to stay in Chicago or go to New York? Yet for me, at that time, it was a crucial decision. It was a choice between remaining in Chicago as a post-office clerk, with all the security that position affords, or taking the risk of heading to New York and having to live by my pen. At that moment, I chose freedom."

"Who are the historical figures that you admire, or that you respect?"

"The heroes of thought, like Marx, Freud, and Nietzsche."

"You know that Stendhal was an admirer of Napoleon . . ."

"Admiring warmongers is a childish and immature trait, in my opinion."

"What books did you read as a child? What books influenced you at that time?"

"First of all was the Bible. Then came Dreiser, who gave me a feeling for realism. After that it was Conrad, because he told such a good story."

"What's your opinion of *Uncle Tom's Cabin*?"

"Well. It doesn't say anything. It's nothing more than a 'document humain.'[9] For the people for whom it was written—the Negro race—it is completely meaningless. It offers them nothing. The feelings and problems of the Negro can only be written about by Negroes themselves."

"Among all the people you have met, who has made the deepest impression on you?"

"People rarely make an impression on me. I'm more affected by places and what I find in books.[10] Moreover, my education didn't go beyond elementary school. No professors ever taught me, so all the knowledge I have has come from books. That's the reason books make a deeper impression on me than people do."

"In your opinion, can the position of the Negro race in America be influenced by events outside America?"

"Definitely! I could give you lots of examples. Let's start with one close to home, the conference that's just been held in Bandung. When the first reports of this conference reached American newspapers, the *St. Louis Post* sent a cable to its correspondent in Bandung, asking him whether he thought that in these circumstances it wouldn't be better to discontinue those columns in the paper that were set aside for Negroes.[11] So even in faraway corners of the country there is an impact. Of course this conference isn't going to come up with something to solve the problem altogether. But it does have an influence."

"When did you develop an interest in the Asia-Africa question?"

"I have an interest because I'm a Negro. Don't forget that I too am a victim of the Western world. People in Europe don't see the importance of events here in Asia. For them, the big issue is the struggle between left- and right-wing groups. Even Sartre is not immune to this. They don't see the potential and the aspirations of the newly awakened nations. It would be wonderful if you here in Indonesia could one day invite someone like Albert Camus to visit. There's a great deal that he would be able to explain to the world of Western thought about events here. And I'm sure he would be extremely enthusiastic about developments here."

"Your country is very beautiful, and your people are very friendly."

I thanked him for these words of appreciation. "And what about America?" I asked.

"America?" he asked. "All I know about America is what I read in the same newspapers you probably read as well. I haven't been there for a long time, and at the moment I have no intention of going there. I love France, and I enjoy Paris. The climate in Paris is ideal for working."

Notes

1. On *Gelanggang*, see Teeuw, *Modern* 115. On Soedjatmoko, see Kahin and Barnett.

2. Other articles in *Gelanggang* during this time almost always bore the author's name along with this standard editorial acknowledgment, hence this particular article should be considered as published anonymously.

3. Wright's handwritten note, clearly scrawled in haste, indicates that his lectures, including for the art league, occurred after the conference ("Retreat"). Yet elsewhere in this book we have suggested that Wright's brief speech to the Jajasan Impresariat Indonesia, delivered before he attended the Asian-African Conference, corresponds to his

reference to the art league. Certainly, this is the moment during which we most clearly see Wright speaking at an event dedicated to the visual arts. And yet, in consideration of Wright's indication that he spoke to the art league after the conference, we are here suggesting that he might possibly have conceived of Gelanggang as an arts group. However, it is speculation to suggest that Wright gave a lecture for Gelanggang.

4. Corroborating *The Color Curtain*'s narrative, the questionnaire itself offers this as its fifty-fourth question (Wright, "Questionnaire" 5).

5. See Wright's "The Artist and His Problems," also in part II.

6. The editorial attribution to Soedjatmoko and Asrul Sani is from 1955.

7. Here, Wright's Indonesian interlocutor is likely referring to Hans de Vaal's 1953 interview with Wright, originally published in Dutch in *Litterair Paspoort*. See de Vaal 159.

8. The reference here is to Vyacheslav Molotov, a historical Soviet politician and diplomat who is discussed in *The Outsider* (248, 258). The phrase *negating . . . the Party* appears in English in the Indonesian-language "Conversation" article. For its original publication in the novel, see Wright, *Outsider* 248. The phrase *its victim . . . power* appears in English in the "Conversation" article. For its original publication in the novel, see *Outsider* 270, which has a slightly different version of the quote.

9. Here, Wright is using a catchword of French naturalism that was in common use in discussions of literature in Indonesia at this time. An example occurs in Asrul Sani's "Richard Wright: The Artist Turned Intellectual," in part III.

10. In the source text, this sentence is jumbled and incomplete, pointing to an error in typesetting. Based on context, we have pieced together the sentence's likely meaning.

11. In his travel journal, Wright noted that the *St. Louis Post-Dispatch* had contacted its correspondent in Indonesia to ask whether it was time to stop using the term *Negro* in its columns ("Jakarta" 199).

9

Konfrontasi's "Synopsis" of Wright's "American Negro Writing" (1955)

During the weekend of 30 April through 1 May, Wright left Jakarta at the invitation of the Konfrontasi Study Club, traveling to the cool slopes of the mountains between Jakarta and Bandung, to lecture at the villa of Konfrontasi leader Sutan Takdir Alisjahbana in the village of Tugu. This type of lecture-discussion event in Tugu was part of the group's regular docket of gatherings, an outcome of the ambition Takdir had harbored since the early 1950s to turn his Tugu villa into a literary or artists' salon on the European model (Asrul, "Sebuah" 70). Another of Wright's associates in Indonesia, Achdiat Karta Mihardja, who had met Wright as a PEN Club representative at the airport in Jakarta, described one of these events in Tugu in a 1951 article, noting that it brought artists, writers, and intellectuals together in a relaxed and convivial environment that was conducive to a productive exchange of ideas on issues of topical concern. Indeed, Achdiat's article "Pertemuan Kebudajaan di Tugu" (A Cultural Meeting in Tugu) suggests that the 1951 gathering he attended even managed to bring ideological opponents face-to-face on grounds of mutual tolerance and trust (241–44).[1] Giving insight into what these meetings looked like by the time of Wright's arrival in the mid-1950s, Beb Vuyk recalled,

"The discussion would take place after dinner on Saturday and sometimes last well into the night. The next morning we would take a dip in the ice-cold water of the swimming pool and then sit in the sun to get warm. Little groups of people would form on the terraces and lawns around the pool, keeping up the discussions and cementing personal contacts." This would be followed by a feast: "Takdir would always have a goat slaughtered on these occasions, and the *sate* [skewered barbecue meat] lunches became a tradition." The study club would stay at the villa until about four o'clock on Sunday afternoon before "we all piled into the pickup for the trip back to the heat of Jakarta."[2]

In Vuyk's account of Konfrontasi's April 1955 weekend at Tugu, the study club scheduled Wright's lecture for the standard time slot on Saturday evening, but between the time of the scheduling and the time of Wright's arrival at Takdir's villa, Takdir had felt compelled to accept an invitation (apparently on behalf of the entire study club, including Wright as their guest) to a dinner party on the Saturday evening in question at a nearby villa occupied by a white American family.[3] Hence, Wright's lecture was rescheduled for the following morning, Sunday, 1 May. At the dinner party, members of the study club who had read about US race prejudice were "interested in observing firsthand how white Americans acted in the company of one of their black compatriots." While Vuyk reported that the party "took on the air of a rather tense display of racial goodwill," Wright in his travel journal did not mention questions of race in his description of the Americans he met in the mountains but rather focused on their concerns about the spread of communism in Asia ("Jakarta" 126).[4]

The next morning, after apparently staying in one of the several rooms in Takdir's villa, Wright gave a lecture titled "American Negro Writing" for an audience that included the study club and other interested individuals. Wright took several photographs at Takdir's villa, presumably during the weekend of his lecture, and the figures in these photographs suggest that his Indonesian audience included some writers whom he had already met during his trip: Siti Nuraini, Achdiat Karta Mihardja, and Sutan Takdir Alisjahbana. Also present were some members of the Konfrontasi circle whom he may have been meeting for the first time, including the poet and short story writer Sitor Situmorang, the essayist and editor Hazil Tanzil, and the future documentary filmmaker Yazir Marzuki. Vuyk also recalled that "a number of Americans" (perhaps some of the guests at the dinner party of the previous evening) were present for Wright's lecture, though they left before lunch was served and the real discussion began. Describing this weekend gathering at Takdir's villa, Mochtar Lubis wrote that Wright "was an animated speaker, and . . . we talked with him about Indonesian literature and the position of American Negroes in the United States" (qtd. in Kiuchi and Hakutani 326).

FIGURE 9.1. Takdir Alisjahbana's villa in Tugu, the venue of Wright's 1 May 1955 lecture "American Negro Literature." Photograph by Brian Russell Roberts (May 2013).

FIGURE 9.2. Patio view of Takdir Alisjahbana's villa in Tugu, the setting for a postlecture discussion between Wright and the Konfrontasi Study Club. Photograph by Brian Russell Roberts (May 2013).

FIGURE 9.3. Set on the back patio of Takdir's villa, Wright's photograph portrays (left to right): Hazil Tanzil, Achdiat Karta Mihardja, and Sutan Takdir Alisjahbana. Though not visible in this reproduction, details on the cover of the book suggest that Achdiat is holding a hardback copy of Wright's novel *The Outsider*. Reprinted by permission of John Hawkins & Associates, Inc., and the Estate of Richard Wright. Courtesy of the Beinecke Rare Book and Manuscript Library, Yale University.

FIGURE 9.4. Wright's photograph, set on the patio with members of the Konfrontasi Study Club, portrays (left to right): Siti Nuraini, Fedja (daughter of Siti Nuraini and Asrul Sani), Sitor Situmorang, and Yazir Marzuki. Reprinted by permission of John Hawkins & Associates, Inc., and the Estate of Richard Wright. Courtesy of the Beinecke Rare Book and Manuscript Library, Yale University.

During the months preceding the lecture and discussion, Siti Nuraini (now sitting among Wright's audience at Takdir's villa) had been giving special attention to questions related to race and African Americans' situation in the United States. Though she had long been exposed to racially suspect representations of blackness such as the Dutch Christmas tradition of Zwarte Piet or Black Pete (Nuraini), in 1955 she had spent time studying and translating a representation of blackness excerpted from the 1940 novel *The Heart Is a Lonely Hunter*, by US southern writer Carson McCullers. This was a work that Wright himself had celebrated, describing it as a novel whose "white writer . . . handl[ed] Negro characters with as much . . . justice as those of her own race" ("Inner"). Nuraini's chosen excerpt focused specifically on the character Benedict Copeland, described in her translation's introduction as "a Negro doctor, who wants to see an improvement in the lives of his people and devotes himself to this cause, only to become alienated and isolated from his people and his family because they do not understand him" (Redaksi March–April 1955).[5] Now, observing Wright speak at Takdir's villa, Nuraini may well have wondered how Copeland's intellectualism-induced isolation corresponded to Wright's exile in Paris. In any case, as she later recalled, the Konfrontasi Study Club was aware that Wright was one of the few black writers in whom white Americans seemed interested, and she had the impression that somehow the United States wanted to claim credit for Wright's accomplishments (Nuraini).

Following the weekend retreat, Wright's lecture "American Negro Writing" appeared in apparently complete form in the May–June 1955 issue of the study club's journal, *Konfrontasi*, which was edited at the time by Takdir, Vuyk, and Hazil. In a highly unusual move, the editors opted to publish the lecture in English. As they explained to *Konfrontasi*'s readers,

> In this issue we are including the text of a lecture on "American Negro Literature" [*sic*] which was given by the famous American Negro writer, Richard Wright, to a meeting of members of the Konfrontasi Study Club and a number of other interested persons. We are publishing the lecture in English, because most of the poems and the characteristics of the language quoted in it make the lecture very difficult, if not impossible, to translate.[6] However, at the end of the discussion we are including a short summary of its contents in Indonesian. (Redaksi May–June 1955)

Konfrontasi's stance on the difficulties of translating poetry from English to Indonesian gave rise to what is the first known English-language publication of the lecture that Wright published two years later in *White Man, Listen!* as "The Literature of the Negro in the United States."

The fact that "American Negro Writing" was delivered and indeed found its first English-language publication in Indonesia prompts questions that promise a reconsideration and reevaluation of *White Man*. Wright dedicated this volume to "*the Westernized and tragic elite of Asia, Africa, and the West Indies*—the lonely outsiders who exist precariously on the cliff-like margins of many cultures—men who are distrusted, misunderstood, maligned, criticized by Left and Right, Christian and Pagan—men who carry . . . the best of two worlds" (vii). Intriguingly, from Wright's own perspective, his lecture for the Konfrontasi Study Club was given for members of the very group to which he dedicated his book of lectures. Wright at one point described this "elite of Asia, Africa, and the West Indies" as generally "more Western than the West" (*White* 56), and, as already noted, he used this same language in his caption for a photograph of Takdir Alisjahbana that was included in the British edition of *The Colour Curtain*.

Given that Wright delivered this lecture to and discussed this lecture with members of the same "tragic elite" to whom he dedicated *White Man*, it is strange to consider that his introduction to *White Man* elides Indonesia from the list of countries where he presented the lectures contained in the book. Indonesia receives no mention as a lecturing venue, but Wright does not neglect to mention that his lectures were given in Italy, the Netherlands, Germany, France, and Sweden (15). Certainly, the book's framing as addressed specifically to the *White Man* is enhanced by Wright's opening list of European venues, while this same framing does not accommodate the image of Wright delivering the volume's lectures to an Indonesian or more generally Asian-African audience. And yet this observation on the book's title further begs the question of why Wright would frame his published lectures as directed toward white people when he specifically chose to deliver at least one among the four to Indonesians. (No doubt the Indonesian venue is also a reminder that in September 1956 Wright gave another of his *White Man* lectures, "Tradition and Industrialization," to another group of seemingly tragic elite at "a kind of second Bandung," the First International Congress of Negro Writers and Artists in Paris [Baldwin, "Princes" 25, 46–48].) In what ways has Wright's framing of *White Man*, as a book of lectures directed toward white people and delivered in Europe, stymied our understanding of his commentary on and interactions with the elite to whom he dedicated his book? In what ways has this framing unnecessarily—and ahistorically—limited our approaches to Wright's exilic commentaries on the postcolonial world? Access to *Konfrontasi*'s synopsis of "American Negro Writing" offers the opportunity to consider how a few of the postcolonial elite grappled with Wright's commentary after the Bandung Conference.

Also contributing to this opportunity is the background and commentary on Wright that the *Konfrontasi* editors provided in their editorial introduction to the May–June issue in which the lecture was published. On one level, this introduction may be seen as a simple effort to offer Indonesian readers, many of whom would have been unfamiliar with Wright, a set of basic contexts for understanding the lecture. Such may be the case with the Indonesian editors' explanation that Wright was

> born in one of the Southern states of the United States of America, where discrimination against the Negro race is more overt than in the North, and where a Negro, if he wants to survive and earn a living, must adopt a servile and self-effacing disposition, or pretend to do so. Like tens of thousands of other colored people, Richard Wright moved to the North, because his inner self would not allow him to accept all the restrictions that white society in the South placed on his people. (Redaksi May–June 1955)

Yet other portions of this introduction extend to commentary that is revealing in relation to the place of the concept of race in modern Indonesia and the universal humanist assumptions held by members of the study club. The editors remark that Wright

> and Bigger Thomas, the tragic protagonist of his *Native Son*, are very similar in the following respects: neither of them will surrender to the harsh realities of the time, and they both seek revenge in the form of an open and honest situation that values all human beings. Bigger fails in his struggle with fate, but Richard Wright has succeeded. Despite his poverty, his tenacity when it came to reading enabled him to amass the knowledge that made it possible for him to explore his rebellious feelings through his intellect. The most important thing was that he was able to channel himself into writing, thus freeing himself from his inner complexities through writing. (Redaksi May–June 1955)

Here we see the universal humanist preoccupation with understanding the types of creative processes that result in mature works of literature. "Rebellious feelings" are mediated by the intellect, and "inner complexities" are resolved in the act of writing, producing a state of clarity that appears to transcend the confusion of emotional fixation. Only in this way, it is implied, does the writer overcome the "harsh realities of the time," seeking to overcome injustice not through rebellion or overt activism but by bringing into being—through one's own writing—"an open and honest situation that values all human beings." These issues are especially apparent in the final sentence of the editors' introductory remarks: "Even though he gained control over his problems in a rational sense, it is clear that in all his writing, as also in this lecture, he is still emotionally fixated on the problem of racial differences" (Redaksi May–June 1955). From the universal humanist point of view, Wright's inability to free himself emotionally from "the problem of racial differences" is an impediment to a breakthrough into genuine humanism in his writing.

The lecture itself as published in *Konfrontasi* is very similar to "The Literature of the Negro in the United States" as it appeared two years later in *White Man*. Indeed, the two versions of this lecture often match up verbatim. The main difference is that the *Konfrontasi* version is somewhat shorter than the version that appears in *White Man*; a handful of passages of poetry and Wright's accompanying commentary are absent from the Indonesian publication. These changes would be consistent with Wright's desire to accommodate suggestions he may have received regarding a preferred time limit for the lecture. And, as would be expected, the *Konfrontasi* lecture is aware of its different rhetorical position in Indonesia. For instance, whereas Wright in *White Man* refers to the United States' first president as "the Father of Our Country" (114), in the *Konfrontasi* lecture he simply refers to him as "Washington" ("American" 7). Similarly, while the *White Man* lecture argues that "the lives of American Negroes closely resemble your own" (108), the *Konfrontasi* lecture argues that "the lives of American Negroes closely resemble those of the other Americans" ("American" 3). Perhaps less expectedly, the *Konfrontasi* lecture elides references to Soviet Russia and communism with such consistency that these elisions can only be considered purposeful, whether on the part of Wright himself or the *Konfrontasi* editors. For instance, while the *White Man* lecture recounts that "Soviet Russia rose and sent out her calls to the oppressed" (141), the *Konfrontasi* lecture credits others: "Trade Union Leaders send out their calls to the oppressed" ("American" 22). Elsewhere, when the *White Man* lecture lists Russians among the groups who have been curious to know more "about the American Negro" (145), the *Konfrontasi* lecture replaces the word "Russians" with "Italians" ("American" 24). It is difficult to ascertain who made the decision to elide references to Soviet Russia from the speech. Might Wright have done so because he knew from previous conversations that his audience members (while largely socialist) were strongly opposed to Soviet-style communism? If so, Wright would have gone out of his way to accommodate this aversion, given that the earliest printed version of the lecture (which appeared in French in Jean-Paul Sartre's journal *Les Temps Modernes* in 1948) conforms to the 1957 *White Man* version in including these references to Soviet Russia (Wright, "Littérature" 218, 220). There is also a possibility that Wright made these changes in response to an overt suggestion by the editors of *Konfrontasi*, who may have been uncomfortable about the publication of positive endorsements of Russian communism in the magazine. This possibility is brought into doubt, however, by the fact that *Konfrontasi*'s "Synopsis" of the lecture credits "the workers' movement of Western Europe and Russia" with energizing African American social engagement.

While the lecture itself is significant to the degree that it represents the first known English-language publication of the lecture Wright later included in *White Man*, it is *Konfrontasi*'s "Synopsis" that is most important to understanding Wright's engagements with and reception by the "tragic elite" to whom he dedicated *White Man*. The synopsis condenses and arranges Wright's words in a way that would have made them seem quite recognizable to an audience familiar with the Indonesian literary debates of the day, and indeed in a way quite germane to the particular stance the Konfrontasi Study Club was advancing in relation to the challenge that was being mounted by the Lembaga Kebudajaan Rakjat (LEKRA, Institute of People's Culture). Founded on 17 August 1950, LEKRA was an association of engaged artists, writers, and intellectuals with institutional links to the Partai Komunis Indonesia (PKI, Indonesian Communist Party). Within a year of its founding, on the first anniversary of the declaration of Indonesian independence commemorated in the sovereign new nation, LEKRA affiliates were actively contesting H. B. Jassin's claim that the spirit of the Indonesian revolution was embodied in the work of the Gelanggang-associated writers and their aesthetic ideology of universal humanism. In reply to Jassin's stance, key LEKRA theorists asserted that the "individualism" of the Gelanggang worldview needed to be replaced by an attitude of *people-mindedness* and an exposure of social ills and revolutionary aspirations through an uncompromising realist aesthetic (Akustia). In July 1955, LEKRA issued a revised version of its original 1950 Manifesto, adding a progressive internationalism to its fundamental outlooks and welcoming all Indonesian artists and cultural workers regardless of class background to its ranks, provided they shared an "emotional commitment to a free and self-reliant Indonesia, formed from a society based on justice and equality" (Foulcher, *Social* 29). Reflecting the Indonesian Communist Party's growing influence over national politics, LEKRA and its spokespeople were soon pursuing a vigorous anti-imperialism, directed primarily against Dutch cultural influence through the activities of STICUSA and against the United States for its perceived promotion of the "American way of life" through commercial cultural exports such as film and popular music (Foulcher, *Social* 34–36).

In this climate of LEKRA's increasing ascendancy, the outlooks associated with universal humanism and groups like the Konfrontasi circle were increasingly being criticized as the expression of an unhealthy bourgeois cultural nationalism. These accusations were keenly felt, and journals like *Konfrontasi* were already under pressure to defend their cultural outlooks through argument and example. Hence, when *Konfrontasi* printed Wright's English-language description of the rise of class consciousness in recent African American literature and Wright's illustration of his "identification with the workers of other lands" in his own poetry (Wright, "American" 23), the journal could well have been seen as endorsing the arguments being put forward at the time by the study club's own ideological opponents. The trajectory of Wright's lecture was potentially particularly troubling for his Konfrontasi audience because his remarks on the origins of African American literature in the shift from "a pre-individualistic culture" to a culture of "strident individualism" (4) established distinct parallels with the way cultural development was conceived in Indonesian thinking at this time. In tracing the ways individualism did not guarantee the African American writers admission into "the culture of their nation" and obliged them to hurl "pleading words again[st] the deaf ears of white America" before turning to a collective identification and outright revolt (13), Wright was suggesting that a writer who identified with the sufferings of his or her people could not turn away from writing that maintained the interests of those people in mind. Rather, a writer must strive to be a part of the people's struggle for justice. This was precisely the call that LEKRA was issuing to Indonesian writers at this time, so in the context of his Konfrontasi lecture, Wright could well have been seen as endorsing the Communist Party/LEKRA aesthetic that his Indonesian hosts had assumed he had abandoned, given what they knew of Wright's anti-Communist statements in *The Outsider* and his contribution to the anti-Communist essay collection *The God That Failed*.

In the Indonesian-language synopsis of Wright's lecture, we see *Konfrontasi*'s response to the challenge the lecture represented. This challenge is met head-on, with an opening reference to Wright's "political-sociological" approach and the suggestion that this "rather limited" viewpoint will provoke a question in the mind of readers as to the true "value" of African American literature. Yet Wright is clearly recognized as an internationally regarded figure hailing from the very center of Western Europe's culture, so the content of his lecture is framed in terms that make it amenable to universal humanist aesthetics. This is achieved first by the suggestion that the value of a work of literature is determined by its honest mirroring of "the life of humankind" and the vicissitudes of human experience. As these qualities are undeniably present in the examples of African American literature Wright quotes in his lecture, the synopsis argues, the reader can be confident that Wright is speaking of the real thing, literature that comes from the heart of the individual author, not programmed according to external demands, as was the case—in the Konfrontasi view—with the "realism" LEKRA was espousing.

When the synopsis reaches the conclusion of Wright's lecture, it is brought face-to-face with Wright's endorsement of engaged writing in defense of an oppressed people. And *Konfrontasi* acknowledges Wright's valorization of African American writers' confrontation with racial oppression and the need for collective action, even though this acknowledgment clearly reveals the lecture's ideological alignment as heading in the direction of LEKRA's stance. However, in a final twist, Wright's description of the call for action to end racial oppression in recent African American writing is recouped in the name of universal humanism (Foulcher, "Bringing" 36). In the words of the synopsis, African American writers are coming to realize that the African American struggle is "the struggle of humanity that was being fought out all over the earth." From the universal humanist viewpoint, the common struggle of humanity is the proper preserve of the writer, even though it may take a specific form according to the writer's honest engagement with his or her own specific experiences. In this way, Wright's defense of politically engaged writing is effectively brought within bounds consistent with *Konfrontasi*'s outlook, in a way that evokes an image of Wright belonging to the universal humanist camp rather than to the Konfrontasi group's opponents.[7]

The "Synopsis" made Wright's lecture seem ideologically familiar enough that when Takdir Alisjahbana shortly thereafter published his study *Sedjarah Bahasa Indonesia* (History of the Indonesian Language), the book's back cover included an advertisement for *Konfrontasi* that mentioned Wright. The advertisement stated, "This young country of ours is faced with a range of issues all at one time, covering political, economic, cultural, social, educational, and legal matters, as well as various other questions." Until now, it explained, "there has been little real effort to make any in-depth study . . . of these issues in relation to . . . Indonesia as well as the world." Pointing toward *Konfrontasi*'s attempt to "fill this gap," the advertisement named six articles it had published during its first year of existence, including "American Negro Writing" by Richard Wright ("Tiga"). The inclusion of Wright's lecture, the only text on the list written by a non-Indonesian, was likely intended to show potential readers that *Konfrontasi*'s concern with issues facing "this young country" also incorporated international perspectives.

Intriguingly, the very issue of perspective had surfaced prominently at the closing of *Konfrontasi*'s "Synopsis," although there would have been some confusion as to how Wright's statements on perspective ought to be interpreted.

In both the 1955 *Konfrontasi* lecture and the later version of the same lecture included in his 1957 *White Man*, Wright concludes by quoting material from his 1941 book *12 Million Black Voices*. In the 1957 version, one of Wright's excerpts from *12 Million Black Voices* appears as follows: "Look at us and know us and you will know yourselves, for *we are you*, looking back at you from the dark mirror of our lives!" (Wright, "Literature" 146; Wright, *12 Million* 146). Though this quote does not appear in the text of Wright's *Konfrontasi* lecture, it appears in *Konfrontasi*'s "Synopsis," as a concluding and apparently informally delivered "rallying cry": "Lihatlah kepada kami, kenallah kami dan saudara² akan kenal diri sendiri, karena kami adalah saudara², kami jang memandang kepada saudara² dari katja gelap kehidupan kami!" ("Synopsis" 28). This is a direct translation of Wright's English-language excerpt from *12 Million Black Voices*. Yet in this case, even a direct translation introduces distortions. When he wrote these words in *12 Million Black Voices*, Wright was speaking to white Americans, asking white Americans to see themselves in the faces and lives of black Americans. Yet the Indonesians in his 1955 audience (whether auditors in Tugu or readers of *Konfrontasi*) would likely have understood Wright to be asking Indonesians to see themselves in the faces and lives of African Americans. This interpretation may indeed have been what Wright intended, given that in the more formal portion of his lecture he had stated that the "voice of the American Negro is rapidly becoming the most representative voice of oppressed people anywhere in the world today" ("American" 24). However, Wright certainly did not intend a second discrepancy in the quotation's interpretation. Whereas Wright's English-language rallying cry has Wright and other African Americans "looking back at you [white Americans or Indonesians] from the dark mirror of our lives," *Konfrontasi*'s literal translation of "dark mirror" (i.e., "katja gelap") may evoke either the image of a dark mirror or a dark pane of glass, such that some of *Konfrontasi*'s readers would have walked away from reading Wright's rallying cry with the understanding that Wright was asserting that there existed a dark pane of glass between himself and his hosts. According to this understanding, the dark pane of glass might permit his hosts to see only an obscured and incomplete image of Wright while reciprocally permitting Wright to see only an obscured and incomplete image of his hosts. This would have been a misunderstanding of Wright's intentions, but, as demonstrated later in this collection by Indonesian commentary on Wright after his visit, the image of colored or distorting glass became a recurring metaphor for the ways some Indonesians understood Wright's views on Indonesia.[8]

Synopsis
from Konfrontasi
SOURCE LANGUAGE: INDONESIAN

In the above essay, the famous American writer Richard Wright lays out the development of Negro literature, which he sees mainly from a political-sociological angle.

Although this rather narrow viewpoint will raise questions and some hesitation in the reader—what really is the value of Negro literature?—we are certain that after reading this strong and convincing account, the reader will feel satisfied. Richard Wright's analysis portrays the life of his community with all its hardships, as reflected in the quotations of poetry and other examples of Negro literature. And isn't the value of a literary creation partly determined by the work's honesty or otherwise, its faithful mirroring of the life of humankind and the vicissitudes of life experienced to the full?

THE AUTHOR, WHO DELIVERED this essay as a lecture to an evening meeting of "Konfrontasi" in early May,[9] began with a comparison between a society he called "an entity" and a society that had begun to assume the individualist characteristics of "identity." The "original" Negro communities (referring to Africa, before Negroes were sold as slaves to America) were actually no different from, for example, French settler communities in Quebec (Canada). They were both holistic and integral communities in which there was no difference between the life of an individual and that of his group as a whole, no difference between life, culture, and politics.

We can add here that this type of holistic community was also familiar in Indonesia in former times.

The organic community was shattered and dispersed in the United States by the forces of modernization in almost all fields in the course of the last two centuries.

The lines of division between the American people in this connection can be termed "Jim Crowism," or, in everyday language, white vs. colored. The causes of this "split" can of course be discussed further, but because this subject has been covered in books by both American and non-American writers, the author did not pursue it here. A discussion of this type would also take him too far away from his exposé.

A phenomenon that is readily apparent in other countries is that a Negro, because of his ability to adapt to his surroundings, can integrate into the culture of the country and the people around him wherever he finds himself living. The author offered the examples of Alexander Dumas and Alexander Pushkin, figures whose names are familiar in the world of literature, as a French writer and a Russian poet.

It is a different matter in the United States.

There it is possible to find a few Negroes who have integrated into white American culture, but these Negroes are exceptions to the rule. In general, the Negroes live separately from their white-skinned compatriots. They are separate, because they have been segregated from the rest of society by white people, both during the time when slavery was rampant and also after it was abolished. They are not allowed to assimilate, not allowed to mix with white people because it is forbidden by law as well as by customary practice within American society. Segregation still exists.

This leaves the Negro to ponder on his unhappy fate, living with suffering and hardship that he can only express in his poetry, in his song and music, and in his church. And even though there have been attempts by the central government to introduce de-segregation (especially in recent times), the old law that says "nature is stronger than nurture" still applies.

Richard Wright gave many examples drawn from poetry to show the suffering of the Negro, portraying the Negro's love for the land where he lived, but also the feelings of hatred and resentment that burn within him toward his tyrannical Great White Master.[10] Negroes have fled from the interior to the cities in the southern United States, and from the cities in the South to the cities of the North. In wave after wave they have fled the misfortune, the suffering, the lash of the whip, and also rape, in search of safety and protection. But it has all been in vain.

The abolition of slavery, emancipation, and later industrialization, have not changed the fate of Negroes generally. On the contrary, they too have been divided up into stratified groups: rich alongside poor, advocates of one cause alongside advocates of another. Negro writers have also been subject to this kind of stratification. The group the author labels "the Narcissists" continue to wade in the mire of their degradation by writing poetry and prose that merely describes how the Negro suffers, how he finds pleasure, how he indulges his passions, and the like.

Alongside this whimpering group there are other groups; from among these we may mention the group that is really still looking for its own forms, which the author calls "The Forms of Things Unknown."

Among them are those who pursue material concerns, but there are also those with spiritual ideals, because they realize that through (Christian) religion, they have entered Western culture. And truly, in religion they feel as though they are crossing the threshold into the culture of their country and people, the American people! But neither can religion bring these two differ-ent skin colors together, because for them it is a Negro church, just as their schools are Negro schools, their hotels and restaurants are Negro establish-ments, and so on and so on.

Unification with the lives and culture of their compatriots is forever out of reach, even though in times of crisis or war they have stood together with whites to defend their country and people. . . . . [11]

There came a point, however, when the socialist movement, the workers' movement of Western Europe and Russia seemed to beckon them, invite them to stand shoulder to shoulder in defense of the oppressed and downtrodden.[12] That call received a warm welcome among the Negroes, as it did also among writers. The Negro began to realize that he was not alone in his suffering, that in other countries as well there was still a great deal of oppression and exploitation of colored peoples by white people, and even of their fellow white people in weak economic circumstances.

And so, on the other side of the literary world from Phyllis Wheatley, there appeared Margaret Walker and dozens of other poets who began to realize that the suffering of their people, the suffering of the Negro, was the strug-gle of humanity that was being fought out all over the earth.[13] And Richard Wright closed his essay with a rallying cry: "Look at us and know us and you will know yourselves, for *we* are *you*, looking back at you from the dark mirror of our lives!"

Notes

1. In the conclusion to his report on this 1951 gathering, Achdiat suggested that ideo-logical tensions between participants were dissipated by the close personal interactions these weekend meetings encouraged (244). Although by 1955 such relaxed interaction between ideological opponents was no longer the norm, Achdiat's comments aptly por-tray the camaraderie that these meetings generated among those who took part in them.

2. See Vuyk's "A Weekend with Richard Wright" in part III.

3. Unless otherwise noted, quotations and narratives in this paragraph are drawn from Vuyk's "A Weekend with Richard Wright," included in part III.

4. Wright's description of this particular trip to the mountains is not the same event as the weekend of his lecture for Konfrontasi. Wright spoke to the study club toward the end of his stay in Indonesia, on Sunday, 1 May. But his journal records an earlier trip, occurring before the Bandung Conference, probably on Saturday, 16 April, or Sunday, 17 April, while en route to Bandung from Jakarta. The 16 or 17 April visit to the moun-tains may be the same as the visit during which Wright spoke with Mochtar, Nuraini, and Vuyk, as recorded in Vuyk's "A Weekend with Richard Wright."

5. Nuraini's excerpt was the fifth chapter of *The Heart Is a Lonely Hunter* and was published in *Konfrontasi*'s March-April 1955 issue, immediately prior to the issue containing Wright's lecture (McCullers).

6. The Indonesian text here is not completely clear. It appears that a word such as *bahasa (language)* has been omitted after *sifat*[2] *(characteristics)*.

7. It is true that Wright himself provided the cue for this interpretation of his lecture in his comment, "I know that many of you are shaking heads and wondering what value there is in writing like that . . . ," and his explanation, "We write only of what life gives us in the form of experience. And [there] is a value in what we Negro writers say" (24). However, the Indonesian synopsis gives these remarks a centrality that is out of proportion to their place in the lecture as a whole, in order to position Wright's words firmly within the universal humanist argument.

8. For further discussion of the difference between *dark mirror* and *katja gelap*, see Roberts 155–69.

9. Here, the "Synopsis" suggests that Wright gave his lecture in the evening, seemingly as a standard Saturday evening lecture at Takdir's villa, as was the typical program for Konfrontasi. This suggestion is inconsistent with Beb Vuyk's memory of the event, in which Wright's place in the standard procession of events gets pushed to the following morning due to a dinner party on Saturday night. Given that it is confirmed that Wright gave his lecture on Sunday, 1 May 1955 (see "Who's Doing What," 4 May 1955, in "A Sheaf of Newspaper Articles," included in part III), it is clear that Wright's lecture was not delivered in a way consistent with Konfrontasi's standard Saturday-evening program. It may be that in the "Synopsis," *Konfrontasi* decided to refer to an "evening meeting" because this phrase best conveyed to its audience the genre of meeting (one of the well-known Tugu meetings at Takdir's villa).

10. In the source text, this sentence includes the ironic term *Sang Kulit Putih*, which we have translated as *Great White Master*.

11. These extended ellipses are present in the source text.

12. Notably, even though *Konfrontasi* discusses Soviet Russia here, it functionally denies that a concern with workers' movements is confined to Communist countries. Consistent with the approach of the CCF, this rhetorical position emphasizes the importance of left-oriented politics that are distinctly non-Communist.

13. The appearance of the spelling *Phyllis* (rather than the correct spelling *Phillis*) occurs in both the *Konfrontasi* synopsis and Wright's English language lecture ("American" 7).

10

Richard Wright's "The Artist and His Problems" (1955)

On the evening of the day following his mountainside lecture for the Konfrontasi Study Club, Wright was back in Jakarta, at the Balai Budaja, or Cultural
Affairs Center, administered by the BMKN. Incorporating a large meeting hall
that also functioned as an exhibition gallery, the Balai Budaja was at this time
a popular meeting place for Jakarta's young artists and writers (Ajip, *Anak*
103). During Wright's few weeks in Indonesia, the building had been the
venue for an Indonesian art exhibition, the screening of a British and a Russian film, and, at the very end of April, an evening commemorating the sixth
anniversary of the death of the great Indonesian poet Chairil Anwar (Program), whose short life had galvanized the universalist ideals of Wright's main
interlocutors. But tonight, at the beginning of May, the Balai Budaja was the
venue for a lecture by Wright himself.

Organized by PEN Club Indonesia and the BMKN, Wright's 2 May lecture was published in Mochtar Lubis's newspaper *Indonesia Raya* on 22 May
1955, two-and-a-half weeks after Wright left Indonesia. It appeared as an article titled "Seniman dan Masaalahnja" (The Artist and His Problems) in the
newspaper's regular cultural and literary column, *Kebudajaan-Kesusasteraan*.[1]

FIGURE 10.1. Exterior of the Balai Budaja (1955), venue of Richard Wright's 2 May 1955 lecture "The Artist and His Problems," for PEN Club Indonesia and the BMKN. This photograph shows the venue during the December 1955 exhibition of work by the Indonesian painter Lee Siang Yun. Photograph by Claire Holt. CHC, record ID 439297. Reproduced with the permission of Daniela Holt Voith. Courtesy of New York Public Library.

FIGURE 10.2. Interior of the Balai Budaja. Photograph by Brian Russell Roberts (May 2013).

Whereas Wright's lecture for the Konfrontasi Study Club was published in English in the club's bimonthly magazine, his PEN Club/BMKN lecture was published only in Indonesian. And whereas Wright's Konfrontasi lecture eventually found its second English-language publication in *White Man, Listen!* as "The Literature of the Negro in the United States," his PEN Club/BMKN lecture has until now never been republished, in either Indonesian or English.

We have prepared this version of "The Artist and His Problems" based on two source texts: the article "Seniman dan Masaalahnja" as it appeared in *Indonesia Raya* in May 1955 and a set of more extensive typescript notes that Wright made in preparation for the lecture, which are held among the Richard Wright Papers in Yale University's Beinecke Library.[2] The *Indonesia Raya* article, which has the quality of polished prose, provides the bulk of the material and is highly valuable for providing a primary account of what Wright said during the lecture and what his Indonesian audience understood of it. And though the *Indonesia Raya* version excludes about a third of the material that Wright included in his notes (and, less often, the notes do not contain some of the material published in *Indonesia Raya*), the two versions of the lecture usually match up sentence for sentence, on the level of ideas, if not word for word. However, the differences between the two versions—ranging from passages in the notes that are missing from *Indonesia Raya* to sentences in *Indonesia Raya* that are missing from the notes and to word-level mismatches between the two versions—provide useful, if inevitably speculative, insight into the process that gave rise to the version of the lecture Wright gave on 2 May 1955 as well as the version of the lecture published by *Indonesia Raya* later that same month.

Reading through Wright's typescript lecture notes, one is struck that they frequently address issues that may not have been well suited for an Indonesian audience of the day. Much of this material is absent from the lecture as published in *Indonesia Raya*. At times, for instance, the notes reference names, ideas, and nuances that only a very cosmopolitan Indonesian audience (or a highly educated European or American audience, for that matter) would have understood in the 1950s. Some of the more involved portions of Wright's notes include remarks on the stark contrast between Gertrude Stein's aesthetics and nuclear-age physics, the question of synthesizing subjective and objective modes of aesthetic expression, and the topic of phenomenology as advanced by Jean-Paul Sartre and Edmund Husserl. Other portions of the notes seem a bit out of tune with Indonesian cultural conditions. At one point, the notes reference Chinese premier Zhou Enlai's Bandung Conference affirmation of his disbelief in God, and Wright subsequently discusses the idea of physics and a godless universe. At another point, Wright singles out the contributions of specifically Jewish writers to the project of integrating morality and art. In Indonesia, where Muslim-based political parties were a part of every ruling coalition during this period of parliamentary democracy, and where acknowledgment of religious faith had been enshrined in the state philosophy (Pancasila), atheism and Jewish aesthetic contributions may have been seen as inappropriate topics for publication in a popular newspaper. Despite *Indonesia Raya*'s own secular nationalism and the open debate encouraged by the lecture's venue at Balai Budaja, these references may well have seemed uncomfortably controversial.

Given that these types of passages were excluded from the version of the lecture that was published in *Indonesia Raya*, one can imagine the following and necessarily speculative scenario occurring at some point between the Bandung Conference's conclusion on 24 April and Wright's 2 May delivery of "The Artist and His Problems." During this time, Wright would have written notes for his lecture and then showed them to his host, Mochtar Lubis, in preparation for the PEN Club/BMKN event. Mochtar may have suggested portions to cut from the lecture, based on his knowledge of audience interest and level of understanding. Importantly, Mochtar also would have been thinking about the lecture's potential for translation into Indonesian as he suggested sections to cut. As Mochtar knew, the Indonesian English-speakers in Wright's audience would speak English as a second or more likely third or fourth language (with English following their regional languages, the national Indonesian language, and—among the older generation—the Dutch language), and some in the audience would speak very little if any English. It is likely that Mochtar suggested it would be best if he himself provided a running Indonesian translation of the lecture as Wright gave it. Based on these suggestions from Mochtar, Wright may have prepared a second set of simplified notes, shorter than the original, to hand over to Mochtar for translation ahead of time. Though obviously speculative, this scenario would be consistent with the recollections of Ajip Rosidi, who attended Wright's PEN Club/BMKN lecture as a young Indonesian writer at the age of seventeen. As Ajip recalled during a 2013 conversation with Brian Roberts, he himself could not follow all of the lecture because Wright delivered it in English, but, looking back on it, Ajip believed Mochtar Lubis translated it into Indonesian so that non-English-speakers could understand it (Ajip, Interview). This scenario, involving two sets of lecture notes (one to hand over to Mochtar and one that Wright kept and that eventually found its way into the Beinecke collection), would also explain the differences between the extant notes and the *Indonesia Raya* version of the lecture, including the sections from the notes that are elided from *Indonesia Raya* and also the sentences included in *Indonesia Raya* (on Wright's trip to the Gold Coast and issues of temporality in *The Outsider*) that are nowhere to be found in the lecture notes.[3]

Whatever the scenario, as we have prepared this English-language version of "The Artist and His Problems," we have relied primarily on "Seniman dan Masaalahnja" as a means of giving readers access to how Wright's Indonesian audience would have understood him in 1955. Based on Ajip Rosidi's 2013 recollections of the event, Wright probably delivered his lecture to about thirty people, but the spoken lecture (even as it was likely supplemented by Mochtar's translation at the event itself) would have been difficult for many audience members to understand or fully absorb, so the translated version as published in Mochtar's newspaper would have helped solidify the understanding of those who were in the audience while also providing a wider Indonesian readership with access to Wright's stances on artists generally and writers in particular.

Yet even as we have been concerned with how Wright's Indonesian audience understood him, we have also been concerned with Wright's intentions. To this end, in back-translating the published version of the talk, we have carefully compared our English-language translation with Wright's typescript notes, working to integrate Wright's English words and phrases whenever this course of action also permits us to convey the meaning of the lecture as it was documented in *Indonesia Raya*. Throughout, we have used explanatory notes to discuss where and how the two versions depart from each other in significant ways at the sentence or phrase level. Finally, wherever the *Indonesia Raya* version of the lecture does not contain material that is included in the notes, we have reinserted the elided material and designated these reinsertions by placing the text in italics. In reinserting this material based on sometimes rough notes, we have followed Wright's own ethic, which he stated in reference to his preparations to publish his *White Man, Listen!* lectures: "In these pages, . . . I've deliberately preserved the spoken tone" (16).

Wright delivered "The Artist and His Problems" in Jakarta at a stage in his public life when he was giving many lectures. From 1950 through 1956, he lectured for the Italian Cultural Association in Genoa and Rome, for STICUSA in Amsterdam, for the CCF and the German publisher Claassen Verlag in Hamburg, for *Présence Africaine* in Paris, and for the Swedish publisher Bonnier in Stockholm, Uppsala, Oslo, Gothenburg, Lund, and Copenhagen. These talks found their way into Wright's four-lecture collection *White Man, Listen!*, as Wright explains in his introduction to that publication (15). Taken together, Wright stated, the four lectures "made a comment, connected and coherent, upon white-colored, East-West relations in the world today" (16). Bringing "The Artist and His Problems" into the orbit of Wright's other lectures from this period—as a sort of lost fifth lecture from the era of *White Man, Listen!*—permits a greater view of his East-West thematic, as this lecture was of course prepared and given specifically for an Indonesian audience in the wake of the Asian-African Conference in Bandung.

While Wright's lecture reflects the larger synthesis he was arriving at through previous travels and writings on Africa and Spain, "The Artist and His Problems" is also distinctly of the time and place of its presentation: modern Indonesia during the months surrounding the Bandung Conference. Notably, Wright refers to his discussions with several Indonesian writers with whom he had been speaking throughout his visit and not simply during his Konfrontasi lecture of the previous day.[4] He reminds his Indonesian interlocutors that the genre of the novel emerged out of specific class conditions in the West. Indonesian writers, Wright suggests, will do well to remember that because of the novel's genesis from within these particular class conditions, the notion of time as showcased in the traditional novel may not resonate with Indonesian senses of temporality. Hence, Indonesia's writers will need to evoke senses of time in their fiction that correspond to Indonesia's specific conditions. Wright predicts that if Indonesian writers work with passion, they may be able to develop new senses of time and new forms. When Wright mentions his "discussions with several Indonesian writers" and his "impression that there are a lot of people in Indonesia asking why the novel is not as developed here as people would like it to be," we have a view of Wright's encounter with a debate that had dominated much of the discussion among literary circles in Jakarta in the previous year or two. At issue was a "crisis" evoked by the supposed loss of the creative élan of the years of national revolution, when both poetry and fiction had blossomed under circumstances of high national drama and optimism about the Indonesian future. Some of the most vocal proponents of the notion of "crisis" in Indonesian literature at this time were associated with the Konfrontasi circle, so it is most likely that Wright's understanding of the debate was mediated through this connection, perhaps even through his recent discussion "about Indonesian literature" with the study club in Tugu (Kiuchi and Hakutani 326). If so, his comments on the problems of form and time at this point in the lecture can be seen as a response to issues that this particular group had raised with him.[5] Wright's direct engagement with specific debates and concerns among Indonesian literary figures seems sharper in the lecture's *Indonesia Raya* version than in the typescript, an effect produced by the elimination (whether by Mochtar's or Wright's own design) of some of the potentially distracting discussions contained in the notes.

In weighing in on the ongoing "crisis" discussions of Indonesian literature, and in discussing Zhou Enlai's recently delivered comments at the Bandung Conference, Wright was in the process of integrating his Indonesian travels into a larger synthesis regarding the international situation and the postcolonial world, bringing these experiences into dialogue with what he had previously experienced in Africa. The Bandung Conference's impress on and integration into his larger synthesis became clear after he returned from Indonesia. Prompted by what he had witnessed in Southeast Asia, he delivered a lecture titled "The Psychological Reactions of Oppressed People," which conceives of the two continents of Asia and Africa as a unitary bloc, as "Asia and Africa" (*White* 31), home to "Asian-African minds" (38). This lecture speaks of the "Western-educated" political figures Wright had met "in Asia and Africa"—Nkrumah, Nasser, Soekarno, and Nehru—and discusses their "negative loyalty" to the West in tandem with African Americans' negative loyalty to the United States (41). And in another *White Man* lecture, "Tradition and Industrialization," Wright again turned to Soekarno, Nehru, Nasser, and Nkrumah, saying that they "will necessarily use quasi-dictatorial methods to hasten the process of social evolution and to establish order in their lands." Here, Wright reminds readers that these Asian and African leaders are only doing what the West has done repeatedly (*White* 101). Wright remarks that "this elite in Asia and Africa constitutes islands of free men, the FREEST MEN IN ALL THE WORLD TODAY" (97). Perhaps not coincidentally, Wright's metaphor of postcolonial leaders as a planet-spanning island chain emerged in a lecture given after he witnessed Asia and Africa's convergence on the Indonesian archipelago for the Bandung Conference.

On the same day that Wright delivered "The Artist and His Problems," Michael Josselson, back in Paris, wrote a letter to Mochtar Lubis, asking, "How did Richard Wright's visit work out?" A week after Wright's departure and a week and a half before publishing the lecture in *Indonesia Raya*, Mochtar replied: "We enjoyed Richard Wright's visit very much. He gave lectures to a small group of Indonesian writers, and to an audience organized by the Indonesian Cultural Association [and] the PEN Club."[6]

The Artist and His Problems
by Richard Wright
SOURCE LANGUAGES: INDONESIAN AND ENGLISH

Editors' Introduction: This article is a lecture given by the famous American Negro writer, Richard Wright, at an event organized by the Council for Deliberations on National Culture (BMKN) and PEN CLUB INDONESIA in the Cultural Affairs Center (Balai Budaja), Jakarta, on the evening of 2 May last.[7]

In discussing these issues confronting the artist, I would like to explain first of all that the artist I have in mind in this lecture is the writer. I am a writer, and I feel that in speaking about the artist and his problems, it would be better for me to limit my discussion this evening to the problems of the artist as a writer.[8]

The writer and his audience

In the contemporary world, one problem is the relationship between the writer and his audience. This is vastly different from the situation in former times, when stories were told among small groups of people who received the stories directly from the mouth of a storyteller, and experiences were passed on to listeners close at hand. Today we see that the connection between the writer and his audience has become distant, and has lost the personal dimension. Now the writer writes not solely to tell listeners about his experiences, but more to convey something to his readers.[9] Modern society has splintered into various different fragments, and the artist is searching for human unity, a unity which economics and politics have sundered.[10] In today's world we also see that the writer cannot know in advance what responses his work might evoke.

Every time he writes, it is like a spark flying into darkness. He hurls a noise out and waits for the echoes to come back. In fact, we might observe that in our world, the artist is someone who exists in solitude. This is very different from the position of the artist in the past; now he does not have people supporting and helping him.[11]

Today, the artist has no personal relationship with his public.[12]

The increasing modernization of human life and the new experiences humanity is undergoing make it impossible for the sensitive artist to accept the old forms of expression.[13]

For example, Walt Whitman, the American poet, left the old forms behind and sought his own new forms. Similarly in France we find that poets have gone in search of new forms. In my opinion, the search for new forms isn't simply experimentation for its own sake. On the contrary, it is motivated by a real necessity. *But new forms quickly became accepted; and this made Gertrude Stein say that classics were what had been classified.*[14] I myself fully accept these innovations, and the search for new forms conforming to new experience. However, I also believe that these new forms of expression must be driven by a passion that the writer wholeheartedly feels, not just by a need to display his technical ability.[15]

Time as an element in art

When I visited the Gold Coast in Africa some time ago, I noticed how time occupied a position in the outlooks of the Negro people there that was quite different from Western people's view of time.[16] Africans, whose way of thinking is calm and static, have a different conception of time.[17] For them, living in a world of tribal allegiances, time is cyclical. This differs, for example, from the Western conception of time, which is linear and progressive, moving from a point in the past toward a point in the future.[18]

The society and religion of a particular region or nation is built on a sense of time. In Indonesia, I feel there are still lingering remnants of the sense of time I just described, *making many times exist in your land*. A writer who is not faced with this problem of time is blessed indeed. I myself, when I was writing *The Outsider*, felt very much aware of it. The main character in that book belongs to a social class whose sense of time is not dynamic and progressive, because it has little hope for the future.[19] In my discussions with several Indonesian writers, I gained the impression that there are a lot of people in Indonesia asking why the novel is not as developed here as people would like it to be. Perhaps one of the reasons is that Indonesia has not yet seen the rise of a middle class, a class that has freed itself from the structures of a feudal society and launched itself on a path toward a new future, consciously in search of experience.

Even though the novel is a form of art, it must not be forgotten that the novel is a distinct form of expression of a particular social class, and that the novel is a form of expression belonging to that class. Perhaps in Indonesia the artist still needs to seek a conception of time that is right for his art, and as long as Indonesia is still in a time of transition, the majority of novels being written will be novels dealing with problems. Nevertheless, who knows? If Indonesian writers are able to perceive their situations keenly, and full of passion, it is possible that they will be able to create a new sense of time, and also new forms of expression attuned to the society around them and its sense of history.

What should the writer write about?

What should a writer write about? What subject matter should he use? There are writers who believe that it is they who choose what they will write about. However, it is actually more often the case that the work itself chooses the writer who will compose it. I'm speaking here of the writer who composes a work on the basis of his emotions, and these emotions are the products of his experiences. In fact, experience constitutes any artist's subject matter.

However, a given experience can mean different things to different people. Someone who seeks experience freely will find that he not only encounters a variety of experiences but also experiences from different levels of human life. The outlook of a Jack London is not the same as the outlook of a Marcel Proust, for example. As is reflected in our modern world, when an artist has no direct connection with his audience, he has to depend more on the way facts imprint themselves on his senses. In relying on his experiences, a writer hopes that what he writes will resonate in the hearts of others. Here we see how subjectivity, when it is thrown forth in art and moves other people, proves the oneness of mankind.

In fact, it is not true to say that a writer who is a genuine artist is able to choose a range of political material and just shape that material into an art form. What actually happens is that the political material takes hold of the artist in the form of his own experiences. For example, a writer may travel all over the world, a journey of thousands of miles, only in the end to write of what concerns him most personally. And that is as it should be.

The professional writer and the part-time writer

These days there are no longer wealthy patrons or royalty who underwrite writers. And except in Spain, there are no longer churches prepared to support an artist. For that reason, in our world the writer has to make a living from his writing, or, if he is unable to exist solely as a writer, he is forced to make a living as a journalist while he continues to write, or to write while working in some other job. Many of my friends have expressed their surprise that I am able to live just from my writing.[20] Actually, this is not because of the way I write; it is possible because of the system of distribution and sale of books that operates at present in the United States. Book clubs, well-financed magazines, and so on make it possible for someone to live as a member of the middle class in America just by writing.[21] In fact, the sale of just four stories to the *Saturday Evening Post*, for example, gives someone the ability to send his son or daughter to a university—Harvard University. To be able to write the kind of stories popular with magazines of this type, however, is harder than you might think.

The writer must produce stories he knows will be liked by the magazines' editors and also by their readers. His personal emotions have very little, if anything, to do with this type of writing. Some writers succeed in writing this way throughout their lives. They are probably very lucky.

It is very rare for a writer to be able to give expression to his deepest emotions and in doing so, to make a living from his writing. There are many who have to work as teachers or journalists and write at night, or on Sundays, when they don't have to go to work. Only those writers who are able to decide for themselves about the really important things in life can avoid the temptation of making a lot of money by writing in the way that those well-financed magazines require. A true artist must be aware that art is a jealous queen. An artist cannot worship her and go picking other flowers at the same time.[22]

A part-time writer has an advantage over the professional writer. Being part of the workforce, he has a connection with society and with humanity. There is no danger he will be out of step with current affairs.

In the end, a genuine and serious writer comes to realize that his subjects are only the outer dress of the emotions he wants to convey. As such, he writes not primarily to make more money, but with the intention of conveying to others the promptings of his heart. When he does this, there is the possibility that he will perform that rare miracle: he will say what he wishes and make money too.

Politics and art

I would like to make it clear that I in no way oppose writers taking sides in political affairs, or writers making use of their art as a vehicle for political ideas. In saying this, it is also not my intention to speak against what people call art for art's sake. There is such a thing as art for the sake of art, and it has its place. *To say that one should not delight in the world as it is, nor write to convey such truth of the world, is to take away from human beings a vital part of existence. Some writers, Gautier, Stein, and a host of others have tried to do this. Stein wanted to make us aware, with words, of what simple existence meant, what it was. This is what I'd call the aesthetic component in life. The universe itself is a spectacle in which one can take endless delight. But to have such a diet of eternal sweetness is to do violence to life; we have also other and deeper needs. Men make theories about the world in which they live; they act to test those theories; and in doing so they learn about the exact nature of the environment. Knowledge of this sort is based on theory. At a time in history when Newton and others started discovering the laws of matter, a split came to be in man's consciousness: there was a public world and a world which was valid only for physics and science. The former was and is the world of our senses, the world we share with our fellow man, etc. This is a world of smiles and immediate beauty;[23] men have made religions out of working out relations of harmony with it . . . Then there is the world which the atom bomb represents, the hydrogen bomb is the apex of. That world came into being slowly, with mathematics and physics as the tools to unearth and discover it. What is the relation between the cold and bleak world of the physicist and the world of the rose is a rose is a rose . . . ?[24]*

One thing is certain: the more that physics reveals that this world contains laws but not for us, that it is neutral, the more we find all concepts from God down to the concept of marriage to be simply man-made artifacts.[25] Chou En-lai told us a few days ago that he did not believe in God; well, it was stating but a fact that millions suspect deep in their hearts and have acted upon.[26] Meanwhile, in human life there are times when tradition, custom, and the old values can no longer provide people with the guidance they once did. At moments like this, leaders arise with new ideologies, and through the use of violence these leaders construct a new society by force.[27] At such times, the position of the writer becomes terribly important. He may find himself in the role of a priest charged with producing replacements for holy scriptures like the Bible, the Qur'an, and so on. In these circumstances, he is hired by those in power to write in a way that leads the people to follow the will of the new government.

For this reason, it is not surprising that writers in Russia constitute the new elite and are the richest class in Russia. *But where God reigns, where marriage is sacred, where traditional values rule, the writer is reduced to writing ads for Lux soap . . .*[28] *No wonder such writers do not respect themselves; and when a writer must write copy to sell the painted beauty of Hollywood movie stars, he must hate himself, and the society in which he lives rightly despises him . . .*

However, if there are readers who would proclaim how lucky the writer-made-priest is, they should remember that there is a great deal of danger in occupying such a position. Suppose, as a writer, you support the man in power in 1950, only to find that in 1955 a new man comes to power. In 1955 you might be shot for having supported the leaders who were in power in 1950. A friend of mine, Louis Adamic, was found murdered some years ago. He was a popular left-wing author, but he wrote for the side that . . . lost. Now he is dead. Two thousand years ago Aristotle said that literature is dangerous work. This is still true today. So, young writers, enter the political arena, go in search of glory and money, but don't be surprised if you end up losing . . . your head!

Subjective and objective and synthetic modes of expression

I'd like to begin by talking about subjectivity, objectivity, and what we'd call mystic visions or synthetic visions which are found in art by telling you a recent, personal experience. Not many weeks ago I was in Toledo and I sat in the Church of St. Thomas before El Greco's great painting, The Burial of Count Orgaz. *I had before my eyes a plastic series of images of how the world looked to one man according to the Catholic relation's [religion's] interpretation of life. I was looking at art and ideology, art and mysticism blended into one declaration thrown up from one man's passion . . . Was it objective or subjective or only mysticism?*[29] *I think from what I've said up to now that you know that I feel that the origins of all art are subjective; if that is so, how can one account for the blazing glory of El Greco's subjective vision being so real and urgent today . . . ? Obviously, we are dealing with relations between the aspects of one central fact. If a writer or an artist, for that matter, chooses to represent what he feels only in terms of the tiny movements of his consciousness, as in the so-called stream of consciousness methods made so famous by Joyce, he can do so; he leaves himself open to vagueness, to many interpretations. Or if he chooses to be objective, to give us a picture of life only in terms of the "facts," as he might call them, he cannot escape choosing his facts, and that gesture alone betrays the bias which he tries to hide but which cannot be hidden. Mysticism is generally such a vision as that painted by El Greco but without the support and sanction of the State or Church; it is a personal vision. The drawback of such visions is that they are mostly held together by arbitrary elements selected by the artist, and not agreed upon or approved by the society. Sometimes such visions carry great validity, such as the visions of Blake;[30] at other times they are just simply the dull daydreams of men out of touch with reality. The moral of all of this is: if you are going to be a mystic, then be sure to get somebody to agree with you beforehand. A church, some government, or you will have a hard row to hoe . . .*

Morality and art

There has been much too much nonsense written on this topic. Art, some people say, ought to be moral; morals, say others, must be artistic. In fact, as a form of knowledge, art is an instrument of the truth, and as such, it is amoral. This does not mean the goal of art is only to affirm moral codes, because this would severely restrict its efforts to expose the truth of human experience. *A while back I referred to the theoretic and aesthetic components of the human outlook. I think that there can be a union of the theoretic and aesthetic components. Many works of art have demonstrated this; I refer to Marcel Proust's* Remembrance of Things Past, *which is a truly enchanting, magical piece of work, a series of novels whose appeal to the senses excludes any message; yet it does carry a deep and meaningful moral lesson.[31] I'd say that it is the East that stresses the aesthetic claim and the West that stresses the moral or theoretic claim. And the fact is that Jews, Proust, Kafka, Stein, have made brilliant contributions in the realm of combining the aesthetic and the moral in great art.[32] In short, beauty is used to float hard facts of life to us. Such art is, of course, close to the pagan ideal. (I'm not talking now of a belief in God, but of the ability of some peoples to admit beauty into their moral notions, beauty such as one sees and feels in Spanish churches—and Spain I claim is the most pagan country of all Western Europe.) The other extreme is to be seen in the stern, bare, bleak Protestant churches of America, especially in the South, Midwest, and New England . . . And it is where these churches exist that industrialization is at its apex of development; and it is where Gothic cathedrals, compelling in their beauty, exist where you find no industrialization at all. Obvi-*

ously, it takes a temperament that can stand outside of these two streams and appropriate the essentials of each and make something that is needed by the human heart, for the heart needs industry as much as it needs beauty, needs moral notions as much as it needs to exercise a delight in the world around it.

The last point

The last point I'd like to touch upon is something that came out of Europe, out of Germany and France. And that is the phenomenology of Sartre, Husserl, and others. William James as much as any of the Europeans called our attention to the fact that we could view the world as innocent people, and Husserl developed a method to make the world be for us something that we could "let be," something which we could contemplate.[33]

Notes

1. The Indonesian title of Wright's lecture, "Seniman dan Masalaahannya," uses gender-neutral language, but Wright's English-language lecture notes have Wright discussing *the artist* as a *he*. Consistent with Wright's own language, which was consistent with the conventions of mid-twentieth-century English, we have preserved the gender of Wright's idealized artist.

2. While "The Artist and His Problems" has not previously been republished, Michel Fabre's *Richard Wright: Books and Writers* (1990) published three brief excerpts from some notes that Wright wrote in preparation for the lecture (Fabre, *Richard* 14, 76, 128). Wright left these notes untitled, but the Beinecke has titled the typescript "[On Writers and their Art]." This typescript has remained virtually unreferenced, and when it has been cited, it has been misunderstood as either "a lecture in Bandung" (76) or an "interview [Wright] gave to a young Indonesian at Bandung" (Miller 178). Thanks to Toru Kiuchi for alerting us to the existence of a copy of these typescript notes in Fabre's personal collection, and for sending us his photographs of the copy held by Fabre; based on the photograph, it is clear that Fabre's brief transcriptions relied on the same typescript as is held in the Beinecke Library.

3. Both the lecture notes preserved in the Beinecke collection and the *Indonesia Raya* version of Wright's lecture have an unfinished feel, with no sense of a conclusion. The Beinecke notes conclude with six lines beginning "The last point I'd like to touch upon . . ." which are struck out in a typewritten deletion, while the *Indonesia Raya* version ends six lines into "Morality and art," the penultimate section of the Beinecke notes. Both written texts thus suggest that Wright extemporized a conclusion to his lecture. The version as printed in *Indonesia Raya* is consistent with our suggestion that the lecture, as delivered at the Balai Budaja, was based on a redacted version of Wright's notes, adapted for an Indonesian audience, which did not include a written conclusion.

4. On Wright's conversations with Indonesian writers, see Wright, "Jakarta" 113–14, 120, 190.

5. In December 1954, H. B. Jassin made a decisive contribution to the "crisis" debate with a challenging address to a symposium in the Faculty of Literature at the University of Indonesia, titled "There Is No Crisis in Modern Indonesian Literature" (Teeuw, *Modern* 141; Jassin 3:1–25). Jassin's address, which was in part a response to the views expressed by Asrul Sani at the 1953 Amsterdam symposium on modern Indonesian literature (Asrul, "Indonesische"), was contested by Beb Vuyk, among others, in an article published in *Indonesia Raya* two weeks later (Jassin 3:29–32). The debate raged in both printed and spoken forums until the end of 1956, and Wright's mentioning of the problems facing the development of the novel in Indonesia is a measure of its centrality in literary discussions at this time.

6. Josselson to Mochtar, 2 May 1955 (IACFR, box 186, folder 3); Mochtar to Josselson, 11 May 1955 (IACFR, box 186, folder 3).

7. This editorial attribution is from 1955.

8. These introductory remarks, *In discussing . . . as a writer*, appear in *Indonesia Raya* but are absent from Wright's notes.

9. *Indonesia Raya* uses the phrase *menjampaikan sesuatu pada pembatjanja* (which we have translated as *to convey something to his readers*), but Wright's notes use the verb *to launch* and use the word *appeals* in place of the vague word *something*.

10. While the *Indonesia Raya* lecture uses the phrase *mentjoba mentjari* (which we have rendered as *searching for*), Wright's notes use the term *reaffirm*.

11. Wright's notes make it clear that when, in *Indonesia Raya*, he references "people supporting and helping [the artist]," he is referring to the patronage system that artists formerly participated in.

12. The sentences *This is very different . . . with his public* are included in *Indonesia Raya*, but the concepts do not appear as smoothly or in the same order in Wright's notes.

13. At this point in the lecture as it appears in *Indonesia Raya*, a confusing misprint appears, with the Indonesian word for *artist* (*seniman*) mistakenly typeset as *sentimen*, a word which roughly equates to the English cognate *sentiment* but may also mean *grudge*. In the version of the lecture appearing in this book, the sentence is clarified based on Wright's lecture notes.

14. For Wright's source, see Stein, "Composition" 454.

15. Whereas the *Indonesia Raya* article uses the term *sepenuhnja* (which we have translated as *wholeheartedly*), Wright's notes use the term *organically*.

16. The sentence *When I visited . . . view of time* appears in *Indonesia Raya* but does not appear in Wright's notes.

17. The *Indonesia Raya* article uses the term *orang² Afrika* (which we have rendered literally as *Africans*), but Wright's notes use the term *African figures*, which may refer to African people but alternatively may refer to African sculpture.

18. This paragraph, translated from *Indonesia Raya*, corresponds to a section of Wright's notes that is quite rough. The *Indonesia Raya* version provides connections and exposition that bring greater coherence.

19. The sentences *I myself. . . . the future* appear in the *Indonesia Raya* article but do not appear in Wright's notes.

20. Wright's remarks on the difficulty of making a living as a writer would certainly have struck a chord with his Indonesian audience. According to Ajip Rosidi's recollections in 2013, only he himself and Pramoedya were able to survive solely based on their writings in 1950s Jakarta. They accomplished this by living very frugally (Ajip, Interview).

21. *Indonesia Raya* uses the phrase *madjalah² jang kaja* (which we have translated as *well-financed magazines*), but Wright's notes use *slick magazines*, a term that came into common use in the United States around 1930, alluding to "the newly invented glossy paper on which the slicks [such as *Vanity Fair*] were printed" (Murphy 67).

22. Wright's notes use the term *mistress* rather than *queen*. Our use of *queen* reflects *Indonesia Raya*'s use of the Indonesian term *ratu*, which in modern Indonesian usage refers to a royal sovereign who is a woman. Whereas the *Indonesia Raya* article extends the metaphor of art as a *queen* by imagining the artist leaving her side to pick flowers, Wright's notes extend the *mistress* metaphor by imagining the artist leaving her side to seek sexual companionship elsewhere.

23. Wright's notes use the phrase *is smile*, which does not fit with the sentence. We have replaced this phrase with *of smiles*, based on the context.

24. Here Wright alludes to Gertrude Stein's famous phrase "Rose is a rose is a rose is a rose" (*Geography* 187).

25. The phrase *the more we find . . . artifacts* was previously published in Miller 178.

26. During an address at the Bandung Conference, Chou En-Lai discussed the topic of "freedom of religious belief." He stated, "We Communists are atheists, but we respect all those who have religious belief" (Ministry 65).

27. Wright's notes convey the image of leaders forcing change at gunpoint.

28. The sentence *But where . . . soap* was previously published in Miller 178.

29. For another of Wright's descriptions of viewing this painting, see Wright, *Pagan* 276.

30. Fabre's *Richard Wright* published the phrases/sentences *it is a personal . . . of Blake* (14).

31. Fabre's *Richard Wright* published the sentence *I think that . . . moral lesson* (128) Probably for stylistic reasons, Fabre's transcription of Wright's notes uses the term *theoretical* rather than Wright's own term *theoretic*, but we have relied on Wright's typescript for the term *theoretic*, which when spoken during a lecture would have been important to Wright for its rhyme with the term *aesthetic*.

32. Fabre's *Richard Wright* published the phrase *the fact is . . . art* (128). In Fabre's transcription of the phrase, it is *Joyce, Proust, Kafka, Stein*, but relying on the typescript we have replaced Fabre's mistranscribed *Joyce* with Wright's actual word, *Jews* (4). Fabre's error in transcription most likely resulted from a rust mark left on the notes by a paperclip, which would cause *Jews* to appear as *Joyce* if read casually or from a low-quality copy of the transcript.

33. This sentence, as it appears in Fabre's *Richard Wright*, mistranscribes the phrase as *we could not "let be"* (76), adding a *not*, while Wright's notes use the phrase *we could "let be."* We have relied on the notes to correct this point.

11

Anas Ma'ruf's "Richard Wright in Indonesia" (1955)

On the heels of Wright's visit, the Jakarta-based monthly cultural magazine *Seni* published in its July issue an article titled "Richard Wright di Indonesia" (Richard Wright in Indonesia), which offered an overview of Wright's travels and also reported on a few conversations with him. Written by Anas Ma'ruf, a prominent translator and contributor to a number of cultural magazines, and appearing as a news item in *Seni*'s regular column *Kronik Kesenian* (Arts Chronicle), this article is intriguing in its awareness of Wright's plans to publish material on Indonesia and also in its suggestion that Wright's lectures at Tugu and Balai Budaja were "part of Richard Wright's attempts to collect material for an article he was planning to write." Wright himself makes no mention of these lectures, either in *The Color Curtain* or in his travel journal. However, in both records he frequently includes statements by Indonesian informants, almost all of them unnamed. In Wright's accounts, the context for these statements remains unspecified, but Anas's comment suggests that they may well derive from discussions that took place during and after the lectures Wright gave for the Indonesian PEN Club, the BMKN, and the Konfrontasi

Study Club, as well as his conversation with *Gelanggang*. If this is indeed the case, the documentary record of these events takes on added importance, as a guide to a more complete understanding of *The Color Curtain* and its depictions of Wright's Indonesian informants.

Anas's observation on Wright's project of collecting material on Indonesia is also significant on another level, because it gives a view of the sense Wright's interlocutors had of being observed. Even as Wright's insights and experiences were on display during lectures with audiences who were listening closely and perhaps taking notes, at least some of the Indonesian audience members were conscious that they themselves were being observed, as Wright seemed to be taking notes on their comments and questions during the discussions.

According to Anas's article, one of these events of apparently mutual note-taking took place at "Taman Siswa," most likely a reference to the Central Jakarta Meeting Hall of the Taman Siswa national educational movement. Originally founded in Yogyakarta by the Javanese nationalist educator and politician Ki Hajar Dewantara in 1922, Taman Siswa was a pan-Indonesian institution, influenced by progressive educational thinkers like Montessori and Tagore, that sought to combine modern European-style education with training in indigenous Indonesian arts. While it played a significant part in the prewar nationalist movement, by the time of Wright's visit internal divisions and increasing competition from the government's own education system had reduced Taman Siswa's influence and left it struggling to maintain a nationwide system of schools and training institutions based on Dewantara's principles (Lee K.). Nevertheless, the organization's reputation was such that Taman Siswa's Central Jakarta Meeting Hall would have been a popular venue for meetings dealing with cultural and educational matters, and the specific venue may well have figured in the schedule of lectures and meetings that followed Wright's return to Jakarta after the conference in Bandung. Anas's article is the only known source that mentions a Taman Siswa venue for one of Wright's meetings, so what is known about this event remains at the level of speculation. Taman Siswa may have been the venue for the conversation Wright had with *Gelanggang*, it may have been the venue for Wright's speech to the divinity students, or it may have been the venue of another event that is only cryptically recorded in *The Color Curtain* or Wright's travel journal.

It is possible that Anas attended the events at Takdir's villa in Tugu and Taman Siswa, but he almost certainly was involved in coordinating and attending Wright's PEN Club/BMKN lecture at the Balai Budaja, as in 1955 he was secretary of the BMKN (Rustapa, Agus, and Bambang 242). As Ajip Rosidi recalled, Anas was a driving force in the organization from the early 1950s through the mid-1960s (*Mengenang* 192–93). Hence, when his article refers to "the conclusions we reached from conversations with him," we should be aware that at least some of the conversations in question took place between Wright and his audience after the delivery of his PEN Club/BMKN lecture. One imagines the audience at this lecture hearing Wright delivering the following words, as documented in *Indonesia Raya*: "What should a writer write about? . . . In fact, experience constitutes any artist's subject matter."[1] Struck by such an idea in relation to the question of Wright's own experiences as a black man in America, an audience member may have, as is suggested by Anas, "asked [Wright] about Negro culture in the United States" during the postlecture discussion, receiving an answer from Wright on the topic of jazz, the development of the New Negro Renaissance, and the 1949 anthology *The Poetry of the Negro: 1746–1949*, edited by Langston Hughes and Arna Bontemps.

Notably, in writing "Richard Wright in Indonesia," Anas clearly had at hand a copy of the Hughes-Bontemps anthology, whose preface says this on the topic of people of African descent in Louisiana:

> [In] Louisiana free men of color . . . sent their youth to Paris to study drama, music, and fencing, and to hobnob with the friends of Alexandre Dumas; to Rome to devote themselves to sculpture and singing. Many of these young people were not inclined to return to their native state, with its oppressive racial attitudes. . . . Their influence in literature was strong enough to produce an anthology of poetry in 1845. The volume was called *Les Cenelles*, and it contained verse by a dozen of the younger French-speaking poets among the free Negroes writing at that time, including Victor Séjour. (viii–ix)

Readers will note that in setting up his analogy between Wright and the Séjour circle, Anas translates nearly directly from the language of Hughes and Bontemps. His analogy, then, sheds a certain amount of light on Wright's self-imposed exile but still more on the ways international texts in general and African American texts in particular were circulating in modern Indonesian literary and cultural circles.

Richard Wright in Indonesia
by Anas Ma'ruf
SOURCE LANGUAGE: INDONESIAN

In early April, a Negro writer arrived in Indonesia to make a visit triggered by the Asian-African Conference in Bandung. Richard Wright, the famous writer in question, made use of his visit to meet with a number of prominent Indonesians and to conduct meetings with the arts community. Among these meetings were events held at Tugu, Taman Siswa, and Balai Budaja, all part of Richard Wright's attempts to collect material for an article he was planning to write.

The conclusions we reached from conversations with him were that he had moved from regionally defined issues pertaining to the Negro, via issues that were national in character, toward wider, more broadly based perspectives. For that reason, the issues he presents in his more recent books have to be evaluated according to different criteria. Along with this, he does not deny that discrimination exists in the United States, even though all trace of it has been removed from the laws. He describes himself as an American citizen who happens to be married to a white woman, something that is still unusual among Negroes, and consistent with his outlook, he will not take the risk of returning to the world of the 48 states. Paris is set to become his second homeland, and a place that offers him the possibility of unencumbered development.

His exile reminds us of those cases of Negroes in Louisiana who sent their sons to Paris to study drama and music and interact with independent artists, to Rome to explore the details of artistic life in fields like sculpture and singing. Many of them never returned to America, because the country was not yet free of the accursed practice of racial discrimination. Those who studied in Europe had a great impact on Negro literature, and in 1845 they compiled an anthology of their work under the title *Les Cenelles*. It includes poetry by dozens of young Negro writers, among them the well-known Victor Séjour.

When Wright was asked about Negro culture in the United States, he mentioned the element of jazz in music and other familiar contributions by the Negro race to American life. More than 200 years of traditional Negro literature in the form of poetry, for example, can be examined in the anthology compiled by Langston Hughes and Bontemps. This is a collection of the work of 150 writers from the time of America's revolution right up to the peak of its strength in 1950. Langston himself produced the words of the manifesto that was adopted by the New Negro movement, or the Negro Renaissance, which was famous in the years around 1920–1927. Names associated with it are those like Claude McKay, Jean Toomer, Countee Cullen, and others.

Bearing in mind the circumstances they face and the achievements they have attained, we get the impression that if the white race regards them as competitors, then it is clear that this competition is offered in a spirit of honesty and seriousness. If their circumstances were equal, it is very likely that the white race would find itself under pressure from the colored race, whose numbers are declining in comparison with white Americans.

Note

1. See Wright's "The Artist and His Problems," also in part II.

Part III   In the Wake of Wright's
Indonesian Travels

12

Beb Vuyk's "Black Power" (1955)

According to Beb Vuyk's essay "A Weekend with Richard Wright," during his visit to Indonesia, Wright at one point spoke with a group of cultural figures at Mochtar Lubis's villa in the mountain town of Tugu. Wright stated, "I always feel immediately at home among colored people," and Vuyk replied, "Though not so with everyone in Ghana, surely?" Sensing that Vuyk was referring to certain scenes in his 1954 Gold Coast travelogue, Wright asked, "You've read *Black Power*?" Vuyk replied, "You sent it to Mochtar, and he lent it to me so I could write a review of it for *Indonesia Raya*."[1] Wright may or may not have sent a copy to Mochtar (perhaps Michael Josselson helped Mochtar obtain *Black Power*), but Vuyk clearly acquired the book in her capacity as a book reviewer for Mochtar's newspaper. The document provided here is Vuyk's review, which appeared in the newspaper's literary and cultural column on 1 June 1955, less than a month after Wright left Indonesia.

By this time, Wright was back in Paris, and his recent Indonesian travels had become a topic of discussion among editors of the Europe-based CCF magazines *Encounter*, *Preuves*, and *Der Monat*. The editors, together with CCF director Michael Josselson and other CCF members, met on 23 May, and the "main emphasis" during the discussion "was on the attractiveness of con-troversial articles, or articles made controversial by inviting discussion and counter-attack." The CCF had hoped to organize a symposium on the topic "Asia Hating the West." The symposium had not materialized, but the editors "felt that the Richard Wright treatment of Bandung and Indo[n]esia might provide the proper point of departure." Hence "all the editors paid a call on Richard Wright who had just returned from South-East Asia. He reported at length on his impressions of the rise of Asian nationalism and especially a 'new and dangerous racism' with strong mystical-religious elements. His man-uscript is likely to run to some two hundred pages, with each of the editors free to make such selections as they like for one or more articles" (Lasky). Before the 1956 publication of Wright's *The Color Curtain*, *Encounter*, *Preuves*, *Der Monat*, and the Spanish-language CCF magazine *Cuadernos* would publish a total of six of Wright's Indonesia-related articles.[2] As we mentioned in this book's introduction, Wright's *Encounter* article did indeed prompt a "counter-attack" from Mochtar Lubis, whose 1956 letter to the magazine spoke on behalf of several of the artists and intellectuals with whom Wright had associ-ated. Mochtar wrote:

> I am afraid while [Wright] was here in Indonesia he had been looking
> through "coloured-glasses," and had sought behind every attitude he
> met colour and racial feelings. The majority of the people with whom
> Mr. Wright had come into contact in Indonesia (one of the best-known
> Indonesian novelists, and others) belong to the new generation in In-
> donesia, and are the least racial and colour conscious of the various
> groups in Indonesia. They are all amazed to read Mr. Wright's notebook
> in which Mr. Wright quotes them saying things which they never had
> said, or to which they did not put meaning as accepted by Mr. Wright.
> ("Through")

Of course, these sentiments came to a head in Indonesia after Wright's articles appeared in the CCF magazines, and nothing of the sort had been published by June 1955 when Vuyk published her review of *Black Power*. Indeed, less than a month earlier, Takdir's wife, Margret, had written of Wright without indicat-ing any perturbation. In a letter to a relative in Bonn, Germany, Margret wrote that the Alisjahbana family planned to spend "probably the whole of July" in Paris, as a side trip in conjunction with Takdir's attendance at a PEN Congress in Vienna: "All depends on getting a house. We have asked Richard Wright to help us rent a house. He is a black American writer who lives in Paris and has just returned from [Indonesia] to Paris. He attended the Asia Africa Con-ference here and spent several weekends with us. I hope that he will find something that would fit us."[3] Whatever may have happened with Wright's efforts to find Parisian housing for the Alisjahbanas, one sees in Vuyk's review of *Black Power* the seeds of later strife already beginning to sprout.[4]

Vuyk's distrust of *Black Power*'s premise becomes a refrain in the review. She avers that although Wright feels an emotional draw based on "skin color," blood and ethnicity provide him with "absolutely no connections" to the Gold Coast. This perceived lack of connection resonates strongly with African American writer George Schuyler's 1926 assertions that "the Aframerican is merely a lampblacked Anglo-Saxon," and "your American Negro is just plain American," "subject to the same economic and social forces that mold the actions and thoughts of the white Americans" (25). Indeed, according to Vuyk, the way Wright "reacts to these things [in Africa] is no different from the way a white American would react." She views the seemingly unanticipated connections between Africans and African Americans that Wright describes in *Black Power* with a degree of skepticism, suggesting that Wright "is wearing glasses that frame the way he sees things." Her use of the "wearing glasses" metaphor seems to set the stage for Mochtar's later criticism of Wright for wearing "coloured-glasses" in Indonesia. In this review, however, Vuyk makes use of the metaphor to suggest that Wright's particular pair of glasses—involving "special feelings for Africa"—have not permitted him to see the "dangerous and frightening path" along which Gold Coast prime minister Kwame Nkrumah is leading his country. According to Vuyk in "A Weekend with Richard Wright," she and Wright had discussed this topic at Mochtar Lubis's villa in Tugu while Wright was in Indonesia. Vuyk had suggested to Wright that Nkrumah's efforts "to give the masses a sense of fulfillment through a national super-belief and a sense of allegiance to party leaders" was "fascism." Wright replied, "It can lead to fascism . . . but you have to take that risk. . . . There has to be something to bring about a new national unity, and that's Nkrumah's goal."[5] In the closing lines of her review of *Black Power*, it seems, Vuyk continued her discussion with Wright, claiming that his glasses interfered with his vision to such a degree that he could not "notice the dangers and problems inherent in such ideals."

Black Power
by Beb Vuyk

SOURCE LANGUAGE: INDONESIAN

The latest book by Richard Wright, the well-known American Negro author, is not a novel but a travelogue. Written on the book's cover below the title is "An American Negro views the African Gold Coast." Richard Wright is both a

Negro and an American. As an American, he is a foreigner in the land from which his ancestors were transported nearly three hundred years ago. However as a Negro, someone of the same skin color, he is emotionally drawn to a country he has absolutely no connections with, either by blood or ethnicity, and whose culture and spirit are foreign to him.

Negroes who set foot on American soil as slaves came from various parts of Africa. They had no connections with each other apart from the fact that they were all slaves. They spoke in hundreds of different ethnic languages, and belonged to different African cultures. To understand each other they had to use the language of their overseer. They adopted his religion and adapted to his culture. The Negro people of America were black-skinned Americans. Spirituals (the songs of Negroes in America) and jazz were Negro contributions to American culture; they came out of America, not Africa.[6]

Anyone reading a travelogue gets to know a country according to the way the writer sees it. As readers, we need to be aware that the writer is wearing glasses that frame the way he sees things, so we have to try to look at things with our own eyes. The lenses in the glasses Richard Wright uses are rather different from each other, conflicted. As an American, and someone who participates in the most technologically advanced civilization this world has ever known,[7] the simple conditions in the Gold Coast are more striking in his eyes than they would be for us, because the problems and conditions in the Gold Coast are in part the same as our problems. The way Richard Wright reacts to these things is no different from the way a white American would react. However, the sentiments he draws on in his approach to this country are very different from the way a white person would approach it.

He was returning to the land of his ancestors. This in itself is not really important. Every year dozens of Americans visit towns and villages in England, Holland, Sweden, and Italy to find out about the places where their forebears were born, three, five, or ten generations ago. They walk the streets of those towns, sometimes stopping in front of an old house or reading their own family names on gravestones in old cemeteries, before coming to realize that they are foreigners without the slightest connection to the past that their ancestors knew. For Richard Wright, the journey was an extended encounter with the past, with the horrifying level of human suffering that had to be endured by his ancestors, who were captured by other hostile tribes and were herded under heavy wooden yokes to coastal destinations several weeks' walk away. Once on the coast, they were sold like cattle by their black owners to white buyers who put them aboard ships as goods for trade and sent them off on sea voyages—lasting weeks—to the slave markets of Boston or New Orleans.

He learned things in Bristol, where slave hunters were outfitted after the slave trade passed from the Portuguese to the British. He learned things along the route that the empty slave ships traveled, south through the Canary Islands to the Gulf of Guinea, where the Gold Coast is located. In coastal towns Richard Wright visited old forts, where the slaves were kept in underground chambers before they were taken away on ships. He was not aware of the place or district his ancestors came from, nor their tribal origins, but when he saw black-skinned women pounding corn in front of their huts, he thought of his forebears, who were probably just like any one of them. Black and white Americans are both foreigners in their lands of origin, but the memory of the way they left that land gives a unique perspective to this black American's report.

"Aren't you an American?"[8] a shop assistant asked him, after he'd only been there a day. Then the African Negro asked the American Negro what part of Africa he came from.

"I don't know."[9]

"Didn't your mother or grandmother ever tell you what part of Africa you came from?"

I did not answer. I stared vaguely about me. I had in my childhood asked my parents about it, but they had no information, or else they had not wanted to speak of it.

I remembered that many Africans had sold their people into slavery; it had been said that they had had no idea of the kind of slavery into which they had been selling their people, but they had sold them . . . . I suddenly didn't know what to say to the man confronting me.

"Haven't you tried to find out where in Africa you came from, sir?"

"Well," I said softly, "You know, you fellows who sold us and the white men that bought us didn't keep any records." Silence stood between us. We avoided each other's eyes.

Richard Wright visited the Gold Coast as the guest of Kwame Nkrumah, the prime minister of the Gold Coast, whom he had come to know in America some years previously. As we understand it, the relationship between the two men was not cordial. Nkrumah is the leader of the Convention People's Party, a grassroots party that is presently in government.[10] Wright was invited on several occasions to attend demonstrations and party meetings, and he had one long conversation with Nkrumah. But it was clear that Nkrumah only wanted to show him and tell him as much as he thought was necessary.

His contact with opposition leaders, members of the intelligentsia who had been educated in England, went more smoothly, although the author was very critical in his approach to them, deploring their unwillingness to identify with the common people. He also visited tribal leaders, the reactionary elements in this society who had held power for centuries. Walking around the markets he made contact with ordinary people and everywhere he went he encountered suspicion, reticence, and deceit. Although there are many pages in the book that indicate his disappointment with the people and conditions in this country, his conflicted feelings urged him to keep on studying the things he saw, to be able to understand and analyze them. The way he felt these things was not based on racial commonality, but rather on the upshot of his specific position as a member of the black minority in America. Through talent and hard work he managed to escape, and this self-liberation is the basis of his sympathy for colored peoples who are struggling for their independence, or have only achieved it in the last few years.

The Gold Coast is a relatively small country, with a population of four and a half million, most of whom still live in tribal communities. Ruling over these communities are kings who hold magical-religious power. They are the intermediaries between this world and the world of the ancestors. They have the knowledge of all the secrets and hidden forces, and in their funeral ceremonies, human sacrifice is still practiced clandestinely. The Gold Coast is a country rich in timber and minerals. It will only be able to develop and establish an economy free from the West if it is able to exploit its minerals itself. However, intertribal relations make technical development impossible. Intertribal relations don't recognize private property, and anyone with money has to share it with members of his own tribe.[11] So any impetus for the accumulation of wealth just doesn't exist. These things are more familiar to us than they are to Richard Wright, as are matters concerning taboos. The only difference is that the percentage of people still tied to the old ways in the Gold Coast is much greater than here, and among 80% of the people, there is still no movement toward integration with modern civilization.

The author sees Nkrumah and his party as a solution in the short term. Nkrumah is trying to capture the emotional vacuum at a time when relations between tribespeople are loosening, not by defending the old beliefs but by giving the people a national superbelief, and a close connection between the party and its leaders.[12]

It is a dangerous and frightening path. It appears to indicate that Richard Wright's special feelings for Africa don't allow him to notice the dangers and problems inherent in such ideals.

Notes

Beb Vuyk. "Black Power." 1955. Translated and published as "Black Power" with the permission of Joke de Willigen-Riekerk.

1. See Vuyk's "A Weekend with Richard Wright," also in part III.

2. See Davis and Fabre 89–90.

3. Margret Alisjahbana to Tante Malchen, 7 [May] 1955, Alisjahbana family papers, quoted by Tamalia Alisjahbana (Tamalia Alisjahbana to Brian Roberts, 18 Sept. 2014, e-mail).

4. According to Vuyk, as relayed to Constance Webb by Margrit de Sablonière, one of Wright's Indonesian interlocutors was furious about Wright's representations and at some point confronted Wright during a visit to Paris (de Sablonière to Webb, 3 Nov. 1966, and de Sablonière to Webb, 12 Dec. 1966). It is possible that this unnamed interlocutor was Takdir Alisjahbana, who, as indicated by the 7 May 1955 missive that is quoted above by Tamalia Alisjahbana, planned to be in Paris in July 1955. In this scenario, Takdir may have seen one of the articles Wright published in the CCF magazines around that time (see Davis and Fabre 89–90). According to de Sablonière, Vuyk reported that Wright's wife, Ellen Poplar, had taken the side of the unnamed Indonesian in this encounter.

5. See Vuyk's "A Weekend with Richard Wright," also in part III.

6. For contemporaneous Indonesian commentary on African American music, see Manik.

7. Vuyk's commentary here quotes almost directly from the lecture Wright gave at Takdir's villa, which speaks of African Americans migrating "from the Southern towns and cities" to "the northern industrial cities," where "they moved restlessly amidst the highest industrial civilisation the world has ever known" ("American" 14).

8. We have added quotation marks to this sentence.

9. This excerpt from *Black Power*, which is marked in italics in this translation, appears in Vuyk's article in English with Vuyk's Indonesian translations in parentheses. Vuyk's English-language quotations from *Black Power* differ from Wright's English in minor ways (Wright, *Black Power* 54).

10. Nkrumah organized the Convention People's Party in 1949. Instrumental in Nkrumah's rise to power, the CPP sought immediate self-determination and self-government and organized boycotts of European goods (Owusu-Ansah 99).

11. We have translated Vuyk's phrase *perhubungan antara suku*[2] literally, as *intertribal relations*. However, the context (which points toward relations among people within the same tribe) suggests that Vuyk meant to use a phrase that could be translated as *intratribal relations*.

12. We are grateful to Paul Tickell for pointing out that Vuyk's reference to a *superbelief* or *super geloof* alludes to a Soekarnoist concept being discussed in *Indonesia Raya* at this time, in which the term *super geloof* signified a form of nationalism that was used as a foil against more sectarian and regionalist ideologies in the run-up to the 1955 general election.

13

Beb Vuyk's "H. Creekmore and Protest Novels" (1955)

In November 1955, a little over seven months after Wright left Indonesia, Beb Vuyk published a second book review dealing with Richard Wright, again in *Indonesia Raya*'s literary and cultural column. Her review of Hubert Creekmore's 1953 novel *The Chain in the Heart* is remarkable for drawing on the work of three writers who were each participants in the mid-twentieth-century community of African American exiles living in Paris: Richard Wright, Richard Gibson, and James Baldwin. The review is also remarkable for being written from the mistaken premise that Creekmore, who was a white novelist and poet from Mississippi, was black.

Vuyk's primary point of entry into Creekmore's novel is her knowledge of Richard Wright. Pointing toward the interest piqued by Wright's recent visit, Vuyk tells readers that she "wouldn't have finished reading" Creekmore's novel "but for the fact that it deals with the Negro problem." And pointing toward her admiration for Wright (notwithstanding her earlier assertion that Wright gave undue tolerance to Nkrumah's dangerous governing tactics), she contrasts Creekmore's allegedly inferior novel with Wright's *Black Boy* and *Native Son*, which "had to be written" and contain "inspirational work." And, importantly, Vuyk takes up Wright's PEN Club/BMKN lecture as a lens through which to understand Creekmore's situation (inaccurate as her view may be) within the African American literary tradition. During his lecture "The Artist and His Problems," Wright had spoken of the large financial rewards that accrue to US writers who fulfill the demands of the literary marketplace: "The writer must produce stories he knows will be liked by the magazines' editors and also by their readers. His personal emotions have very little, if anything, to do with this type of writing. Some writers succeed in writing this way throughout their lives. They are probably very lucky." And yet in his discussion of "the professional writer," Wright had warned against "the temptation of making a lot of money by writing in the way that those well-financed magazines require." Now, half a year later, Vuyk disparaged Creekmore as one of many "third- and fourth-rate writers" who write for the marketplace, benefiting from "the popularity of novels by Negro writers that discuss the Negro problem" to "gain easy popularity and at the same time make a lot of money as writers." In Vuyk's assessment, "Hubert Creekmore writes to make a living." And she indeed seems to have been recalling Wright's warning against the temptations of the marketplace when she offered her mordant conclusion that Creekmore's novel is "sensationally successful" because as an allegedly African American writer he dexterously deploys "the Negro problem" according to "the 'successful novel' formula."

The day prior to his PEN Club/BMKN lecture, Wright had spoken to the Konfrontasi Study Club, tracing the transition in African American literature from earlier "complaints and pleas" to current "statements and demands" (Wright, "American" 23). After Wright's departure, Vuyk's related reading on this topic provided her with additional information on the way African American literature's orientation toward social action intersected with the term *protest* during the mid-twentieth century. In the review, Vuyk refers to the winter 1953 edition of *Perspectives USA*, a magazine published by the Ford Foundation in British, French, German, and Italian editions with the ambition of "promot[ing] peace by increasing respect for America's non-materialistic achievements among intellectuals abroad" (qtd. in Barnhisel 738), an initiative consistent with the Foundation's deep involvements and investments "in the U.S. project of cultural diplomacy" (737). Reading *Perspectives USA*'s 1953 republication of Richard Gibson's essay "A No to Nothing" (1951) and James Baldwin's "Everybody's Protest Novel" (1949) helped Vuyk further her thinking on African American literature and social action. Bringing Creekmore's novel into the orbit of these African American writers, Vuyk asserts, "*The Chain in the Heart* made me understand the meaning of protest." Such a statement suggests that Vuyk, before reading Creekmore's novel, was already interested in exploring the place of the keyword *protest* within the African American literary tradition, likely in relation to Wright's own work and his narrative of African American literature's progression from "pleas" to "demands."

Vuyk's peers, Asrul Sani and Soedjatmoko, had already grappled with the meaning of *protest* when they included the article "A Conversation with Richard Wright" in their column *Gelanggang*. This May 1955 article had referenced James Baldwin's "Everybody's Protest Novel." However, the *Gelanggang* article had misunderstood Baldwin's scathing view of the protest tradition to such a degree that Baldwin is portrayed as asserting that Wright's efforts at protest are an advancement over Stowe's efforts at protest. In November 1955, however, as Vuyk published her review of Creekmore, she was in the position to present a more accurate understanding of Baldwin's view. As she knew from reading "Everybody's Protest Novel," Baldwin had asserted that "the failure of the protest novel [in both Wright and Stowe] lies in its rejection of life, the human being" (Baldwin, "Everybody's" 100). And now, in Creekmore's *The Chain in the Heart*, Vuyk saw a clear example of Baldwin's definition of protest, leading her to assert that Creekmore "doesn't create work from the depths of his humanity, rather, it is contrived." Ironically, then, the white southern US writer Hubert Creekmore helped bring additional clarity to the Indonesian conversation Wright had contributed to with his lecture to the Konfrontasi Study Club on African American literature's relation to social action.

Meanwhile, Vuyk's reading of journalist Richard Gibson's "A No to Nothing" seems to have provided her with her own pair of glasses, prompting her to misidentify Creekmore as black. In Gibson's essay, she had read of US newsstands full of "cheap pocket editions of novels" by African American writers "all picking away industriously at the great [Negro] Problem" (Gibson, "No" 90). From Gibson she had learned of an archetypal "paranoiac" African American writer who "may even be so deluded as to think himself clever when he decides to throw in his lot with the motley band of puerile imitators of Richard Wright—a doubtless sincere but defective thinker" (91). Vuyk was in agreement with Gibson on Wright as a thinker, and Gibson's discussion seems to have structured her vision so that when presented with a pocket-edition novel taking up African American themes, she was prepared to assume that its writer was one among Gibson's puerile horde of Wright-imitators. Echoing Gibson, Vuyk writes of Creekmore's novel: "It's all just an imitation of Richard Wright, and like all imitations, inferior to the original."

In faraway Paris, less than a year after Creekmore seemingly helped Vuyk learn the meaning of the term *protest*, Wright's relationship with the author of "Everybody's Protest Novel" further unfolded, now bearing the impress of the

Bandung Conference and Wright's experiences in Indonesia. In September 1956, Wright and Baldwin participated in the First International Congress of Negro Writers and Artists, which was framed by one of the principle organizers as "a kind of second Bandung" (Baldwin, "Princes" 25). In speaking at this putative second Bandung, Wright drew on the perspective he wove out of his experiences at the Bandung Conference: "Nkrumah, Nasser, Sukarno, and Nehru, and the Western-educated heads of these newly created national states, must be given *carte blanche* to modernize their lands without overlordship of the West, and we must understand the methods that they will feel compelled to use" (Wright, *White* 100). He continued: "Yes, Sukarno, Nehru, Nasser and others will necessarily use quasi-dictatorial methods to hasten the process of social evolution and to establish order in their lands—lands which were left spiritual voids by a too-long Western occupation and domination" (101). Baldwin listened to this speech and, following a precedent he had set years earlier, criticized Wright publicly, this time in a 1957 *Encounter* article titled "Princes and Powers." Portions of Wright's speech, wrote Baldwin, were undoubtedly "tactless," but Wright's acquiescence to the use of "dictatorial methods" by Nkrumah, Nasser, Sukarno, and Nehru was "even stranger" (48). In this way, Vuyk (at the time of the Bandung Conference itself)[1] and Baldwin (during this "second Bandung") were in unknowing agreement with each other over the ideas that Wright was developing on governance in postcolonial nation-states.

H. Creekmore and Protest Novels
by Beb Vuyk
SOURCE LANGUAGE: INDONESIAN

Appearing as a double volume in the Signet series is *The Chain in the Heart* by Hubert Creekmore. This novel tells the story of three generations of a Negro family in a small town in one of the Southern states of the United States.

Hubert Creekmore himself is a Negro, born in Mississippi and according to the information on the cover of the book, also the writer of several other novels. Among them is "The Sensationally Successful *Cotton Country*." I don't know that book, but *The Chain in the Heart* is no more than moderately successful, and but for the fact that it deals with the Negro problem, I certainly wouldn't have continued reading past the first few pages. We have here a follower of Richard Wright, but without Wright's expertise and wild-eyed intensity. *The Chain in the Heart* wouldn't be being discussed here if it were not an example of a tendency initiated by a number of serious Negro writers in

America, that is, the popularity of novels by Negro writers that discuss the Negro problem and the reaction of third- and fourth-rate writers who make use of the problem of their race to gain easy popularity and at the same time make a lot of money as writers.

We find a reaction to this type of novel in the second issue of *Perspectives* 1953, where, under the title "Two Protests against Protest," two Negro writers, Richard Gibson and James Baldwin, discuss this issue extensively. Gibson's protest, entitled "A No to Nothing," begins with an imaginary conversation between a liberal American publisher and a young Negro writer with a novel to offer. The publisher's first question is: "What aspect of the problem does your novel discuss?" When the writer replies that he doesn't discuss the racial problem in his book, the publisher's attitude changes. He asks several more questions about the possibility that there might be some discussion of the racial problem in the book, and sends him away with a vague promise. This is Gibson's way of explaining why the quality of what is called Negro literature is mediocre and the books themselves are tedious.

Discrimination as an obstacle

American publishers expect writers who happen to be of the Negro race to go some way toward writing about the Negro problem because they feel certain that this will be popular with their readers.

Gibson advises people of his race not to become Negro writers, but writers who "happen" to be Negroes, human beings and not clichés. He acknowledges that as long as racial discrimination persists, Negro writers cannot be totally free because that type of racial distinction has an influence on the soul. But at the same time this is no reason for Negro writers to write just what white publishers expect of them. "There is always and only 'The Problem,' his (the Negro's) private domain, his privileged preserve. About it however he may soon learn, is a high wall, and that young writer would do well to realize his real problem is finding a way out over that wall, no matter how lush may appear the pasture within."[2]

Comparison with the works of Richard Wright

The Chain in the Heart made me understand the meaning of protest. This book doesn't shed any new light on the problem and doesn't offer a personal viewpoint on it. Its theme repeats the themes of Richard Wright's novels, or perhaps better, filters them. Bigger Thomas, the main character in Richard Wright's *Native Son*, commits murder as a result of the circumstances in which he is forced to live. Taffy George, in the last section of *The Chain in the Heart*, steals money from a white man who gave him financial assistance to continue his education, in a moment of hatred, resentment, and rebelliousness. One of them commits murder because he is forced to live in certain conditions because he is a Negro, and the other steals, but the reader can sympathize more with Bigger Thomas's murders. Though recoiling in horror, the reader accepts them as the consequence of racial conditions in a particular society. Taffy George is a thief, not a murderer. But his crime leaves no impression on the reader, because he ends up giving in to his fiancée's urging and returning the money anyway.

Richard Wright's *Native Son* and his autobiography *Black Boy* were written because indeed they had to be written. That is what makes these books such inspirational work. The writer writes about himself in a way that is both a protest at his own fate and the fate of his race.

Hubert Creekmore writes to make a living

Hubert Creekmore creates protest novels. This doesn't mean that his protest has no foundation or that circumstances and relationships in the novels are described untruthfully. However it does mean that he doesn't create work from the depths of his humanity, rather, it is contrived. He is someone who makes a living from his writing, like thousands of other American writers who write historical novels, detective stories, family sagas, and adventure tales because they are popular. Creekmore is a Negro, and the novels most Negroes read are protest novels, so he writes what they want to read.

But he coasts along, making no effort to create new situations or portray new contexts, let alone shed light on "the problem" from another angle. It's all just an imitation of Richard Wright, and like all imitations, inferior to the original. The context is the South, with Negroes who faithfully live out their traditional religious practices in their homes, such as we know from *Black Boy* and the backstreets of Chicago that we know from *Native Son*. Elderly people who are faithful to their religion inside their homes and city people suffering loneliness and alienation. We even find the theme of a well-intentioned white person who helps out a Negro youth but is in fact the very reason that the youth loses his way.

The Negro problem has become a topic that fits the "successful novel" formula. The sensationally successful novel by Hubert Creekmore.[3]

Notes

Beb Vuyk. "H. Creekmore Dg. Roman² Bantahan." 1955. Translated and published as "H. Creekmore and Protest Novels" with the permission of Joke de Willigen-Riekerk.

1. See Vuyk's "A Weekend with Richard Wright," also in part III.

2. Vuyk's quote from Gibson appears in English in her original Indonesian-language article. Vuyk's quotation is only slightly changed from Gibson's original (Gibson, "No" 92). In Vuyk's Indonesian-language article, the English-language quote from Gibson is followed by a rough Indonesian translation.

3. This final sentence of the review appears in English in Vuyk's original.

14

Asrul Sani's "Richard Wright: The Artist Turned
Intellectual" (1956)

Some twelve months after meeting Wright in Jakarta and probably interviewing him for the cultural column *Gelanggang*, Asrul Sani published an extended
review of Wright's 1953 novel *The Outsider*, also in the *Gelanggang* column. As
mentioned in part I, Wright's novel was available in Indonesia in its Dutch
translation as early as September 1954, and as Asrul notes in his review, by
April 1956 the English-language publication could be bought in its pocketbook edition (apparently New American Library's Signet Giant edition) in at
least one major bookstore in Jakarta.

Asrul's review is a remarkable document from a number of points of view.
It conveys Asrul's impressions of meeting and speaking with Wright several
months earlier, an experience that left him fascinated—as he believed anyone would be—by Wright's "naïveté": "His laughter is the kind of laughter
that many intellectuals have forgotten how to produce, and I had the feeling
that the soul of this writer was as straight as a bamboo tube, that he was unburdened by the kinds of complications we generally find in representatives
of peoples with very powerful traditions and who, as a result, come into this
world with almost unbearable burdens." Readers familiar with Wright, whose

writings indeed reveal a writer burdened with intense complications, may be struck by Asrul's misreading of Wright's soul here.

The question of laughter was at the center of mutual misreadings between Wright and Asrul. According to his narrative in *The Color Curtain*, Wright himself began noticing Indonesian laughter on his February 1955 visit to the Indonesian consulate in Paris. Here, Wright asked the consulate's press and cultural attaché about the world press's reaction "to the Africans being invited to this conference," and the attaché laughed in response, saying, "They don't understand it." Wright interpreted this laughter as a celebration of the world press's bewilderment (441). This scene points toward the way laughter becomes a theme in Wright's travel journal, which has him laughing with an Indonesian official at the consulate ("Jakarta" 7) and commenting that Indonesians remind him of Africans because of their readiness to laugh (12). The journal also has him interviewing Mohammed Natsir, the former Indonesian prime minister, and noting his uproarious laughter while discussing imperial mercenaries, missionaries, and militaries (115). At another point Wright attends a dinner with Indonesian cultural figures during which there was a substantial amount of laughter (190). As Wright's Indonesian sojourn was coming to a close, his journal conveyed an uneasiness regarding Indonesian laughter, as he believed this laughter frequently seemed to happen at the wrong moments (210). Like Wright, many non-Indonesians have been confused by the conventions of Indonesian laughter, which often reflects nervousness or embarrassment rather than comfortable sociability, as Wright had assumed at the dinner with Indonesian cultural figures (190).[1] Indeed, it seems that as Wright laughed along with what was for him the disorienting laughter of his hosts, his own laughter also became disorienting to them, leading Asrul to assume Wright's soul to be "as straight as a bamboo tube."

Such mutual misreading is not confined to the issue of laughter. Probably drawing on the moment from the 1955 *Gelanggang* "Conversation" during which Wright stated that the Bible was the first book to influence him, Asrul's 1956 article avers that "as a Christian, [Wright] is guided by the Gospel." The article's assessment on this point may cause readers to consider that although Asrul's 1956 article mentions Wright's autobiography *Black Boy*, Asrul may not have read the portions outlining young Richard's struggles against the strict religious orientation of his grandmother.[2] However, even as Asrul is unaware of the misunderstandings in his own article, he is nonetheless aware of Wright's misunderstandings of Indonesia, as conveyed by Wright's Indonesian travel writings, particularly as published in the CCF-sponsored magazine *Preuves*. Having read Wright's 1955 French-language article "Le monde occidental à Bandoeng," Asrul recounts Wright's narrative of toilet paper and Indonesian lavatories and calls it "ignorance." In thus commenting on Wright's CCF-published Indonesian travel writings, Asrul joined Mochtar Lubis, whose own letter to *Encounter*, "Through Colored Glasses," had criticized Wright's inaccurate portrayals of Indonesia just one month earlier.

Yet even if Asrul's review does not see Wright through rose-colored glasses, and even if he uses the term *document humain* (Wright's own derisive term for Stowe's *Uncle Tom's Cabin*) to describe Wright's *Native Son* and *Black Boy*, he hastens to declare Wright to be "a true writer . . . an artist deserving of respect," indicating the high regard in which Wright continued to be held in Indonesia a year after his visit, even in the face of his former interlocutors' discontent with how they and their country were being represented in Wright's post-Bandung narratives. Balanced between admiration and pique, Asrul's review embodies the self-confidence articulated in his famous "Gelanggang Testimony of Beliefs" of 1949. "We are the true heirs of world culture" (Asrul, "Surat" 3), Asrul and his peers had announced, laying claim to a sense of equality and commonality with artists and writers at the centers and peripheries of world culture in the aftermath of World War II. Similarly, the review articulates the workings of the "universal humanist" attitude that came to be seen as the hallmark of Gelanggang, both as an aesthetic principle and a literary-critical approach. It takes as its starting point the endorsement of the universal humanist outlook that Asrul finds in Wright's statement "my hero could have been of any race . . . ," and it agrees with Wright's premise that "freedom from social constraints does not mean freedom from metaphysical constraints." In its critical analysis of the novel, however, the review suggests that a focus on "the human condition"—the universal—may result in a disconnect between heart and mind on the part of the author and a concomitant failure in aesthetic judgment and achievement. In this respect it adds an extra dimension to the criticism of Wright's emotional "fixation" on the problem of racial difference in the synopsis of his lecture to the Konfrontasi Study Club in April 1955. There, it was implied that it is only through the processing of unruly emotion through the intellect that the writer moves beyond partisanship into "an open and honest situation that values all human beings" (Redaksi May–June 1955). Here, however, there is an added nuance. In taking Wright to task for abandoning the "promptings of his heart [that] are still tied to the situation of the Negro in America today," Asrul makes clear that in his view, the processing of inner turmoil should not necessarily mean that the writer's intellect comes to dominate and override emotional complexity. Indeed, the "greatest achievements in literature" are those in which the "complexity and confusion" is not eliminated but mastered, through control of language and clarity of thought. This results in "the literary phenomenon referred to as the 'genius' of a simplicity of thought and feelings that proceeds out of very deeply embedded complexities" and that stands in marked contrast to those "lofty works" that are driven by the intellect alone. This is the crux of Asrul's critical assessment of Wright's novel: so anxious is Wright to convey a message about "the human condition," Asrul suggests, that he loses touch with the prompt-ings of his emotional convictions. This means that Wright's judgment of his own talents as a writer has faltered, and *The Outsider* is poorer in consequence.

Finally, Asrul's review indicates the easy familiarity with contemporary Euro-American literary culture that characterized this section of the Indone-sian literary world in the early post-independence period. Asrul and his com-patriots at this time were multilingual and well-traveled, as much at ease in international circles as they were committed to the work of nation-building at home. Indeed, during 1952 and 1953, as a recently married couple, Asrul Sani and Siti Nuraini had spent time in Europe on a STICUSA scholarship, dur-ing which they read contemporary Dutch, French, and German literature and interacted with figures as diverse as the German writer Hans Werner Richter and the Greek novelist and philosopher Nikos Kazantzakis.[3] Unsurprisingly, then, Asrul's 1956 review reflects his cosmopolitan outlook, comfortably and convincingly situating Wright in his own intellectual and aesthetic milieu, even as it takes him to task for perceived failures of judgment and an aban-donment of his true calling as an artist. The review suggests that Wright has been led astray by his "existentialist friends," becoming so enamored with the philosophy of existentialism he has come to know through his personal as-sociation with Jean-Paul Sartre and Simone de Beauvoir, that his protagonists become spokespeople for all the "big questions," rather than acting out the logical consequences of their decisions and actions as characters in a novel.

Recalling an aspect of *Gelanggang*'s 1955 interview with Wright, Asrul's review reflects a preoccupation with existentialism in Indonesia at this time. The critic H. B. Jassin had identified existentialist thought as a leitmotif in the dramas of Utuy T. Sontani in 1953 and 1954 (Jassin 2:149–50), and in his sur-vey of contemporary Indonesian literature at the end of 1954 he had vigorously defended Indonesian poets against a 1952 accusation that they were unhealth-ily preoccupied with existentialist themes in their work (3:23). Furthermore, articles in literary and cultural magazines at the time indicated existential-ism's currency and perceived relevance to Indonesian cultural and literary debates.[4] At this stage, the Indonesian interest in existentialism tended to focus on its concern with the individual human subject and the experience of human freedom and responsibility, themes central to the work of Sartre, de Beauvoir, and Camus and that resonated with the universal humanist out-looks. More broadly, however, they touched on the cultural-political concerns

FIGURE 14.1. Portrait of Asrul Sani (left) and Siti Nuraini (right), during their early 1950s residence in the Netherlands. Unknown photographer. Used with permission of Siti Nuraini. Courtesy of Anya Robertson.

that underlay so much of the cultural debate in Indonesia at this time—the meaning of freedom and the role and responsibility of the artist in shaping the culture of a newly emerging nation.[5]

In the work of later generations of Indonesian writers and dramatists, the 1950s interest in existentialism was to evolve into an aesthetic response to absurdism, in particular a concern with questions related to the futility and meaninglessness of existence under harsh and oppressive authoritarian structures, be they political or metaphysical. The result of this development was a genre of antirealist literature and theatre that was at times playful and experimental but could also have a sharply political edge, in its evocation of dream-like or nightmarish worlds that carried clear metaphorical allusions to political and social conditions that robbed life of its meaning (Hatley, "Cultural" 222–24).

In 1956, when Asrul published his review of *The Outsider*, a concerted response to absurdism was still something for the future. Intriguingly, however, it was Asrul Sani himself who later that same year began publishing texts that anticipated the subsequent emergence of this genre in Indonesian literature and theatre. In September 1956 he published an Indonesian adaptation of Camus's absurdist play *Caligula*, based on its 1944 edition by Editions Gallimard in Paris.[6] This adaptation was published just two months after Asrul produced an absurdist work of his own, an indication of his fascination with the genre and his interest in adapting it to an Indonesian setting. This was the short story entitled "Museum," which appeared in *Konfrontasi* in July–August 1956. Highly unusual in Indonesia at this time, "Museum" begins as a realist narrative but quickly shifts onto a symbolic, dream-like plane where events and their meanings are unclear and fear and confusion begin to undermine the rational mind's apprehension of reality. In the story, an Indonesian civil servant on holidays in Jakarta finds himself under the control of a godlike "guide," who confronts him with the meaninglessness of his life as an employee in a government department that has no more life than a museum of dead objects, a tourist in a city where an architect cannot conceive of any possible way of completing a truncated monument to the national revolution against colonialism. In this city, anyone who stands apart from the crowd faces imminent destruction. The allusions to disillusionment with the outcome of the struggle for national freedom, which Asrul famously elaborated as a condition besetting Indonesian literature (Asrul, "Indonesische"), are here expressed in metaphorical form, inviting the reader to respond intuitively to a set of underlying political and intellectual concerns. Thus, unlike *The Outsider*, where questions of "being and nothingness" are topics of dialogue in a realist narrative, Asrul's short story explores questions of meaning and responsibility through metaphor and allusion. Perhaps Wright's novel was already far from his mind when Asrul composed his story, but it is tempting to see "Museum" as an illustration of one possible way that Indonesian writers might remain true to their vocation as creative artists, rather than becoming intellectuals who made use of fiction as a way of engaging in rational argument, the accusation Asrul's review of *The Outsider* made against Wright.

Richard Wright: The Artist Turned Intellectual
by Asrul Sani
SOURCE LANGUAGE: INDONESIAN

There are some novels that, after reading, we hold onto with a twinge of sadness and sympathy for the characters whose stories the authors tell. The books that affect us in this way are those that in literary criticism are often assessed under the category of the *document humain*.[7]

An example from close to home is Suwarsih Djojopuspito's novel *Buiten het Gareel*. If I were to evaluate this book according to its literary worth, I could only say, with the utmost respect, that it fails to reach even a fourth-rate level in its pursuit of literary merit.[8]

Most of Richard Wright's books, like *Native Son* and *Black Boy*, can also be included under the category of the *document humain*. I hasten to add, however, that the author of these books is a true writer, a painter of clear images, an artist deserving of respect.

There is something particular that we find in the best of these books, and that is a call aimed at the human heart. They speak not primarily to the mind, but to the heart. And in their writers, we find a kind of gripping honesty, a voice that rises up from the depths of the heart (even though behind it there lurks an urgent sense of protest) and an absence of spiritual complexity. The characters in these books find themselves in situations of extreme emergency, which is the source of everything in them.

I FOUND THESE QUALITIES in Richard Wright's latest work, *The Outsider*, which has now been published as a pocket book, and with a bit of luck can be bought in the "Pembimbing" bookstore in Jalan Kebon Sirih, Jakarta. In it, Richard Wright takes a new turn. He is no longer setting out to write about a Negro—as he says, "My hero could have been of any race . . ."—but a human being, because the human being is even more important than the Negro.

Nevertheless, by doing this, Wright has curtailed his voice as an artist and has instead taken on the role of an intellectual. And this intellectual has constructed a theory and then tried to speak to the mind of his reader—even though he chooses to do so through the medium of the novel, because previously, he was a writer of novels.

Now this is how things stand. I once met Wright and had the opportunity to talk with him. Anyone who does so will immediately be fascinated by the amount of "naïveté" in him. It is a naïveté that is accompanied by an evaluation of his surroundings that subsequently reemerges as a reaction that is essentially physical in nature.

His laughter is the kind of laughter that many intellectuals have forgotten how to produce, and I had the feeling that the soul of this writer was straight as a bamboo tube, that he was unburdened by the kinds of complications we generally find in representatives of peoples with very powerful traditions and who, as a result, come into this world with almost unbearable burdens.

He has two very simple points of reference. As a Christian, he is guided by the Gospel, and as a modern man he believes in the truth revealed to us by science.[9]

TO MY MIND, writers can be divided into two groups. The first includes those whose spirits are highly complex and who are unable to solve their own spiritual problems, while the second consists of those whose outlooks are straightforward, practical, and uncomplicated. Both groups can attain high standards in their own ways. But the greatest achievements in literature are the books produced by those who are almost incapable of coming to terms with the complexity and confusion of their personal problems and yet can write about them in straightforward language and with simplicity of thought.

In this category I would include people like Dostoyevsky, Tolstoy, Kafka, Rilke, and other similar writers. They seem to display the literary phenomenon referred to as the "genius" of a simplicity of thought and feeling that proceeds out of very deeply embedded complexities. By contrast, the greatest failures in literature are those lofty works produced by writers in the second category who, in one way or another, are endeavoring to show that they are dealing with complex and profound personal issues.

This is what Richard Wright does, and as a result, we find ourselves with a book that proves that his talents and skills as an artist or a writer are too thin for such weighty matters. The artist has become an intellectual tout court, and the intellectual subsequently takes up a tendency toward oratory.

THE OUTSIDER TELLS the story of a 26-year-old Negro youth called Cross Damon. He marries a girl of his own race who gives him two children before they go their separate ways. He then goes to live with a 16-year-old Negro girl, who becomes pregnant by him and threatens to take him to court for having sexual relations with a minor, unless he marries her. This he is unable to do, because he is only separated from his wife, not officially divorced.

His wife, who hears about his predicament, turns it to her own advantage by making a number of demands that throw him into confusion. But then something happens that comes to his aid. The subway train he is riding is involved in an accident, and though he escapes unscathed, he is presumed dead. He sees this as a chance for "freedom" and goes to New York to start a new life. But before he leaves, he murders another Negro who might possibly reveal that he is still alive.

In New York, he acquires a new name and quite by chance finds himself mixed up in Communist circles. He gets into a fight and kills two people, a Communist leader and a fascist, and then murders another Communist leader, Hilton, whom he suspects of knowing his secret. He falls in love with the wife of the first Communist leader he has killed, but after his secret is revealed, she commits suicide.

AS WE SEE, there is quite a lot of blood in this book, although it is the work of someone who is driven by metaphysical and philosophical motives, not someone who is mentally disturbed. I don't deny the possibility that these murders are symbolic, but even symbolic actions have to have a minimum of truth about them and be inherently convincing. To me, this is what is lacking here.

Cross Damon is a young man and an intellectual, and as an intellectual he is of course a reader. His friend says that you find books all over Damon's house, from the bedroom to the lavatory, and the most important of them are: Nietzsche, Hegel, Jaspers, Heidegger, Husserl, Kierkegaard, Dostoyevsky. This list makes plain in which direction the wind is blowing. The book was written after Wright became associated with Jean-Paul Sartre, and after he had taken the empress of the existentialists, Simone de Beauvoir, to see the slums of Harlem, in New York.[10]

But his existentialist friends didn't lead him to the true source of his strength. And this is not because Wright is a Negro (skin color has nothing to do with this), but because he is an American Negro.

Damon and Houston—a disabled district attorney who because of his disability also sees himself as an "outsider" (as you see, a person doesn't need to be of the Negro race to be an "outsider," a white man can be so as well—in short, ". . . could have been of any race")—who are Richard Wright's spokesmen, have learned their philosophy lessons well. The philosophy is sometimes brought out in the dialogue—which is indeed quite well structured—but once a writer loses the ability to make ideas an integral part of his novel (as is the case here), Wright has no hesitation in allowing Damon to hold forth for thirteen whole pages in front of Blimin, Menti, and Hank, three members of the Communist Party.

But it appears this philosophy isn't the compelling force behind the actions of Richard Wright's characters. When Damon wants to separate from his wife, he looks for excuses. You would expect him to be consciously acting out the unavoidable consequences of his way of seeing the world, such as, for example, we find in the character of Meursault in Albert Camus's *L'Etranger*.

BUT NO. FULLY AWARE of what he is doing, he looks for excuses. Wright has found the motive that works best for the American public (and that perhaps he himself is convinced is the right motive). Isn't it so that in America now, everything is determined by psychology? That's what everyone believes. Anyone who exhibits odd behavior in public is said to be someone suffering from "paranoia." That explanation seems perfectly understandable.

Damon too finds his excuse in mental illness. He usually returns home at five in the morning, but one day he suddenly appears at four, slaps his wife's face, and then goes out again to return at five. When he sees her again, he pretends to be unaware of what happened earlier and asks her why she is crying. He behaves in a caring way, lifting his son up off the floor and carrying him around in his arms. His wife understands the situation straight away. Damon needs to see a psychiatrist. He refuses. Later, he repeats his actions, and at that point, it is clear to his wife that Damon really is suffering from a mental illness and there is a reason for them to separate.

This is Wright's cunning trick. And it's not the only one he employs in his book. And all of them are tied up with the big questions, the question of human existence and so on.

ONE VERY INTERESTING aspect of the book is the way Wright portrays the communist characters. If Wright can be believed, the Communist Party in America is a collection of gangsters. The way it is organized and the prominent people in it all belong to the gangster world. Blimin, who represents the party in his conversation with Damon, and who is answered by Damon in his thirteen-page-long philosophical disquisition, is no different from the crime boss who does the thinking and is always in the background of the action in every American gangster movie we ever see. In fact, the way he behaves is so much in that mold that we can't escape the thought that Wright has picked him up in an idle moment, like a flower off the silver screen, and placed him into his book. His sidekick Menti is a totally loyal believer in the gang, someone who is willing to fight for it, while Hank is just a robot. He is the type of person whose brain has been removed—such as we saw previously in the films of Bela Lugosi—who only awaits the order to go out and kill.[11]

What Richard Wright presents to his reader in this book—apart from the first chapter, which is indeed written with great skill—is a calling card dressed up with bits and pieces that identify him as an intellectual who, as is usually the case, is struggling with a variety of weighty spiritual matters that cling to his body like a disease.

But in fact, Richard Wright is still the same writer who gave us *Black Boy* and *Native Son*. It's just that this time, he wants to be different. He writes well, and he is a skilled storyteller, but he wants to be something more than that.

He wants to convey a message about the human condition. And the message is that in the Negro's present situation, his freedom is not ultimate freedom. Freedom from social constraints does not mean freedom from metaphysical constraints. I would not hesitate to agree with this. But it is clear from pages and pages of *The Outsider* that the promptings of his heart are still tied to the situation of the Negro in America today. His total being is focused on the injustice suffered by his fellow Negroes. But his mind tells him that this isn't enough. He needs to say something about a bigger cause, to convey a message about the human condition. At this point his mind parts company with his heart. And the hapless Richard Wright blows up the description of a flea into something the size of an elephant. The body has tusks and a curving trunk, but the soul just crawls around in the dirt.[12]

RICHARD WRIGHT ONCE MADE a visit to Indonesia. After he left, he wrote in the French magazine *Preuves* that in Indonesian lavatories all you found was a bottle or bucket filled with water, because the Indonesian people were no longer willing to import toilet paper from Europe at exorbitant prices.

This was just ignorance. Reporters make even more ignorant remarks in the reports they file from Indonesia. But *The Outsider* is a failure of judgment. And failures of this kind are very dangerous for a writer.

Notes

Asrul Sani. "Richard Wright: Seniman jang Djadi Intelektuil." 1956. Translated and published as "Richard Wright: The Artist Turned Intellectual" with the permission of Yayasan Asrul Sani.

1. On the disorienting ways Indonesian conventions of laughter have occasionally circulated internationally, see Farouque.
2. See Wright, *Black Boy* 102–44.
3. On their fellowships with STICUSA, see Jassin, Asrul, and Nuraini. Nuraini's correspondence with Jassin during the fellowships, held in SNC, is dated 1952 and 1953.
4. See for instance Dubois; Lemaire; and Jassin, Asrul, and Nuraini.
5. The challenge these questions posed in independent Indonesia was the theme of Soedjatmoko's much-cited rationale for the appearance of *Konfrontasi*, published in the magazine's first issue of July–August 1954 (Soedjatmoko).

6. Asrul's adaptation of *Caligula* was published as a special edition of the BMKN-sponsored journal *Indonesia: Madjalah Kebudajaan*, in September-October 1956 (Camus).

7. The term "document humain," which was part of the vocabulary of French naturalism (Heehs 168–69), was used in Indonesian discussions of literature from the early 1950s as a description of writing that could be seen as a faithful and unflinching record of human experience. In Indonesia, the genre largely avoided naturalism's insistence on "the sometimes sordid uniqueness of the particular human being" (168) and concentrated instead on naturalistic style and realist observation. A typical example of the Indonesian use of the term occurs in a 1955 survey of modern Indonesian literature in English by James S. Holmes in which Holmes describes the early novels of Pramoedya Ananta Toer as "one continuous, obsessed *document humain* of a people in fratricidal revolution" and suggests that these novels derive their strength from their "naturalness, their lack of artifice" (Holmes 34).

8. This extraordinarily harsh criticism of Suwarsih Djojopuspito's Dutch-language autobiographical novel of life as a nationalist (Taman Siswa) schoolteacher in the 1930s reflects the unwillingness of Indonesian writers and critics, both at this time and later, to accord this Dutch-language novel a place in the national canon. Foreign critics have tended to view *Buiten het Gareel* (Out of Harness), published in the Netherlands in 1940, much more positively. In the work of non-Indonesian critics, it has often been seen as a literary milestone and a pioneering expression of Indonesian feminism (Hatley, "Postcoloniality" 160–67). For a recent discussion of the novel, see Sears 88–119.

9. In the 1950s, Wright said, "I'm nothing in matters religious" (Wright, *Black Power* 36).

10. On Wright and de Beauvoir's visits to Harlem, see Fabre, *Unfinished* 309.

11. As reflected in the references to film history in his review of *The Outsider*, Asrul was not only a writer but a major figure in the world of Indonesian film. In the 1950s, he was one of a small number of Dutch-educated Indonesian filmmakers who went on to study overseas (in Asrul's case in the Netherlands and at UCLA) and whose work exhibited the strong influence of Western individualism (Heider 131).

12. Asrul's elaborate metaphor seems to suggest that Wright unduly enlarges the particular or putatively small story (the flea) of African American oppression in the United States so that it becomes a universal or putatively large story (the elephant) about the human condition. Asrul's suggestion is that rather than telling the story of the elephant (with which Wright identifies intellectually) Wright would have been better off telling the story of the flea (with which his soul truly identifies).

15

Frits Kandou's "Richard Wright's Impressions of
Indonesia" (1956)

In May 1956, a year to the month after Wright lectured at the Balai Budaja to PEN
Club Indonesia and the BMKN, the *Sebaran B.M.K.N.* (the BMKN newsletter)
published a two-part article on Wright's *Bandoeng, 1.500.000.000 d'hommes*,
which was the French-language translation of his book on Indonesia and the
Bandung Conference.[1] The article was written by Frits Kandou, who was a
regular contributor to Indonesian cultural journals of this period, particularly on issues related to French culture.[2] Kandou's facility with the French
language permitted him to mediate Wright's travelogue to his Indonesian associates based on *Bandoeng, 1.500.000.000 d'hommes*, which was published
in December 1955, a few months before *The Color Curtain*'s publication in
March 1956.[3] Kandou's translations of Wright's words are notable for being
at two removes from *The Color Curtain*'s language, as Wright's French translator, Hélène Claireau, converted his English to French, and Kandou converted
Claireau's French to Indonesian. Our own English translations of Kandou's
Indonesian quotations of Wright constitute a return to English via three layers
of translation.

Kandou opens by telling his readers, "It is not my intention here to offer a critical review of Wright's work, but just to give a summary of his experiences and impressions in Indonesia. To avoid misunderstandings, the summary presented to the reader will be as complete as possible, and wherever I can, I will let Wright speak for himself." Clearly, Kandou anticipated his audience would be less interested in what he himself had to say about Wright and more interested in news of what their former guest had to say about his impressions of Indonesia. Hence, the article offers comparatively little of Kandou's commentary but provides readers with several pages of translated quotations from *Bandoeng, 1.500.000.000 d'hommes*. In fact, in Kandou's Indonesian-language article, his quotations and translations of Wright are so dominant as to qualify "Richard Wright's Impressions of Indonesia" as a previously unknown republication of excerpts from Wright's Indonesian travelogue, similar to the excerpts that appeared more prominently in the CCF magazines.

In publishing this English-language version of Kandou's two-part article, we are offering it in altered form. Rather than providing translations of Kandou's very extensive excerpts from *Bandoeng, 1.500.000.000 d'hommes*, we are including a few highly truncated and representative quotations from these excerpts. Because our selected quotations are English-language translations of Kandou's Indonesian-language translations of the French version of *The Color Curtain*, the quotations included in our translation often do not line up neatly with Wright's English. However, the goal here is not to produce a neat correspondence between the two but to offer readers an approximation of what Kandou's Indonesian readers found in 1956. Throughout the translated article, we have used notes to refer readers to the specific pages in *The Color Curtain* and *Bandoeng* where they may find the full passages quoted by Kandou. In the same way, we also indicate notable alterations or discrepancies produced by the circuitous translation history of these excerpts.

Condensing the Wright quotations permits our version of the article to highlight the significance of Kandou's commentary on Wright. Kandou's commentary is a subtle but significant addition to the story of Wright's reception in Indonesia. The bulk of Kandou's excerpts from Wright's travel writing involves Wright's discussions with three unnamed Indonesian figures: an interlocutor whom Wright refers to as "a well-known Indonesian writer," an educator whom Wright refers to as "Mr. X," and a student whom Kandou (following Wright's cryptic naming conventions) dubs "student Y." Kandou's denomination of the unnamed student as "student Y" points toward the way Wright's former Indonesian interlocutors approached representations of themselves and their compatriots in Wright's travel writing. In Beb Vuyk's recollection of her circle's frustration with Wright in her essay "A Weekend with Richard Wright," Wright's general refusal to identify his informants was a cause for suspicion. According to Vuyk, Wright composed his travel writing in such a way that "each [interlocutor] was discreetly referred to by an initial, such as 'Student A' and 'Engineer P,' so that however suspicious we might have been about the authenticity of most of these 'confessions,' we were powerless to do anything about it."[4] If Vuyk is to be believed, Wright's erstwhile interlocutors did not know who this "student Y" was.

Yet Indonesians in the Konfrontasi, Gelanggang, and BMKN circles certainly would have recognized "Mr. X," who appears in so much detail (both in Wright's *The Color Curtain* and Kandou's excerpts) that he can only be identified as the senior Konfrontasi figure Takdir Alisjahbana. As noted in the introduction to this book, Wright alleges in *The Color Curtain* and *Bandoeng* that he conducted his interview with Mr. X/Takdir in Europe before leaving for Indonesia, even though it is clear from Wright's travel journal that he conducted this interview in Indonesia after the Bandung Conference. Ignoring Wright's assertion that he conducted the interview in Europe, Kandou presents the interview as having taken place in Indonesia. And while reading Kandou's excerpt, Wright's former interlocutors in Indonesia would have been confused by Wright's assessment of Takdir, which describes Mr. X/Takdir as responsible for the introduction of Indonesian as a replacement language for Dutch during the years of the Japanese Occupation but nonetheless maintains that his contributions to Asia's development would be meaningless.

According to Vuyk, furthermore, Wright's Indonesian circles saw disconcertingly garbled shades of both Takdir and Sitor Situmorang in the figure that Wright identifies (including in Kandou's excerpts) as the "well-known Indonesian writer." Mochtar Lubis certainly saw distorted shades of Takdir in Wright's well-known Indonesian writer. After reading of Wright's exchange with this writer, Mochtar wrote that "one of the best-known Indonesian novelists . . . and others . . . are all amazed to read . . . Mr. Wright quot[ing] them saying things which they never had said" ("Through"). Almost certainly, it was in light of Kandou's sense of how his peers would receive Wright's willingness to alter contexts and splice conversations that Kandou decided to remain cagey in presenting the material in the BMKN newsletter, as if to remind his readers that he himself was not offering these descriptions but rather was reporting the facts of what Wright had written. Again, Kandou wanted to "avoid misunderstandings" by letting "Wright speak for himself." Later, after letting Wright speak for himself, Kandou seems to advance a generous rationale for (or, by Indonesian convention, a polite mask for barbed criticism of) the anomalies he anticipates his readers will find in their former visitor's words: "As Wright didn't stay long in Indonesia, he wasn't able to pursue his observations more deeply."

Wright may not have stayed long in Indonesia, but Kandou's article takes up one of the long-running themes surrounding his visit. This theme has to do with questions of Indonesian sanitary practices. As reported repeatedly in the Indonesian daily press, Wright had not been pleased with sanitary conditions in his room at the Hotel Shutte Raaf. And in his travel writing, he had stated, "Instead of toilet paper, the Indonesians use water. . . . Toilet paper is hard to come by, having to be imported from Europe. Families not well-off enough to afford buckets will place several beer bottles of water discreetly beside the commode" (*Color* 522). By the time "Richard Wright's Impressions of Indonesia" appeared, Asrul Sani's 1956 *Gelanggang* article had already related Wright's narrative of toilet paper and lavatories and remarked, "This was just ignorance." Now, Kandou also referred to Wright's commentary on this topic and saw larger implications for Wright's narrative of Indonesia, taking it as "proof that this writer's attitude is not always objective." Even if Kandou appreciated *Bandoeng*'s documentation of colonial mentality and commentary on the Indonesian leaders Natsir and Sjahrir, Wright's representations of Indonesian sanitary practices could tell readers something about how they should approach the book more generally.

Significantly, this article's publication in the BMKN newsletter brought Wright's Indonesian travels into close proximity with Pramoedya Ananta Toer. At this time, Pramoedya was closely associated with *Sebaran B.M.K.N.* (published fortnightly), and during the newsletter's run from around January 1956 through June 1957, he wrote the entire copy for over a quarter of its issues. No one else except Ajip Rosidi came close to this level of involvement.[5] Certainly, Pramoedya and Ajip would have read Kandou's article, with Pramoedya likely having a hand in its commissioning or selection. One wonders what Pramoedya might have thought as *Sebaran B.M.K.N.* published an article about a writer whom he had admired but whose visit to Indonesia had revolved around universal humanist figures such as Mochtar Lubis and Takdir Alisjahbana. Given Pramoedya's ideological distance from institutions aligned with the Indonesian Socialist Party, such as Mochtar's *Indonesia Raya* and Takdir's Konfrontasi Study Club, and given Pramoedya's public conflict with Takdir over copyright issues, one may imagine a certain satisfaction on Pramoedya's part, as Kandou's article highlighted the portion of Wright's Indonesian travelogue that predicts Takdir's contribution to "reality in Asia was likely to be nil."

Richard Wright's Impressions of Indonesia
by Frits Kandou

SOURCE LANGUAGE: INDONESIAN

I

As we know, Richard Wright spent several weeks in Indonesia. A full report of his experiences was recently published in French by the publisher Calmann-Lévy in Paris, under the title *Bandoeng, 1.500.000.000 People*. When Mochtar Lubis suggested to Wright that he visit a volcanic crater, thinking he might like to see the sights, the Negro writer replied, "No, let's not. Human craters are what excite me . . ."[6] That short sentence accurately portrays Wright's dedication to the task he assumed when he took the decision to attend the Asian-African Conference. At the beginning of his report he notes his surprise that his friends in Paris were unable to tell him anything about the part of the world he was about to visit: the only thing people knew was that the country had some connection with . . ."spices." . . . It is not my intention here to offer a critical review of Wright's work, but just to give a summary of his experiences and impressions in Indonesia. To avoid misunderstandings, the summary presented to the reader will be as complete as possible, and wherever I can, I will let Wright speak for himself.

When Wright first set foot on Indonesian soil on the afternoon of 12 April 1955, his initial impression was, and I quote: "the way customs was handled was extremely chaotic . . ."[7] He understood that this was the result of a lack of experience in this area, but he couldn't help feeling this was something really striking: "ten minutes was enough to indicate the vacuum left behind by the Dutch imperialists . . ."[8] On the way from the airport into the city, Wright observed the scene laid out before him as he crossed several canals: "I passed over those famous canals that for some reason the Dutch had dug in this hot and muddy environment. . . . I saw a young man squatting on the bank of the canal, defecating into the dirty water in broad daylight; I saw another one, then another. . . . Children using a canal as a urinal; a few meters away a woman was washing clothes."[9]

Wright stayed in the home of an Indonesian engineer, a house he described as "modern as modern can be."[10] This engineer had lived for a while in America, and when Wright asked his host whether he had also visited Harlem, the following conversation took place between them: "I never went to Harlem. In fact I never went anywhere . . ." "What do you mean? Did you have some unpleasant experience because of your nationality?"[11] "No, I avoided it. I was scared. . . . I came home from work and stayed in my room. I never went anywhere."[12] Wright understood. He says, "Fear prevented him from becoming a target for expressions that are part of American life . . ." So, the writer of *Black Boy* was forced to conclude, somewhat regretfully, ". . . he avoided all of it, without giving it the slightest try . . ."[13]

Wright found himself uncomfortable with the way Indonesian servants worked. On page 110 of his book we read: "While I was in Jakarta and also in places outside the city, I heard here and there that if an Indonesian servant finds himself working for a white American, for example, he displays an embarrassing degree of subservience [. . .].[14] I was told this custom is not a Dutch invention, but the remnant of a Javanese feudal tradition."[15]

Wright went out of his way to make contact with prominent figures in the political and cultural fields in Indonesia. He found it wasn't always easy to meet up with someone. Wright formed the opinion that in Indonesia, "time is not divided into hours but periods when one sleeps, eats, works, and so on."[16] So Wright concluded: "There are no real work hours there; if you want to see someone you have to fit in with human biological needs."[17]

As for Wright's conversations with prominent people, I will confine myself to three unnamed figures: the first a cultural educator, the second a university student, and the third a well-known writer. On Mr. X, the cultural educator, Wright writes as follows: "Mr. X is an extraordinary man, one of the most important educators in his country. As he is more Westernized than most Westerners, self-made, partly self-educated, and rich, he is unique among his compatriots."[18] I won't keep Wright's own observations of this Indonesian he describes as "more Westernized than a Westerner" from the reader here. On page 51, he comments as follows: "Asia, Africa, or even Europe have never been ruled by compassionate aristocrats; instead millions are caught in nets of fear, hunger, and impossible dreams . . ."[19] Wright could admire Mr. X, but he was forced to make the following judgment: "He was logical, but his logic wasn't applicable to the life around him."[20] So Mr. Wright's overall conclusion was: "It was sad to realize that the influence of this intellectual on reality in Asia was likely to be nil . . ."[21]

II

The following conversation is between Wright and a university student I will just call Y, to make it easy. Again to avoid any misunderstandings, I will convey the translated conversation to the reader in its entirety.[22]

In relation to his conversation with student Y, Wright wrote as follows: "He is a native Indonesian, unmarried, energetic, and a student of political science on a government scholarship."[23] His political awareness arose during his early schooldays: "Unaware of what I was doing, I colored in the face of Queen Wilhelmina on the exercise book in front of me with my pencil; suddenly I realized I'd made her the same color as me. . . . When the [Dutch] teacher saw it, he beat me."[24] Wright's comment on his conversation with this Indonesian goes as follows: "I got the impression that for him, the struggle was not yet over, even though he had his own government."[25] The conclusion Wright drew from his conversation with this Indonesian is as follows: "Everything I knew about Asia from books and daily newspapers told me that this man represented the true Asia, today's Asia . . ."[26]

The third conversation I will now transcribe is between Wright and an Indonesian writer. On page 175, we read as follows: "In a conversation with a well-known Indonesian writer, I asked without any warning, 'Do you consider yourself to be colored?' 'Yes,' he replied. 'Why?' I asked. 'Because I feel inferior.' [. . .] This writer is the head of a powerful cultural organization; he is very religious and is highly respected by his colleagues. Nevertheless, he is passionately against the Japanese: 'Those yellow monkeys!' he says, when we talk about them."[27]

As Wright didn't stay long in Indonesia, he wasn't able to pursue his observations more deeply. However he was able to document various matters rather well. For example, his way of illustrating the colonial mentality in his report was very original. Writing about a little textbook, he observed: "This little book was designed to teach the Indonesian language to Dutch employees, Dutch women, or European tourists. [. . .] This publication, entitled *Bahasa Indonesia: Lessons in Elementary Malay*,[28] is the work of S. van der Molen and was published in 1949 in The Hague by W. van Hoeve. Really 'impressive,' for example, is lesson 24 on page 56, entitled 'The boss is angry.' It goes like this, word for word:

Who is it?
Where do you come from?
Where are you going?
What are you looking for?
Don't pass along here!
Stop there!
You are not very clever!
You are stupid!
You'll be in trouble in a minute!
You should be ashamed!
I want information!
I don't understand.

I think you are lying.
I don't believe you!
Don't talk nonsense!
Speak freely!
Don't be afraid, answer!
Why are you silent?
Why don't you dare?
I don't want to hear that nonsense. Be quiet!"[29]

Wright comments as follows: "The sentences I have quoted are based on the maintenance of: 'law, order, peace, and tranquility.'"[30]

In conclusion, I will quote a few sentences from Wright's book *Bandoeng, 1.500.000.000 People* on a subject where it can be said the writer was entirely off the mark. It serves as proof that this writer's attitude is not always objective. The matter concerns toilets, and what Wright found was quite unexpected. On page 110 we read the following: "Indonesians do not use toilet paper, but water. . . . Toilet paper is hard to obtain, because it must be imported from Europe. Poor people place beer bottles filled with water by the commode. . . ."[31] This is what Wright wrote. Unconsciously, the writer went looking too far for an interpretation, because any Indonesian, even one living in Europe, could have explained to Mr. Wright that he preferred to use "toilet bottles" rather than paper, and this preference has nothing to do with poverty or imports. And any Muslim would be able to assure Mr. Wright that the use of toilet paper is in fact forbidden. . . . Unfortunately it is not possible to relate everything concerning the impressions Wright formed in Indonesia. What he had to say about Moh. Natsir and Sjahrir, for example, is very interesting.[32] For those who are interested, I will mention in conclusion that the publisher of this short book of Wright's is Calmann-Lévy, 3 Rue Auber, Paris.

Notes

1. The French edition was published in Calmann-Lévy's "Liberté de l'Esprit" series, which also published a French edition of *The God That Failed*.

2. Kandou's 1955 articles on French culture include essays on Henri Matisse and André Malraux in *Siasat*'s *Gelanggang* column (Kandou, "Henri" and "André"). His interest in French culture and his knowledge of French can be traced to his mother, Augustine Magadalena Wawo Runtu (1899–1987), who studied in Paris on a French government scholarship in the early 1950s and taught French at the University of Indonesia in Jakarta between 1953 and 1958 (Vreede-De Stuers).

3. On this publication history, see Fabre, *Unfinished* 422.

4. See Vuyk's "A Weekend with Richard Wright," also included in part III.

5. Information on Pramoedya's and Ajip's involvement with *Sebaran B.M.K.N.* is drawn from our own tallies of the periodical's content.

6. For this exchange, see Wright, *Color* 534; and Wright, *Bandoeng* 122.

7. For this comment, see Wright, *Color* 503; and Wright, *Bandoeng* 88.

8. For this comment, see Wright, *Color* 503; and Wright, *Bandoeng* 88.

9. For this description, see Wright, *Color* 504; and Wright, *Bandoeng* 89.

10. See Wright, *Color* 508; and Wright, *Bandoeng* 95.

11. We have translated Kandou's term *kebangsaan* according to its modern-day meaning of *nationality*, which was already its standard meaning in the 1950s. However, its use here contains a possible ambiguity, in that the base word, *bangsa*, was also used during the colonial era to translate the European concept of *race*. It is possible that Kandou was using *kebangsaan* here and elsewhere in his article to translate Wright's references to race.

12. For access to the full extent of the conversation included by Kandou, see Wright, *Color* 511: *Mr. P looked at me. . . . Then I left*; and Wright, *Bandoeng* 97: *M. P. me regarda. . . . Puis, je suis sorti.* Kandou's translation is missing text corresponding to a sentence that is present in the English and French versions of *The Color Curtain*: "*He was as dark as I was. I understood. He could not take it*" (*Color* 511); "*Son teint était aussi foncé que le mien. Je comprenais. Il n'avait pas voulu l'affronter; il n'en avait pas eu le courage*" (*Bandoeng* 97).

13. For access to the full sentence included by Kandou, see Wright, *Color* 511: *Fear had kept . . . without even trying*; and Wright, *Bandoeng* 97: *La peur l'avait empêché . . . sans même essayer.*

14. Because Kandou uses ellipses extensively, our own ellipses in the text of the translation are represented with brackets.

15. For access to the full extent of the description included by Kandou, see Wright, *Color* 521–22: *In my goings and comings. . . . upper-class Indonesians*; and Wright, *Bandoeng* 110: *Au cours de mes allées et venues. . . . des Indonésiens de la classe dirigeante.* A mistake appears in the French translation, which refers to *Japanese* rather than *Javanese* feudal traditions (*Bandoeng* 110), but Kandou's translation corrects this to *Javanese*.

16. For access to the full extent of the description included by Kandou, see Wright, *Color* 523: *The day is divided. . . . be in soon*; and Wright, *Bandoeng* 112: *La journée se divise. . . . qu'il ne tardera pas.*

17. See Wright, *Color* 523; Wright, *Bandoeng* 112.

18. For access to the full extent of the passages included by Kandou, see Wright, *Color* 464–70: *Mr. X was an extraordinary man. . . . origin of most of our trouble*; and Wright, *Bandoeng* 42–50: *M. X était un homme extraordinaire. . . . l'origine de la plupart de nos difficultés.* Kandou's version is missing two passages that are present in the English and French versions: *He first heard the word "lynch." . . . baleful effects* (*Color* 466); *Il a entendu pour la première fois le mot "lynch." . . . douloureux effets* (*Bandoeng* 44–45), and *That part of the past. . . . the whole of history* (*Color* 466–67); *La partie du passé. . . . la totalité de l'histoire* (*Bandoeng* 45).

19. For access to the full passage included by Kandou, see Wright, *Color* 471–72: *If the future. . . . social conditions about him*; and Wright, *Bandoeng* 51: *Si l'avenir. . . . les conditions sociales du milieu.*

20. For access to the larger quotation included in Kandou's translation, see Wright, *Color* 470: *He had an acute mind. . . . no valid reality*; and Wright, *Bandoeng* 50: *Il possédait une vive intelligence. . . . pas de réalité valuable.* Kandou's translation omits the following material, which appears in English and in slightly altered form in French: *. . . and he ruefully admitted it. But, as drastic as he sounded; . . . et en convenait avec tristesse. Malgré la rigueur de ses raisonnements.*

21. See Wright, *Color* 472; and Wright, *Bandoeng* 51–52.

22. Kandou's use of the phrase *Untuk menghindari salah faham lagi* is ambiguous in this context. While one straightforward translation would be *To avoid any further misunderstandings*, implying that the article's first installment had produced a degree of controversy, we believe it should be seen as parallel to the phrase *Untuk menghindari salah tampa (To avoid misunderstandings [on my part])*, which occurs in the introduction to the first installment. For this reason, we have chosen to translate the phrase as *Again to avoid any misunderstandings*.

23. For access to the full extent of the description included by Kandou, see Wright, *Color* 472–74: *He is full-blooded Indonesian. . . . German doctor to be found*; and Wright, *Bandoeng* 53–54: *Age d'une vingtaine années. . . . n'était disponible.* A few passages are missing from Kandou: *Yes; the state should support religion* (*Color* 473); *Oui, l'État devrait soutenir la religion* (*Bandoeng* 53); *". . . You are a new country and without experience"* (*Color* 473); *". . . Vous êtes un nouveau pays sans expérience"* (*Bandoeng* 53); and *it has religious sanction. . . . married out of the clan* (*Color* 473); *il s'agit de la diversité des religions. . . . marié en dehors de son clan* (*Bandoeng* 53); and *At the last moment the boy's parents said that I could come along* (*Color* 474); *Ils finirent par lui céder* (*Bandoeng* 54).

24. For access to the full extent of Wright's description as included by Kandou, see Wright, *Color* 474–76: *I colored the face of Queen Wilhelmina. . . . ". . . just getting rid of them"*; and Wright, *Bandoeng* 54–57: *Sans savoir ce que je faisais. . . . ". . . que de nous en libérer."* Kandou notably excludes one passage that appears in Wright's English and French: *It seemed natural. . . . what I had done* (Wright, *Color* 474); *Il me semblait naturel. . . . ce que j'avais fait* (*Bandoeng* 54–55).

25. For access to the full extent of this passage as included by Kandou, see Wright, *Color* 476–78: *What struck me first of all. . . . West was his enemy!* and Wright, *Bandoeng* 57–59: *Ce qui me frappa tout d'abord . . . l'Occident était son ennemi!* Kandou's version departs from the English and French versions in a few notable instances. Kandou's excerpt is missing the phrase *the "given" in his environment* (*Color* 476); *des données de son entourage* (*Bandoeng* 57). Kandou's translation changes the English and French versions' phrase *to hoist the West off of his back* (*Color* 478); *pour se débarrasser de l'Occident* (*Bandoeng* 59) to *of acquiring greatness of spirit*. Kandou's version elides Wright's *Of Western values he wanted none . . . Great Men?* (*Color* 478); *Il ne voulait d'aucune des valeurs occidentales . . . Des grands hommes?* (*Bandoeng* 59).

26. See Wright, *Color* 476; and Wright, *Bandoeng* 57.

27. For access to the full extent of this passage as included by Kandou, see Wright, *Color* 583–84: *In an intimate interview. . . . replied proudly*; and Wright, *Bandoeng* 175–76: *Dans un entretien. . . . répliqua-t-il fièrement.* Although Mochtar seems to have seen shades of Takdir in this figure, and although Vuyk's account suggests it may also be

influenced by a remark conveyed to Wright by Sitor Situmorang, Wright's representation of the "very religious" and well-known Indonesian writer does not correspond directly to any writer with whom he is known to have interacted. Wright's journal description of an unnamed Indonesian novelist he apparently spoke with on 16 April resembles the exchange regarding color and inferiority ("Jakarta" 120).

28. Kandou's translation positions Wright's description of the book, "a book of elementary Malay" (Wright, *Color* 575), as if it were a subtitle, *Lessons in Elementary Malay*. The 1949 volume's actual title is *Bahasa Indonesia: A Textbook of Elementary Indonesian Malay*.

29. For access to the full extent of this section as included by Kandou, see Wright, *Color* 575–77: *This booklet was designed. . . . Be quiet!* and Wright, *Bandoeng* 166–68: *Ce petit livre était destiné. . . . Taisez-vous!* In Kandou's translation of the commands from master to servant, he follows the French translation of the English phrases Wright quoted from the booklet. Oddly, in translating the angry master's orders and insults directed at the servant, the French translation converts the informal Indonesian *kamu*— which in this context is the second person pronoun for a person of inferior status— into the formal and polite French *vous*. Correspondingly, in Kandou's retranslation the master addresses the servant as *tuan*—the second person pronoun for a male of superior status and, almost invariably in the colonial and immediate postcolonial period, a European. The use of second person pronouns in the extract thus constitutes a reversal of the master-servant relationship, so Kandou's retranslation (whether knowingly or not) evokes a postcolonial image of the servant yelling at the master.

30. For access to the larger quotation included in Kandou's translation, see Wright, *Color* 577: *And today there are Dutchmen. . . . peace, and tranquility*; and Wright, *Bandung* 168: *Et aujourd'hui, il y a des Hollandais. . . . la paix et la tranquillité*.

31. See Wright, *Color* 522; and Wright, *Bandoeng* 110.

32. For these discussions, see Wright, *Color* 515–18 and 523–28.

16

Beb Vuyk's "A Weekend with Richard Wright" (1960)

In the few years following *Sebaran B.M.K.N.*'s 1956 article on Wright's *Bandoeng, 1.500.000.000 d'hommes*, political conditions in Indonesia changed rapidly and in ways that placed new pressure on the Indonesian institutions with
which Wright interacted during his Bandung Conference travels. Decisive
change was signaled as early as December 1956, when regional army commanders in various parts of Sumatra staged a civilian-backed rebellion against
central government control. Their actions were the beginning of a political
crisis that by 1958 had broadened to a full-scale revolt involving not only most
of Sumatra but also another regional rebellion based on the island of Sulawesi
in eastern Indonesia. Backed by regional army commanders and politicians
hostile to Soekarno, the rebellion was fueled by local perceptions that the
wealth of Indonesia's regions was being exploited by the central government
in Jakarta. Later, as Mochtar Lubis himself acknowledged, it became clear
that the United States, through the CIA, was also heavily involved in funding
and supporting the movement, as part of the effort to stem the influence of
Communism in Indonesia at this time (Hill, *Journalism* 50). When an American civilian pilot was shot down on a bombing run in support of the rebels in

eastern Indonesia in May 1958, relations with the United States immediately soured, and in the words of one historian, the Indonesian Communist Party (PKI) was "quick to capitalise on anti-American feelings" (Ricklefs 319). By mid-1958, the central government and central army leadership were again in control, and the United States was struggling to repair the damage to its relations with Indonesia. However, the rebellion had strengthened the influence of the PKI on the direction of Soekarno's thinking and added to a sense of crisis that supported his call for change in Indonesia's internal and external political affairs. On 5 July 1958, with the backing of the army's chief of staff, General Nasution, Soekarno dissolved the Constituent Assembly, which had failed to produce a new Indonesian constitution, and declared a return to the Constitution of 1945, which placed supreme executive power in the hands of the president. On Independence Day, 17 August 1959, Soekarno formally announced the end of parliamentary democracy in Indonesia. It was to be replaced with his own concept of "Guided Democracy" and a "'retooling' of the institutions and organisations of the nation in the name of ongoing revolution" (323). Politicians, newspaper editors, and public figures who resisted the changes, especially those associated with the modernist Islamic Masyumi party and the Indonesian Socialist Party (PSI), came under intense pressure and were ultimately deprived of freedom of expression and movement.

Meanwhile, and in the same climate, relations with the Netherlands, already under strain since the foundation of the unitary republic in 1950, had all but collapsed. Dutch refusal to negotiate the surrender of Irian, the western half of the island of Papua, to Indonesian control inflamed nationalist sentiment and played directly into the revolutionary fervor of Soekarno and his allies, particularly the PKI. Less than eighteen months after the Bandung Conference, in August 1956, the Indonesian government repudiated the agreement struck with the Dutch at the Round Table Conference of 1949 over the payment of Indonesian debt to the former colonial power. In 1958, Dutch commercial interests in Indonesia began to be nationalized, often falling under control of local army commanders, and Dutch expatriates who had remained in Indonesia after independence began leaving the country in large numbers and under conditions of duress. With the backing of the PKI, Soekarno began to promote a spirit of radicalism and anti-imperialism over economic pragmatism, moving ever closer to the image that Wright, after leaving Indonesia, was projecting of him.[1]

As cultural and political changes in Indonesia put new pressures on the PSI and other institutions, many of the individuals with whom Wright associated in Indonesia found themselves under threat, in a climate of increasing Cold War hostilities. In December 1956 Mochtar Lubis was arrested on charges of support for the regional rebellions and attempts to undermine the authority of the central government through his activities as a newspaper editor and journalist. Two weeks later, and without trial, he was placed under house arrest in Jakarta, where he remained until being temporarily released between April and July 1961 (Hill, *Journalism* 57, 62).[2] For a time, Mochtar's newspaper *Indonesia Raya* continued to appear, but after a series of temporary bans, the paper was finally banned outright in September 1958 (58–59). At the same time, between 1958 and 1960, the journal *Konfrontasi* gradually came to be a mouthpiece for anti-Communist Cold War cultural politics, taking on more and more of the character of CCF journals published elsewhere in the world and regularly including translations of articles sourced from these journals that illustrated the allegedly pernicious effects of Communist cultural influence (Foulcher, "Bringing" 49–53). The relaxed gatherings of Takdir Alisjahbana's Konfrontasi Study Club, such as Wright had experienced in 1955, were now a thing of the past, and the journal's final issue, dated May–August 1960, appeared sometime in 1961, after a twelve-month delay securing printing permission and paper supplies (54). Indeed, the journal's demise at this time was symptomatic of the increasing marginalization of the PSI and its affiliated institutions in the new political climate of Guided Democracy. After failing to secure any representation in the new parliament inaugurated by President Soekarno on 5 July 1960, the PSI was finally banned in August of the same year, an act that spelled the end of its political influence and ushered in a period of extreme duress for those organizations and individuals associated with the pro-Western cultural outlooks it had been seen to represent.

The political conditions of 1956–1960 also brought about painful readjustments in the life of Beb Vuyk. When she had sailed from the Netherlands for Indonesia in 1929 at age twenty-four, Vuyk was seeking greater ties to the Indonesian ancestry she had inherited from her paternal grandmother. In Indonesia during World War II, Vuyk spent three years in Japanese concentration camps, and after Indonesia emerged as a sovereign nation in 1949, she chose to become an Indonesian citizen.[3] Among her fellow citizens, she was an active participant in discussions of the developing Indonesian literary culture. But in 1957, as Dutch businesses came under threat of appropriation and—in Vuyk's view—the situation of intellectuals in Indonesia came to resemble that of German intellectuals in the 1930s, she and her husband, Fernand de Willigen, arrived at the painful realization that they would have to leave Indonesia, at least temporarily (Scova Righini 326–39). Finally, at the end of 1957, when it was reported that Soekarno was intending to cancel the Indonesian passports of "former Dutch people" (Scova Righini 330; Kloek 1339), Vuyk and de Willigen fled to the Netherlands. There, Vuyk continued as a long-distance member of *Konfrontasi*'s editorial board and began writing for *Vrij Nederland*, a left-wing Dutch periodical, in which she published a two-part article on Richard Wright titled "Weekeinde met Richard Wright" (A Weekend with Richard Wright).[4] Although this article has been overlooked by commentators on *The Color Curtain* and missummarized by Wright's biographers and bibliographers,[5] it represents the most significant account given of Wright's Indonesian travels by any of his interlocutors in Indonesia.

As Vuyk mentions in the article, by the time she published "A Weekend with Richard Wright" in November 1960, she had read Wright's 1955 *Encounter* article "Indonesian Notebook," as well as his more extensive *Der Monat* article of the same year, "Indonesisches Tagebuch." Though she does not mention doing so, it is likely that she would have also read *The Color Curtain*. Furthermore, as an Indonesia-watcher with a circle of acquaintances who kept track of such things, she was also likely aware of an interview with Wright published in the French weekly *L'Express* in August 1960 in which he had commented on his experiences in Indonesia:

> I went to Indonesia to report on the Bandung conference, and on that occasion I was sometimes told atrocious things. I checked them and was able to establish that they were strictly true. For example, during the Japanese occupation, the Japanese put all the Dutch—men, women, and children alike—into concentration camps. . . . They used natives, i.e. Indonesians, to guard the camps. . . . Someone assured me that the Dutch told the native guards, "If you touch any Dutch women, if you rape them, we shall kill 1,000 Indonesians for every single white woman." I was told the Indonesians were so incensed by that insult . . . that they tried to redeem themselves in the eyes of the Dutch in a way which seems strange at the least. They ordered all the white women out of the camp, lined them up against a palisade, set up a machine gun and shot every one of them. Then they asked the Dutch, "Well, now, have we touched your women? Have we raped them?" Wasn't this a most horrible incident? . . . They were deeply incensed and they wanted to convince the Dutch: "We are not what you believe; we are not interested in white women, but in freedom." Now, can you really consider that the cleanest form of action should be murder? I pondered this and told myself: "No, I cannot relate such atrocities. The West is not able to listen to such things without contemplating revenge." (Fabre, "Interview" 203–4)

Vuyk's article makes no comment on this inevitably incendiary account, but its appearance in August 1960 may have helped trigger her writing and publication of "A Weekend with Richard Wright" just three months later in November 1960. Over five years had passed since Wright's visit to Indonesia, and it seems perhaps strange that Vuyk would spontaneously reopen the public record of his Indonesian travels. Yet if she did read Wright's *L'Express* interview, and noted his assertion that the story he was recounting was "strictly true," it is possible that her article was prompted by the desire to offer another perspective, a corrective seeking to undercut Wright's claims regarding the strict truth of his accounts of Indonesia and Indonesians in his travel writing more generally.

The first installment of "A Weekend with Richard Wright" was published on 19 November and its second installment on 26 November. The article offers an intimate view of the literary and cultural exchanges evoked by Wright's travel to the Bandung Conference, particularly as Wright's travel brought him into engagement with the Konfrontasi Study Club. Indeed, although historical scholarship on the Asian-African Conference has tended to focus on questions of official international politics (as played out on the ground in Bandung and as inspiring later movements in nonaligned and third world international-isms),[6] "A Weekend with Richard Wright" is a strong reminder of the ways the Bandung Conference, as an occasion that brought Wright and other cultural figures into dialogue with Indonesian and international interlocutors, played an immediate though little-researched role in the development of transnational modernism's cross-pollinating literary and expressive cultures.

Vuyk's essay—as it complements and competes with Wright's account of Indonesia—offers a valuable case study of the quandaries and misrecognitions involved in global intellectual exchange in a climate marked by growing Cold War tensions. Here we have portraits of some of Wright's major Indonesian interlocutors: Mochtar Lubis, Takdir Alisjahbana, Nenni (Siti Nuraini), Rul (Asrul Sani), Sitor Situmorang, and Beb Vuyk herself, together with allusions to each figure's status vis-à-vis the political tensions prompted by the effects of the Cold War in Indonesia. Misrecognitions between Wright and his hosts come to a head in Vuyk's representation of the events surrounding their guest's lecture at Takdir's villa in Tugu. During the postlecture discussion, Wright (apparently without grasping the intensity of his interlocutors' bitterness at Japan's World War II occupation of Indonesia) suggests that the Indonesians and Japanese ought to feel a sense of commonality because they are both peoples of color.[7] In response to this suggestion, we see in Vuyk's essay a scornful rejoinder from study club members and an emphasis on Japanese wartime atrocities in Indonesia. Yet these are met with Wright's apparent minimization of the horrors of the Japanese Occupation. He points out that his Indonesian hosts are Western-educated intellectuals, and he wonders how the Japanese treated the common people. To illustrate the hatred ordinary Indonesians felt for the Japanese as a result of their wartime occupation of Indonesia, the writer Sitor Situmorang tells the story of a Javanese village leader who referred to the Japanese as "yellow monkeys." Vuyk's article describes the study club's outrage on seeing that Wright, in his subsequent travel writings, seemed to attribute the phrase "yellow monkeys" not to a village leader but to his host during the weekend meeting and the study club's most senior figure, Sutan Takdir Alisjahbana.

The "yellow monkey" incident is one of several misrecognitions and apparent misrepresentations Vuyk discusses.[8] Ultimately, she tells readers, incidents like this one led Mochtar to write a letter to Wright. After reading Wright's response to his letter, which, according to Vuyk's account, alleged that Mochtar still embraced a colonial mindset, Mochtar pronounced Wright to be "color crazy."[9] Though Vuyk's representation of the Wright-Mochtar letters may refer to personal correspondence between the two, it is likely that Vuyk's narrative on this point is a reconstruction (remembered impressionistically three or four years after the fact) of a discussion she had with Mochtar regarding Mochtar and Wright's 1956 exchange of letters in the pages of *Encounter*. During this exchange, Mochtar had stated that in Indonesia Wright "had sought behind every attitude he met colour and racial feelings" (Mochtar, "Through"), with Wright making no explicit mention of a colonial mindset but rather replying that Mochtar should read *The Color Curtain* for details on "the *nature* of the racial feeling I found not only in Indonesia, but in the Asian personality as a whole." Wright counseled Mochtar to "think hard" about their conversations while driving in the mountains between Jakarta and Bandung (Wright, "Mr. Wright").

One of the remarkable—and truly tragic—aspects of Vuyk's "A Weekend with Richard Wright" is that it was published at the very end of Wright's life, as he was dealing with health problems that Wright's daughter Julia and others believe were the result of foul play and that Wright's biographer Hazel Rowley hypothesizes may have been liver poisoning brought on by excessive bismuth treatments (Rowley 522–24). During these final days, he was on penicillin for a fever, and just sitting down to type made him tired, wanting to return to bed.[10] When Wright's Dutch translator, Margrit de Sablonière, read Vuyk's 19 November installment of the article, she telephoned Wright, observing that Vuyk appeared in one of the photographs included in *The Colour Curtain* (British edition) and asking Wright if he knew her.[11] De Sablonière then sent Wright a document that apparently gave a cursory and at times inaccurate summary of Vuyk's first installment, prompting Wright to write back to his friend and translator, contesting several points he believed were made in Vuyk's article.

In an effort to set the record straight for de Sablonière, Wright stated that he never made any comments to Vuyk about people of mixed blood, that he never referred to Nkrumah as "my president," that he did not endorse fascism in Ghana but acknowledged that Nkrumah's actions would be perceived as fascism by the West, and that he did not remember asking Vuyk or any woman to call him "Dick."[12] As will be apparent to readers of "A Weekend with Richard Wright," the first three of Wright's objections (on mixed blood, Nkrumah as president, and fascism) stem from misunderstandings of either nuances or major issues in Vuyk's article, whether due to de Sablonière's own misreading and missummarization of Vuyk's article or a subsequent miscommunication between Wright and de Sablonière by telephone or in writing. With these misunderstandings in hand, and without pointing to evidence, Wright suspected that Vuyk was in league with American interests and that her article constituted an American attack against him, and by extension Pan-Africanism, by the CCF, which had (perhaps desiring a repeat performance of Wright's trip to Indonesia) unsuccessfully approached him with a request to speak on Tolstoy in India earlier in 1960.[13]

In the interim between Vuyk's first installment and her 26 November installment, de Sablonière told Wright that, in case the article's second half continued with the same tone, she was hard at work putting together notes for a counterattack against Vuyk—something concise and well-documented, something to establish the truth.[14] Wright and de Sablonière must have been distressed when the second installment appeared and, especially in its conclusion, seemed dedicated to setting the historical record straight, citing chapter and verse from Wright's CCF articles on Indonesia and asserting that Wright at some points had misunderstood the scenes he recounted. At another point, according to Vuyk, he had played fast and loose with the truth, eliding crucial contexts and condensing the views of three separate people into the words of one vaguely defined informant. Although The Color Curtain's subtitle describes the volume as a report rather than a piece of creative writing, de Sablonière felt it was Wright's right as an author to "kind [of] create figures"; it was a convention frequently used by authors, even if they often got into trouble for it.[15] With the appearance of this second installment, de Sablonière telephoned Wright again and recommitted to write an attack against Vuyk.[16] Given that issues of Vrij Nederland became available on the Friday prior to their stated Saturday publication dates, this telephone call may have happened either on Friday, 25 November, or Saturday, 26 November.[17] In any case, by the afternoon of 26 November, Wright was checking into the small, private, and nearby Eugène Gibez medical clinic.[18] De Sablonière completed her counterattack and arranged to have it published, but when Wright died of a reported heart attack on 28 November—just two days after the second installment's stated 26 November publication date—her publisher refused to print it. Because the publisher had sent Vuyk a prepublication copy of de Sablonière's answer to "A Weekend with Richard Wright," Vuyk wrote to de Sablonière saying that she herself had penned a sharp retort, but now Wright was dead, and she did not want to continue with the argument.[19]

Looking back on these agonizing final days of November 1960, de Sablonière in 1966 explained that Wright's trip to Indonesia had been financed by the CCF and that when he arrived in Indonesia "he was received by a group of people who were CCF."[20] Indeed, like Wright during his Indonesian travels, Mochtar and Takdir had ties to the CCF. And given her close association with Mochtar and Takdir, Vuyk also undoubtedly had ties, though these were less prominent.[21] In any case, the conflict surrounding Wright's travel writing and Vuyk's response was consistent with the CCF magazine editors' emphasis on "the attractiveness of controversial articles, or articles made controversial by inviting discussion and counter-attack" (Lasky).

Even if Wright's own objections to Vuyk's article pivoted largely on his misunderstandings, he was correct to suggest that as a factual record, it was not completely accurate. Notably, it implies that Wright's lecture for the Konfrontasi Study Club took place the weekend before the Bandung Conference—on Sunday, 17 April—rather than on Sunday, 1 May, which is the date confirmed by the daily press during Wright's actual visit.[22] Vuyk's article also contains a scene during which Wright says he is planning on staying with the American ambassador until Monday, 18 April, the day of the Bandung Conference's opening session. This seems inaccurate because according to *The Color Curtain* and Wright's travel journal, he stayed at the home of one "Mr. P," an Indonesian engineer, during the week before the conference (*Color* 509; "Jakarta" 104). Perhaps Vuyk misunderstood Wright when he explained to her that he had an appointment *to visit* the American ambassador? He indeed called on and spoke with the American ambassador during his time in Indonesia ("Jakarta" 194). Or perhaps when Vuyk spoke with Wright sometime close to the day after his arrival, he was between accommodations, certain he did not want to return to the substandard Hotel Shutte Raaf but not yet having solidified arrangements with Engineer P and hence believing that he might need to depend on the hospitality of the ambassador or another official at the US Embassy? Wright's travel journal indicates that he called on the American Embassy and had a long discussion with an unnamed official, apparently on the same day that Mochtar made arrangements for him to stay with the engineer (99–100). At another point, Vuyk's narrative seems to suggest that after disembarking from the plane on 12 April, Wright proceeded directly to the Ministry of Information to obtain a press card. Yet according to Wright's journal, this event certainly did not occur on 12 April but more likely on 13 or 14 April ("Jakarta" 98–106).

In spite of the essay's inaccuracies and status as a narrative reconstruction, several of Vuyk's recollections may be corroborated, speaking to the larger, though always qualified, reliability of her essay. According to Vuyk, Wright directed the conversation toward questions of "great men" and the most important event of the twentieth century, both topics that appear on the questionnaire Wright prepared in the run-up to his Indonesian travels (Wright, "Questionnaire"). Vuyk also depicts a discussion with Wright regarding her upcoming review of *Black Power* for *Indonesia Raya*, and indeed *Indonesia Raya* published this review less than a month after Wright's departure.[23] Vuyk's essay further narrates Wright's Konfrontasi lecture as taking place on Sunday rather than conforming to the club's standard Saturday schedule, and indeed the daily press during Wright's visit confirms this is what happened.[24] Also related to Wright's lecture at Takdir's mountain villa, Vuyk recalls that during the talk Wright placed particular stress on the alliterative set of *s*'s in the phrase "captured, chained, and sold into slavery." The published transcript of this lecture reveals that even if Vuyk's rendition of the phrase was not precisely correct, Wright's rendition of it was even more alliterative than she recalled: "transported across the Atlantic in crowded, stinking ships, and sold into slavery" (Wright, "American" 3–4). Just as Vuyk's account of the lecture offers valuable insight into Wright's performance of what we may otherwise engage with as a written text, her larger essay offers another—and crucial—entrance into the events that scholars have typically understood exclusively through Wright's own narrative in *The Color Curtain*.

If one may point toward several details corroborating Vuyk's account of Wright's past Indonesian travels, one must also acknowledge the fundamental accuracy of Wright's predictions regarding Indonesia's future. In November 1960, while discussing Vuyk's article, Wright told de Sablonière that while in Indonesia in 1955 he had warned Mochtar, Takdir, Vuyk, and others that they were too cozy with the American ambassador and that if they distanced themselves from the Indonesian populace while stubbornly following the Americans, they would find themselves in exile. In addition, in Wright's eyes his former hosts were naïve to insist on Western-style democracy in a land where it had no precedent.[25] Though his Indonesian interlocutors might have seen such comments as an overreaction in 1955, his commentary seems prescient in retrospect. With Vuyk's departure for the Netherlands in 1957, Wright's earlier predictions on exile were beginning to come to pass. Indeed, his statements on the problems associated with Western-style democracy in Indonesia anticipated both scholarly debate on Indonesian political history and the trajectory of that history itself.[26] Still more striking is the fact that although Vuyk and Mochtar cast aspersions on the ways they perceived Wright conflating the categories of color and colonialism, their own position was later further marginalized as President Soekarno himself began making similar analogies. In his 1963 Independence Day message to the Indonesian people, Soekarno analogized antiracism and anticolonialism, now linking the two categories via the concept of a general "social conscience of man" (Sukarno 234). He declared:

> Our Message of the [Indonesian] People's Sufferings is interlocked with the Message of the Sufferings of Mankind, the Message of the Sufferings of Mankind is interlocked with our Message of the Sufferings of the [Indonesian] People. The Indonesian Revolution is interlocked with the Revolution of Mankind, the Revolution of Mankind is interlocked with the Indonesian Revolution. . . .
>
> The Indonesian Revolution does not only demand food and clothing! . . . The Indonesian Revolution demands many other things. It encompasses all the aspirations of mankind. It is congruent with the social conscience of man. . . .
>
> The Negroes in America are now in a Revolution,—the Revolution of the Social Conscience of Man. Do they demand food and clothing? No! They demand treatment as equal human beings, treatment which is "congruent with the social conscience of Man."
>
> Therefore, Sisters and Brothers, never forget for a moment that our ideals are noble. Noble ideals which are really the ideals of the whole of Mankind, noble ideals which resound in the souls of the whole of Mankind! (234–35)

In framing African American antiracist activism as emblematic of the planet-wide revolution of which the Indonesian Revolution was a constituent part, Soekarno in 1963 was coming close to—if not fully agreeing with—a statement articulated by Wright at Takdir's mountainside villa in 1955: "The voice of the American Negro is rapidly becoming the most representative voice of oppressed people anywhere in the world today" ("American" 24). In a few short years, Indonesia had undergone significant change, and by 1963 Wright's words were in keeping with its president's thinking. Mochtar Lubis may have been correct to say that Wright saw Indonesia through colored glasses in 1955, but those glasses offered a glimpse into an Indonesian future in which the president would incorporate similar perspectives into his vision of the ongoing Indonesian Revolution.

A Weekend with Richard Wright

by Beb Vuyk

SOURCE LANGUAGE: DUTCH

I

Mochtar came by to pick up an article I had written for his newspaper. "I won't come in," he said. "I have to collect Richard Wright from the airport."

"What's he doing here?" I asked. His lively, youthful features contorted into a grimace: "He's covering the Bandung circus."

Mochtar's *Indonesia Raya*, one of the most prominent opposition papers, had reacted sharply against the planned Bandung Conference. "Get your own house in order before you take on world politics" was his sober judgment.

He turned around and was gone, waving "bye" with his hand above his head.

"Where's he staying?" I wanted to ask. But the car was already out the gate. Mochtar was always in such an un-Indonesian hurry. I decided to give Takdir a call.

Takdir is one of the most fascinating figures among the Indonesian intelligentsia. A poet, novelist, and essayist, he studied law while working with the Institute for Popular Reading (Balai Pustaka) before the war. He felt more drawn, however, to linguistics, philosophy, and sociology, subjects that in Indonesia at that time you couldn't specialize in. At the same time he began to publish under his own directorship the magazine *Pujangga Baru* ("The Young Literati"), a literary, cultural, and political monthly, the only independent Indonesian journal of the period. *Pujangga Baru* attracted the participation of virtually all the Indonesian intellectuals who took up writing, and it had an enormous influence on the development of the new Indonesian language.[27] It stopped publishing during the Japanese Occupation, because Takdir found it impossible to write about culture under a fascist administration. That's the kind of man he was. After the war it appeared again in Batavia, where after the first police action Takdir organized the officially prohibited Republican education system.[28] With a natural talent for business, he had taken over the Unity printing office the year before and set up a publishing firm and bookshop. Alongside the all-important *Pujangga Baru*, he began publishing two popular-scientific magazines. After the transfer of sovereignty, his activities increased. He set up an after-hours university where he lectured, and as a member of Sjahrir's Socialist Party he took an active part in political life, holding seats in parliament, the city council, and the Constituent Assembly. In between his political and publishing activities, he traveled to Europe and America, on business and to participate in conferences.

Takdir was someone who could work twenty hours a day, sleep well for the other four, and then start another twenty-hour day. Active, energetic, and incredibly versatile, he was a typical Renaissance figure, one of several that Indonesia has produced. Tragically, the culture from which people like him have derived their cultural renewal is highly specialized, which means they are confined to one subsection of it. Takdir's unbending choice of the West—first digesting Western culture and then going back to square things up with his cultural heritage—made him controversial in a society that finds its ideal in the notion of compromise. He had many friends, even more enemies, but at that time his financial independence made him invulnerable. Later, after political disintegration became so great that political opposition was equated with incitement to rebellion, he was placed under city arrest, even though a few months later he was granted permission to travel overseas. At the moment he is in America.

IN APRIL 1955 the political unraveling hadn't yet reached that point. The year before, Takdir had turned *Pujangga Baru* into *Konfrontasi*, which concerned itself primarily with issues that were surfacing in the wake of Indonesia's recently obtained independence. This meant that the new magazine adopted a raison d'être different from that of *Pujangga Baru*, which was established as a nationalist journal when *merdeka* ("independence") was still something that had to be wrested from the Dutch. There was a study club attached to *Konfrontasi* that met monthly to explore a topic of cultural-political significance, following which the topic would be worked up into an item for publication in the journal. It wasn't easy to pin down a speaker every month to give an introduction to the topic, and as secretary to the editorial board it was my job to find someone.

It took me more than half an hour to get hold of Takdir by phone. He's even more mobile than Mochtar.

"Get on to him right away and ask him for a lecture," he said, after hearing about Wright's arrival. "Invite him up to Tugu for a weekend, and get the whole study club to come. That could be interesting."

Right after the war, Takdir's ability to smell a bargain led him to buy up a piece of land in the Puncak Pass area with two half-burnt-out houses on it. At that time the area was still highly unsafe, and he got it for a good price. With the help of a bricklayer and a carpenter from the local village, he rebuilt the two houses as a pair of bungalows, joined together by a covered walkway. Now, a few times each year, he would invite a group of people up there to exchange thoughts about some particular issue. That was what he had had in mind for the place. The discussion would take place after dinner on Saturday and sometimes last well into the night. The next morning we would take a dip in the ice-cold water of the swimming pool and then sit in the sun to get warm. Little groups of people would form on the terraces and lawns around the pool, keeping up the discussions and cementing personal contacts. After lunch—Takdir would always have a goat slaughtered on these occasions, and the *sate* [skewered barbecue meat] lunches became a tradition—we would hang around until about four o'clock in the afternoon, when we all piled into the pickup for the trip back to the heat of Jakarta, traveling down to Bogor through the lovely, green, and park-like West Javanese landscape that murmured with the sound of flowing water. These weekend gatherings, to which both Indonesians and foreigners were invited, were relaxing and friendly affairs in a pleasant rural setting. However fiery the discussions could be on occasion, everyone who took part in them came away with the happiest of memories. "Just ask him if he could give a lecture about American Negro literature," I heard Takdir say.

"Which weekend?"

"This coming one. The Bandung Conference starts next week, and he'll be tied up."

"I can't get it together for this weekend. I haven't got his address, and phoning is so hard with all those overloaded lines. And there's no time to write letters back and forth."

"Mochtar will know his address. Go and invite him yourself. Go to Bandung if you have to. But I think it's likely he's up at Tugu with Bill Palmer or one of the other Americans.[29] Nenni might be interested in going with you. You'll be going through Bogor anyway."

I DIDN'T MANAGE TO get hold of Mochtar. His wife, Halli, wasn't home, and at *Indonesia Raya* they said he was on his way to Puncak. I took the train to Bogor, where luckily Nenni was at home.

Nenni is the wife of a poet and a poet in her own right. An attractive and graceful woman, aware of the impact she has on other people, she is nevertheless often hesitant and unsure of herself in company because she tends to be the victim of her husband's wrongheaded belief that every word an intelligent woman speaks must be as intelligent as she is. What's more, she has saddled herself with the tiring business of having to be the modern, intellectual Indonesian woman whenever she is around people she doesn't know, especially around foreigners. With me, she gave it up long ago. She is pleasant, really intelligent despite her little affectations, and in certain situations she's as helpless as a caged bird in a primeval forest. She comes from a very religious

Minangkabau family, and during the turbulent years of the Japanese Occupation she was the clever little daughter her parents hid away in a strict Islamic boarding school. She came straight out of that school into the chaos of the revolution and married Rul just before the transfer of sovereignty. With her husband she fell into the hands of institutions, like the Dutch Foundation for Cultural Cooperation and the Rockefeller Foundation, that carted them off all over the world. She saw and learned a great deal at that time, but she came out of it a bit breathless, especially when she found herself wedged in between what she used to be and what she is now. This was one of those occasions. She really wanted to come with me, but at the same time she put up a fight against going—unless it was all a little show of being a good wife and mother for her own mother, who could hear everything we said from the adjoining room. In the end I won her over, and, an hour later, as we clambered up the narrow stone path toward Mochtar's bungalow in Tugu, she was so enthusiastic that she would gladly have taken on a dozen more steep tracks in her high heels, if finding Richard Wright meant we had to go looking among the scattered houses of the American colony up there.

This time, however, luck was on our side. On the open terrace behind Mochtar's house sat Mochtar and Halli with a plump little man in a much too correct light-gray suit. "He's only a bit browner than us," was all Nenni managed to say, because Mochtar was already on his feet and it was time to shake hands and say our how-do-you-dos.

"CALL ME DICK," he said straight off, so Dick it was, however hard it was for us to get the name out at first. In Indonesia, even friends of twenty years use the word *Mas* ("elder brother") in front of a man's name (although since the revolution young people tend to prefer *Bung*, another word for "brother"). It's only foreign friends, especially Americans, whom Indonesians address by their first names; even then, they don't do so five minutes after meeting them.

"You got here quickly," I said.

"It all went smoothly," Mochtar replied. "A whole crowd of foreign journalists arrived on that same plane, and they all headed off first to Information to get themselves accredited. When we arrived there was already a long line. Luckily, I knew the man at the desk, so I went round the back and we were finished in five minutes. We picked up Halli and came straight here."

"Yes," said Richard Wright. "It all went quickly and smoothly. I'm so pleased to have made it to Indonesia. I feel at home here already." He looked around our little group and smiled. "I always feel immediately at home among colored people."

At the time I had no idea how the others reacted. But it gave me a vaguely unpleasant feeling, even though I couldn't say why.

"Though not so with everyone in Ghana, surely?" I replied.

"You've read *Black Power*?" he asked.

I nodded. "You sent it to Mochtar, and he lent it to me so I could write a review of it for *Indonesia Raya*."

Black Power isn't a novel; it's a travel diary. Richard Wright made a visit of several months to Ghana, on the invitation of Nkrumah, whom he met in America. It was a rather disappointing sort of pilgrimage to his racial origins. "An American Negro views the African Gold Coast," it says on the cover. As an American, he is a stranger in the land where his ancestors were abducted nearly three hundred years ago, but as a Negro, someone of the same skin color, he still has an emotional interest in this land, to which the ties of blood and ancestry no longer bind him. Even though much of the book testifies to his bewilderment over people and circumstances he encounters, his emotional attitude toward race helps him push on through suspicion, deception, and lack of openness to try to make sense of what he sees there.

"I HOPE TO SEE Nkrumah again in Bandung."[30]

"I was quite shocked by what I read about him in your book. His solution to the emotional vacuum created by the loosening of tribal ties and the loss of the old beliefs in the protection of the ancestors is to give the masses a sense of fulfillment through a national super-belief and a sense of allegiance to party leaders—it makes me shudder. This is fascism."

"It can lead to fascism," he admitted, "but you have to take that risk. You can't build a modern state out of tribal communities. There has to be something to bring about a new national unity, and that's Nkrumah's goal. Everything depends on him. He is a great man; if anyone can make a success of it, he will."

"He is a great man," he repeated. Then he looked around at all of us, and said, "Your president is also a great man. I look forward to meeting him. He's the one who came up with the plan for this conference. For the first time in the history of humanity the colored races will come together in an international conference. That is an event of great historical significance."

We were silent. Then he turned to Mochtar. "You don't agree, you said during the drive up here."

"It has everything to do with internal politics," Mochtar ventured in reply. "To drown out the noise of its weakness and blunders, the Ali administration needs a big political success story.[31] That's why it's doing everything it can to make sure this conference succeeds."

"That's possible," replied Richard Wright. "I'm not up on internal Indonesian problems. I'm a foreigner, and I see this conference the way the rest of the world sees it."

He went quiet for a moment, and then said, "What do you think is the most important fact of this century, from a historical point of view?"

"The liberation of the colonies," answered Mochtar without hesitation.

He nodded. "Definitely. The distinguishing feature of this twentieth century will be the coming into independence of the colored peoples."

Nenni noticed the use of the future tense. I wasn't sure about Mochtar.

"Mochtar, do you think the shared colonial past is a tie stronger than color?" I asked.

"Of course. The peoples of Asia and Africa have all been colonized in one way or another. They all gained their freedom in the same period, and they all have the same problems to solve."

"And have to undergo the same acculturation process," Nenni added.

II

It began to drizzle, so we had to move inside. Mochtar asked if we were staying for lunch and called out to the boy working in the garden, telling him to kill a chicken.

His bungalow is very basic, but it is spacious and comfortable, made up of just a bedroom and a big living room that is divided from the kitchen by a couple of waist-high cupboards, which gave Halli the chance to take part in the conversation while she prepared the chicken. Mochtar built the house himself, with the help of a couple of workmen and a kind of building pattern that you can buy in America, just like the patterns we buy to make a skirt or blouse. Everything here is Mochtar's own work, right down to the furniture. Apart from the Miró reproductions, the walls are hung with his own paintings, since he's a painter as well as a writer. He's fond of primary colors, especially yellow. Yellow is Mochtar's color, bright, open, and in-your-face, dangerous attributes for someone involved in politics in a country where, more than anywhere else, politics is a game of intrigues and hidden meanings lying behind a lot of yelling and shouting.

Mochtar is someone with the urge—very rare in an Indonesian—to work with his hands, which explains why he built a house, furniture, toys for his children, and a swimming pool in his garden. He also needs to spend a lot of time outdoors, pounding tennis balls across the net, swimming in ice-cold water, escaping city life in the world of nature. Maybe he learned to fly to escape into the heights, to lift himself far above the petty racket of politics and journalism. It will be four years this coming 13 December that he was detained, held in a prison cell for several weeks, and then, without trial or sentence, placed under indefinite house arrest. Since then he has been confined to his small house in the city, watched over by a guard in his large front garden. Just before my departure from Indonesia, I paid him a visit. He had set up a small bedroom at the back of the house as a study. It looked out on a window-high blank wall, and it seemed to me like a cell.

"Why don't you sit in the front of the house?" I asked. "Have they forbidden it?"

"When I'm here I don't have to look at the guard, and I can imagine that I'm free," he said proudly. He went on to tell me he was doing lots of writing and painting, had taken up his French grammar, and was learning Spanish with the help of a linguaphone. That was more than two years ago. The other day, I had a letter from a friend in Indonesia that reached me via America. "Mochtar is busy driving himself crazy. He suffers from a persecution complex," he said.

After lunch, I made an appointment with Richard Wright for the upcoming weekend. He said he was staying with the American ambassador until next Monday, but it was no problem to leave a couple of days early. Something about his tone of voice made me ask, "What sort of a fellow is he, your ambassador?"

"A southern gentleman whose grandfather owned slaves," he replied, hissing the s of "southern" and "slaves." I asked no more questions.[32]

EVEN THOUGH WE HAD scheduled Richard Wright's lecture for Saturday evening, Takdir had accepted a dinner invitation to the Hollingers on behalf of us all.[33] I suspected Richard Wright would not have been pleased, but he gave no indication either way. Bill Hollinger is a sociologist with one of the technical aid projects, and his wife Flora works with him in the office.[34] They and their three children live in one of the bungalows directly above Takdir's.

Most of us had read enough about the Negro problem to be interested in observing firsthand how white Americans acted in the company of one of their black compatriots. But I fear that Richard Wright's black-and-white view of the world was beginning to have its distorting effect on us, because of course when it came to the point there was nothing to observe. Bill and Flora included him in the invitation as their guest and ours. But they were probably aware of our suspicions, because this busy dinner party—there were more than thirty people there, half of them Americans—took on the air of a rather tense display of racial goodwill. It was all the more unreal because both the Hollingers' house and the bungalows of the other Americans were regularly the scene of enjoyable gatherings between Indonesians and foreigners— whites and coloreds, to use Dick's terminology. It was the same thing the next morning at the lectures—there were a number of Americans in the audience. Takdir had found it difficult to refuse, when they asked if they could attend. The tension here in Takdir's house wasn't as strong; it was only recognizable in the taut lines of Richard Wright's face when he stood up to speak. He gave a first-rate lecture, demonstrating through examples taken from two centuries of poetry how Negro literature in America is American literature, written in the same language and in forms that correspond to the dominant poetic forms of the time. The poetry's content changes with the way the poets see their position as Negroes, moving from grievances to accusations. He introduced his lecture with a brief historical survey of the origins of the Negro population in America, beginning with the slave expeditions. When he spoke the words "captured, chained, and sold into slavery," I heard that same hissing sound on "sold" and "slavery." His bottom lip went up, his face tightened, and his eyes burned with hostility. The s in *slave* and *slavery* was the same as in *sold* and *southern*. His grandparents had been born slaves, and there in the south his grandmother had fed and raised him. It still burned inside him.

LATER, WHEN THE Americans had left and lunch was served, he relaxed. He sat on the bench with a plate piled high with food and tried to pronounce the names of the Indonesian dishes.

"It's nice that we're on our own again," he said, but this time I didn't take offense at his "us and them" approach.

"He asked me if I felt inferior to whites," Takdir told me. "'Why should I feel inferior?' I asked him."[35]

"It's his youth, Mas," I said. "Read *Black Boy*, his autobiography, and you'll understand."

"But he's not a 'black boy' anymore. He's become a writer of international renown. He has an apartment in Paris, and a farm in Normandy. He's on friendly terms with people like Sartre and Simone de Beauvoir."

"He lives in France because he and his white American wife don't want to live in America. He won't even live in New York, where there are dozens of Negro intellectuals, writers, and artists. He can't forget his youth. Didn't you hear the way he hisses when he pronounces the words *slaves* and *slavery*?"

After lunch we all lazed around drinking coffee. Even high up in the mountains it gets warm around two in the afternoon, and we were all feeling sleepy. I dozed off, and was woken up by Sitor's voice, sounding loud and angry.

"I do not feel inferior to whites. I was born a 'native,' and I've lived with racial discrimination. But we are free now. I'm no longer a 'native' but an Indonesian."

FIGURE 16.1. Wright on the patio of Takdir's villa with members of the Konfrontasi Study Club. This photograph portrays (left to right): Richard Wright, Siti Nuraini, Fedja (daughter of Siti Nuraini and Asrul Sani), and Sitor Situmorang (arm only). Photographer unknown. Courtesy of the Beinecke Rare Book and Manuscript Library, Yale University.

Sitor really belongs to our group in an emotional sense, even though outwardly he distances himself from us and cozies up to what is called—in back-veranda conversations—the "palace clique." He has a wife and five children, and he is undoubtedly the most important of our young writers. But he also harbors a burning ambition that doesn't always find sufficient social and financial outlets in his life as a writer. Just before I left Indonesia, his enemies took vicious delight in spreading a rumor that he was going to be appointed minister of cultural affairs. It gave them a great deal of pleasure, because for two weeks Sitor went about telling everyone how happy he was at the news. These days, he is the only one of my friends who's doing well. For Sitor there

FIGURE 16.2. Wright on the patio of Takdir's villa with members of the Konfrontasi Study Club. This photograph portrays (left to right): Sitor Situmorang (arm only), Richard Wright, Fedja, and Siti Nuraini. Photographer unknown. Courtesy of the Beinecke Rare Book and Manuscript Library, Yale University.

are no publication bans, no house arrest or self-imposed exile, but a decent income and a finger in the pie as a member of various advisory bodies.[36] Back then in 1955, people were already saying that he had ten faces and ten tongues, but the tongue that voiced those shrill, angry words was unmistakably sincere.

"Do you think that whenever I'm talking to someone I'm conscious of whether he is 'white' or 'colored'? I don't feel inferior to whites, and I don't hate them either." He took a deep breath and went on, somewhat more composed, "Feelings of racial inferiority can give rise to a racial-superiority complex. The Japanese were prone to that, and it was pathetic to see. They tried to spread it among us as well. They had little success, and absolutely none at all among the intellectuals." And then, raising his voice again, "We are against colonialism, but we are not against whites. We struggled for racial equality, not for the belief in another superrace, a colored superrace."

RAISING ONE'S VOICE IN such a way to convey harsh truths to a guest is highly unusual in Indonesia. One hardly ever contradicts a guest, and certainly never does so discourteously. But Richard Wright was totally unmoved. I don't think he realized what had happened.

"What were the Japanese like?" he asked in all innocence.

"Frightful," answered two or three voices together.

The look on his face clearly showed that he found it hard to believe. "But they are also a colored race."

At that, there were several among us who laughed out loud.

"You are all Western-educated intellectuals. How did they behave toward the ordinary people?"

"They behaved like bloodsuckers and oppressors of the worst kind," someone said. Someone else cut in: "Like a superior race toward lesser beings." Then it was Sitor again:

"I'll tell you a story, Dick, that'll show you how the ordinary people still think of them. The government sent a friend of mine to a village where there was a plan to build a Japanese-made factory and install Japanese foremen to run it. His job was to report on the local people's reaction to the plan. My friend went to see the village head and told him why he was there.

"'Japanese,' the village head said, 'those yellow monkeys here in our village?' then he spat on the floor."

Many months later those same yellow monkeys appeared again, in an article on Richard Wright's Indonesian journey that Wright published in the August edition of *Encounter* and the August and September editions of *Der Monat*. In the article, he took on himself the role of a sort of father confessor, to whom numerous Indonesians had confessed feelings of bitterness and unease that came out of a racial-inferiority complex. Each confession contained a short, well-constructed anecdote, and each penitent was discreetly referred to by an initial, such as "Student A" and "Engineer P," so that however suspicious we might have been about the authenticity of most of these "confessions," we were powerless to do anything about it. Except in two cases: the assistance that Mochtar's friend had rendered in expediting Richard Wright's press card so that Wright would not have to stand in line is in this article transformed into a touching little story about one colored man helping out another in a display of mutual solidarity. A man with a face "as dark as mine" is bent over his desk bored stiff as he listens to the request of a white American journalist: "But the moment he saw me his whole manner changed. While the white American waited, I got my press card. I was a member of the master race. And I thought of all the times in the American south when I had had to wait until the whites had been served before anyone would help me."[37]

Even more painful is the way Takdir's denial of any sense of racial inferiority here comes across as a confession of just the opposite, an illustration of the strong racial feelings that may exist even among intellectuals in Indonesia. He has Takdir, described as the most important Indonesian novelist, speak as follows: "'Of course I feel inferior. I can't help it. It is so difficult to come into contact with the Western world and not feel it.'"[38]

Even so, remarks Richard Wright, Takdir takes a strong position against the Japanese—and, thereupon, the "yellow monkeys" of Sitor's village leader spring to life out of Takdir's mouth, complete with the spitting and all: "'Those yellow monkeys!' He spat as he referred to them."[39]

Mochtar sent him a complaint and received in reply a short letter, which he showed to me: "I note from your criticism of my article that you are still not free of the colonial past."

That was all. "What does he mean?" I asked. Mochtar shrugged his shoulders. "The fellow is color crazy," he replied angrily.

Notes

Beb Vuyk. "Weekeinde met Richard Wright." 1960, 2011. Translated and published in 2011 as "A Weekend with Richard Wright" with the permission of Joke de Willigen-Riekerk. Reprinted by permission of Joke de Willigen-Riekerk and The Modern Language Association of America.

1. For a brief account of the increasing political and economic role of the military and the development of Soekarno's vision for Indonesia at this time, see Cribb and Brown 78–87.

2. The detention of Mochtar Lubis in December 1956 was the first instance in independent Indonesia of a writer (who in this case was also a crusading journalist and editor) being imprisoned for political motives. Mochtar himself believed his arrest was the direct result of Communist influence on President Soekarno (Hill, *Journalism* 50), and it was marked in *Konfrontasi* by the publication of an article by Beb Vuyk on the antifascist "White Rose" movement of 1942 and its exposure of Nazi war crimes (Foulcher, "Bringing" 45).

3. For more on Vuyk's background, see the introduction to Beb Vuyk's "Stories in the Modern Manner" in part I.

4. Vuyk's "A Weekend with Richard Wright" first appeared in English in the translation we published in 2011 in *PMLA* (Vuyk, "Weekend").

5. See Kinnamon 454–55; and Webb 381.

6. See for instance Ampiah; Tan and Acharya; and McDougall and Finnane.

7. Decades after the appearance of "A Weekend with Richard Wright," Siti Nuraini ("Nenni" in Vuyk's essay) thought back on Wright's visit and her attitudes during the 1950s. She was adamant that she never consciously felt color differences between herself and the Dutch, though she indeed felt them during the Japanese Occupation (Nuraini). Nuraini's sense of the absence of racial discrimination under the Dutch was not shared by all Indonesians, even among those of elite status like herself. However, hostility toward the Japanese, and resentment at Japanese attitudes toward Indonesians during World War II, was indeed widespread.

8. For a discussion of the yellow monkey incident in relation to Javanese prophecy, see Roberts 164–65.

9. The term *color crazy* appears in English in Vuyk's original article.

10. Wright to de Sablonière, 23 Nov. 1960 (MFP, Richard Wright Letters Project, boxes 30–31, folders 23 and 1–3).

11. De Sablonière to Webb, 3 Nov. 1966 (CWP, box 5, folder 10).

12. For reference to the document and for Wright's objections, see Wright to de Sablonière, 23 Nov. 1960. On the question of his nickname, Wright seems to have been objecting to what he believed was an inference on Vuyk's part that his alleged request to be called "Dick" represented something sexual, but Vuyk's essay explains that the Indonesian discomfort stemmed from being asked to address a stranger by any form of his given name within five minutes of their first meeting. Wright's misunderstanding apparently stemmed from de Sablonière's cursory summary of the article.

13. On Wright's suspicion of Vuyk as involved with the CCF, see Wright to de Sablonière, 24 Nov. 1960 (MFP, Richard Wright Letters Project, boxes 30–31, folders 23 and 1–3); and Wright to de Sablonière, 23 Nov. 1960. On Wright's refusal to travel to India on behalf of the CCF, see Wright to de Sablonière, 8 Oct 1960 (CWP, box 5, folder 15).

14. De Sablonière to Wright, 21 Nov. 1960 (RWP, box 105, folder 1594).

15. De Sablonière to Webb, 26 Dec. 1966 (CWP, box 5, folder 10).

16. De Sablonière to Webb, 3 Nov. 1966; and de Sablonière to Webb, 6 Dec. 1966 (CWP, box 5, folder 10).

17. On *Vrij Nederland* issues becoming available on Fridays, see de Sablonière to Wright, 21 Nov. 1960.

18. See Rowley 522; and Kiuchi and Hakutani 392.

19. De Sablonière to Webb, 3 Nov. 1966.

20. De Sablonière to Webb, 3 Nov. 1966.

21. On Mochtar's and Takdir's CCF ties, see this book's introduction. Multiple folders are devoted to Mochtar and Takdir in the University of Chicago Special Collection's records of the International Association for Cultural Freedom, but Vuyk has no folder ("Guide").

22. See "Who's Doing What" (4 May 1955) in "A Sheaf of Newspaper Articles," in part II.

23. See Vuyk's "Black Power," also included in part III.

24. See "Who's Doing What" (4 May 1955) in "A Sheaf of Newspaper Articles," included in part II.

25. For these opinions, see Wright to de Sablonière, 23 Nov. 1960; and Wright to de Sablonière, 24 Nov. 1960.

26. The doubts regarding Western-style democracy's suitability for Indonesia attained prominence in Indonesian studies in the highly visible 1964–1965 dialogue between Harry J. Benda and Herbert Feith. See Benda; and Feith, "History." In Indonesia itself, Western-style constitutional democracy began to crumble as early as early February 1957, with the announcement of Soekarno's "Presidential Conception," which explained Indonesia's problems in terms of an "imported democracy" that needed to be replaced with "the democracy of Indonesia" (Feith, *Decline* 541–42). When the Soekarno regime collapsed in the wake of the coup and counter-coup of September-October 1965, the aversion to Western-style (or "liberal") democracy continued for another thirty-two years under the regime of President Suharto (Bourchier and Hadiz 37–55; Elson 263–66). It was not until the first decade of the twenty-first century that Indonesia instituted reforms reflecting Western-derived democratic norms.

27. *Pujangga Baru* was founded by Sutan Takdir Alisjahbana, Armijn Pane, and Amir Hamzah in July 1933. Until the coming of the Japanese in March 1942, it was the major independent forum for debate on matters related to Indonesian language and culture and was credited with helping to keep alive the nationalist vision in the politically repressive conditions of the late 1930s. It resurfaced under a newly constituted editorial board in 1948 during the war of independence and continued publishing until 1953. For many, the appearance of *Konfrontasi* in 1955 was a continuation of the *Pujangga Baru* mission in the changed circumstances of national independence. On the prewar *Pujangga Baru*, see Teeuw, *Modern* 28–46.

28. The term *Republican* in this sentence refers to the Republic of Indonesia, the official designation of nationalist-held territory during the war of independence against the Dutch between 1945 and 1949. The term *police action* was the Netherlands' official description of two military assaults that Dutch forces launched on the Indonesian Republic during this conflict. The first of these assaults took place in July 1947; it resulted in a military victory for the Dutch but ultimately an increase in American goodwill toward the Republic. The second "police action" in December 1948 had the same effect, and hastened the negotiations that led to the recognition of Indonesian independence in December 1949 (Ricklefs 276–77, 282–85).

29. In the 1950s and 1960s, William Palmer represented the American Motion Picture Association in Indonesia (AMPAI). A Jakarta socialite, Palmer introduced Hollywood's new releases to private audiences and frequently had Soekarno as a guest. Eventually, pro-Communist publications in Asia accused Palmer of being a CIA agent. PKI supporters subsequently ransacked the AMPAI office in Jakarta and apparently entered Palmer's mountain villa by force (Conboy 42–43). During Mochtar Lubis's detention from 1961 to 1966, Palmer's rental, paid in US dollars, of the Lubis family's Tugu bungalow—the site of Vuyk's first meeting with Wright—was a crucial element in the family's financial survival (Hill, *Journalism* 81).

30. Gold Coast prime minister Kwame Nkrumah did not attend the Bandung Conference but rather sent his friend Kojo Botsio as an observer (Vitalis 267). Robert Vitalis has traced the prevalence of scholars' inaccurate assertions of Nkrumah's presence at the conference, but Vuyk's account suggests that some onlookers, even while visiting Indonesia for the conference, anticipated or assumed Nkrumah's presence.

31. Mochtar refers here to the cabinet headed by Prime Minister Ali Sastroamidjojo, which governed Indonesia between July 1953 and July 1955. The Indonesian Socialist Party was excluded from the coalition that formed the cabinet, which explains Mochtar's negative view of the administration (Ricklefs 300).

32. In *The Color Curtain*, Wright meets an unnamed "highly competent official" who exhibits "elementary honesty; this particular man was a reformed American of the Old South. His grandfather had owned slaves and he was eagerly willing to own up to what had happened in history" (600).

33. It seems as if Vuyk is incorrectly remembering Wright's lecture as occurring before rather than after the Bandung Conference. It may well be that she misremembered on this point. Yet it is also possible that Vuyk may have originally indicated here that Wright's lecture was subsequently rescheduled for a postconference weekend. For reasons of space or relevance, an editor at *Vrij Nederland* may have decided to drop such an explanation.

34. William C. Hollinger, who received his PhD in economics at MIT, began teaching at the University of Indonesia in 1954. He left Indonesia during the height of Sukarno's anti-Americanism and returned in 1968 as a leader of the Harvard Development Advisory Service. Hollinger eventually became an independent consultant in Indonesia (Wells and Ahmed 49).

35. It is unclear from the source text whether this exchange between Takdir and Vuyk took place in Wright's immediate presence during the weekend retreat. However, it can be assumed that Takdir and Vuyk were speaking to each other in Dutch or Indonesian, not a language Wright understood.

36. As Vuyk's comments here indicate, Sitor Situmorang's career followed a trajectory that placed him apart from the other Indonesian writers and intellectuals who figure in her narrative. In 1959 he became head of the Lembaga Kebudajaan Nasional (LKN; Institute of National Culture), a cultural political organization affiliated with the Partai Nasional Indonesia (PNI; Indonesian National Party) that promoted Soekarno's thinking through cultural activities of all kinds. In 1962 he produced a collection of poems in the manner of Chinese-style socialist realism titled *Zaman Baru* (The New Age), in striking contrast to his poetry and prose of the 1950s. Like Pramoedya Ananta Toer, Sitor was arrested in the wake of the coup and counter-coup of 1965 and spent the years between 1967 and 1974 under detention (Goenawan, "'Cultural'" 35).

37. The quotation is drawn from Wright, "Indonesian" 28.

38. The quotation is drawn from Wright, "Indonesian" 31.

39. The quotation is drawn from Wright, "Indonesian" 31.

17

Goenawan Mohamad's "Politicians" (1977)

Goenawan Mohamad is one of contemporary Indonesia's most prominent and influential media and cultural figures. Born in 1941 to parents who had suffered three years of internal exile in remote West Papua for their nationalist involvement during the colonial period, Goenawan himself experienced the full force of colonial brutality when his father was executed by Dutch forces in 1947, during the revolutionary war. At the age of eighteen, in 1959, he moved to Jakarta from his home in Central Java to take up studies in psychology and philosophy at the University of Indonesia. Already drawn to creative writing, he soon became part of the literary world of Jakarta, initially as a contributor to the literary magazine *Sastra*, which was edited by H. B. Jassin, among others.[1] Significantly, the year of Goenawan's arrival in the capital was the same year that President Soekarno announced the abandonment of the 1950s experiment with parliamentary democracy and a return to the Constitution of 1945, as the basis for the system of Guided Democracy under a powerful president dedicated to the promotion of national pride and an ongoing struggle against neocolonial exploitation.

The shift to a more authoritarian system of government in a climate of heightened nationalist and anti-imperialist sentiment had dire consequences for the increasingly beleaguered proponents of the universal humanist approach to Indonesian literary and cultural development. After an inexorable decline in the face of the growing strength and assertiveness of the Communist-affiliated cultural organization LEKRA, cultural and literary institutions associated with the pro-PSI outlooks became the targets of vilification and personal attack, and many of the individuals who belonged to the circles Wright had interacted with in 1955 either chose, or were compelled, to withdraw from direct participation in Indonesian cultural affairs. At the end of April 1961, with no official explanation, Mochtar Lubis was unconditionally released from the house arrest he had endured since January 1957. One month later, he traveled to Israel to attend a congress of the International Press Institute in Tel Aviv, where he spoke of the threat to democracy brought about by Communist propaganda and "the susceptibility of national leaders to sacrifice free speech and democratic principles" in their drift toward "'totalitarian systems' for models for their countries" (Hill, *Journalism* 62). Immediately on his return to Indonesia he was rearrested and was held in military detention from 14 July 1961 until rerelease under a new regime led by General Suharto on 17 May 1966 (61–63). In this political climate, other members of the Konfrontasi circle chose self-exile. In 1960 Beb Vuyk acquired permission to remain permanently in the Netherlands (Kloek 1339), and both Sutan Takdir Alisjahbana and Achdiat Karta Mihardja moved into self-imposed exile shortly thereafter.[2]

In the face of such political risks, resistance against the imposition of political exigencies in the Indonesian arts continued to be waged by some of the original proponents of universal humanism and their younger generation heirs. Among them was Goenawan Mohamad. On Independence Day, 17 August 1963, representatives of this group issued what turned out to be a defiant last stand in the face of LEKRA ascendancy, in the form of a declaration titled "Cultural Manifesto" (Manifes Kebudayaan), a restatement of the Gelanggang ideals in a hostile political climate.[3] Reanimating the Gelanggang association between humanism and freedom of artistic expression, the manifesto declared a belief "that culture represents the struggle to perfect the conditions of human existence" and called for a conception of Indonesian national culture as "our way of struggling to defend and enhance our dignity as the people of Indonesia living amidst a community of nations" (qtd. in Goenawan, "'Cultural'" 1–2).

As a signatory of the manifesto, Goenawan quickly became persona non grata of the Soekarno regime. With the help of friends, in 1965 he too fled

Indonesia into self-imposed exile in Belgium, where, with funding from the CCF, he obtained a scholarship at the College of Europe in Bruges.[4] After General Suharto assumed power in 1966, Goenawan returned to Indonesia in 1967 and immediately became a prominent crusader for freedom of the press and cultural regeneration. In 1971, he founded the weekly news magazine *Tempo*, which was to become one of Indonesia's most respected media outlets. *Tempo* maintained a tradition of investigative journalism for more than twenty years, until it was banned in 1994 after running afoul of President Suharto and his New Order government. In 1999, however, *Tempo* was revived in the wake of Suharto's May 1998 resignation, and it remains a prominent and influential weekly publication today. Goenawan retired as chief editor in 2000 to concentrate on his writing, but he has continued to contribute the weekly short essays he began to publish in *Tempo* in the late 1970s under the column title *Catatan Pinggir* (Notes in the Margin). As Goenawan's longtime English translator, Jennifer Lindsay, has remarked, the column's title is significant. It suggests that the essays are to be taken as "marginalia," notes from the sidelines by a writer who presents himself as an observer, "one who can see the good and bad points of both sides of an argument, and is reluctant to be forced into exclusive commitment to either of them" (Lindsay, "Introduction" xi). Highly literary in style, the essays embody the original universal humanist principles reconceived as a commitment to intellectual debate, democratic ideals, and cultural pluralism, often against the tenor of political developments in their author's homeland. As Lindsay notes, these essays are also masterful illustrations of the capabilities of the Indonesian language and its often unacknowledged potential for complex critical commentary and observation ("Translator's" xi–xvi).

"Politicians" is one of the earliest of Goenawan's *Catatan Pinggir* essays.[5] The column first appeared under the title *Fokus Kita* (Our Focus) in 1976 and was renamed *Catatan Pinggir* in March 1977, only six months before "Politicians" was published. The tone of the essay makes it clear that although Goenawan was a cultural heir of Gelanggang and other PSI artists and intellectuals, he was not an heir to the resentment that many of them felt when they saw themselves and their peers misrepresented in Wright's refashioning of them as personae rather than people. It seems that little if any cultural memory of these earlier disappointments was preserved in Indonesia through the 1970s. In any case, the tenor of Goenawan's article is not one that accommodates accusations of "coloured-glasses" or post-aesthetic intellectualism.[6] Rather, "Politicians" appeared on the occasion of the 1977 publication of Wright's *American Hunger* (the posthumous sequel to his earlier autobiography), and it draws on *American Hunger*, *Black Boy*, *The God That Failed*, and

The Color Curtain to suggest that Wright's life and writings offer a template for understanding the purpose of politics and politicians in Indonesia.

In 1955, as Beb Vuyk recalled, Wright had surprised his Indonesian hosts with his belief that Nkrumah and Soekarno merited the title "great man."[7] Yet in voicing this opinion Wright had been articulating an attitude shared by many African American intellectuals of the 1950s. For these intellectuals, the anticolonial struggles waged by people like Soekarno and Nkrumah provided an inspiration and a model for their own struggles at the time. As one commentator in the National Association for the Advancement of Colored People's official magazine, the *Crisis*, suggested in 1953,

> the Negro intellectual who chooses racial protest will find that his own self-conception is indirectly reinforced by the achievements of colored men in the emerging states of Africa and Asia. I doubt that many Negro intellectuals in this country have failed to experience at least vicariously a sense of power and an understandable feeling of revenge against whites in observing Soekarno, a Dutch-schooled intellectual, toss his teachers and masters out of Indonesia, or . . . in watching Kwame Nkrumah, a graduate of Lincoln University in Pennsylvania, being released from jail to become Prime Minister of the Gold Coast, while old-line colonial administrators rubbed their chins, stared at their tea, and wondered how far it would all go. (Record 334)

Among the artists and intellectuals aligned with the PSI in the 1950s, such a view of Soekarno's role overlooked the broader context of the Indonesian struggle against colonialism, and to the degree that Soekarno himself embraced it, this view also prompted the president's drift toward authoritarianism and self-aggrandizement, a trend Wright's hosts believed needed to be strongly resisted. By 1977, however, the Indonesian response to Wright was no longer dogged by personal recollections of his admiration for a president whose political thinking and actions were provoking deep-seated skepticism and opposition. Rather, as Goenawan's essay demonstrates, the response to Wright had reverted to the same kind of textual admiration that Pramoedya had expressed in the early 1950s. In Goenawan's eyes, Wright's literary work pursued questions of the human heart in a way that had something to teach Indonesian society about politics and even politicians. Goenawan's stance does not endorse the color-colonialism connection that Wright's interlocutors had felt their guest was trying to insinuate in 1955; indeed, Goenawan makes no equation between African American antiracism and postcolonial anticolonialism. Rather, he writes in praise of Wright as an individualist who appreciated the expediency of political movements, whether of the Communist Party in the service of antiracism or of the Asian-African Conference in the service of anticolonialism. Goenawan acknowledges the differences between Wright's beginnings "as a destitute Negro child on the banks of the Mississippi River" and the upbringing of his Indonesian readers, but he also posits that Wright's inclinations are instructive for someone seeking to redefine politics beyond a top-down approach to political power. Wright's case—as an individualist who saw the benefits of political collaboration—speaks to those who are treated unjustly and must cultivate support among the masses, rather than the powerful, if they are to change their circumstances.

Politicians
by Goenawan Mohamad
SOURCE LANGUAGE: INDONESIAN

"Politics was not my game; the human heart was my game."[8] So wrote Richard Wright in *American Hunger*, the continuation of his autobiographical narrative that was published seventeen years after he died in Paris on 28 November 1960. Do his words hide a certain arrogance? Maybe. Richard Wright felt that the proof of what he said lay in his own life.

His life journey seems to have its beginning in his grandparents, who were Negro slaves in the American South. Richard was born emancipated, but as a black child on the banks of the Mississippi, his was a miserable world. In the end, he escaped. As he wrote in *Black Boy*, the first part of his autobiography, which was published in 1945, he headed north, with the vague hope that there "men should be able to confront other men without fear or shame."[9]

He ended up in Chicago. This is where the main part of *American Hunger* plays out. But if there is one part of the story that will be of interest to Indonesian readers, it is his experiences with the Communist Party of America. For it appears that this black man, who never felt at home in a life overshadowed by white men, finally found something he hadn't encountered before. He joined the Party in 1932.

The rest of the story was one of disillusionment, as we know from the book *The God That Failed*, which was translated into Indonesian. He turned out to be someone who wasn't suited to the Party. He was too much of an intellectual, an "individualist" who "talked like a book."[10] The sense of constant suspicion and the strictures surrounding the way the Communist Party of America operated caused him to leave the Party in 1936. Forever.[11] In *American Hunger*, however, he does not condemn people's need and yearning to be part of a political movement. In 1955 Richard Wright visited Indonesia to witness the Asian-African Conference in Bandung. The result was *The Color Curtain*, a report on the meeting—an event he may not have fully understood, but whose significance he attempted to evaluate properly.

"Politics was not my game; the human heart was my game." However, he added: "But it was only in the realm of politics that I could see the depths of the human heart."[12]

MAYBE WE SHOULD rehabilitate the concept of "politics"?

Not everyone begins life as a destitute Negro child on the banks of the Mississippi River, but imagine what it would be like if we happened to be one of those people who feel they are treated unjustly and want to change their circumstances. Or imagine we had a program, or a plan, or aspirations that involved the interests of the masses and for that reason needed their support. In that situation we would need something to make our voices heard and start improving things. In other words, we would need some kind of "political action"—however straightforward and peaceful it might be.

This is because a country doesn't function according to the strictures that govern a soldiers' barracks or a home for novice Buddhist monks. The relations that emerge between people on the top and those on the bottom cannot proceed solely on the basis of power. A family planning program isn't going to be successful if it relies on sticking up photocopied instructions. Environmental conservation plans can't be promoted just through a single 17 August speech. Neither can the prospects of peasant farmers or becak drivers be aided just by mobilizing bureaucrats and officials.[13] Regulating the relationship between "top" and "bottom" requires a procedure that goes beyond the mentality of a chief supervisor. Maybe we do need politicians . . .

Unfortunately, here in our country, politicians are unpopular. It may be because we think all we need are technocrats, people who are occupied with solving problems, and don't need to concern ourselves with the people actually involved in the problems and their solutions . . .

Notes

Goenawan Mohamad. ["Politikus"]. 1977. Translated and published as "Politicians" with the permission of Goenawan Mohamad.

1. For biographical information, see Grant.

2. Takdir left Indonesia and served as a professor of Malay studies at the University of Malaya in Kuala Lumpur between 1963 and 1986. Achdiat became a lecturer in Indonesian literature at the Australian National University in Canberra in 1961, where he

died in 2010 (Pamusuk 6, 174). Of those who remained in Indonesia during the years of ideological conflict, the most actively involved in cultural political affairs was Asrul Sani, who, in the late 1950s, became an influential figure in the burgeoning Indonesian film industry. In 1962, along with other film professionals, Asrul helped found the Lembaga Seniman Budayawan Muslim Indonesia (LESBUMI, Institute of Indonesian Muslim Artists and Cultural Figures), an organization established under the aegis of the traditionalist Islamic party Nahdlatul Ulama to counter LEKRA influence in the arts (Sen 30; Pamusuk 31; Choirotun 284). Asrul's ten-year marriage to the poet and translator Siti Nuraini came to an end in 1961, and Nuraini moved to Europe on a second Dutch government scholarship. In 1969 she began working for Radio Australia in Melbourne, where shortly thereafter she married Peter Barnett, a senior journalist in the organization (Barnett 339–48).

3. On the Cultural Manifesto of 1963, see Goenawan, "'Cultural.'"

4. On Goenawan's links to the CCF, see Lindsay, "Goenawan" 32.

5. When it was initially published in 1977, this article appeared without a title. However, on its republication in a 1982 collection of Goenawan's *Catatan Pinggir* essays, it appeared as "Politikus" (Politicians). Though our translation relies on the earlier publication as the source text, we have drawn the translation's title from the 1982 republication. Another republication of the essay appears on Goenawan's blog as "Politikus Juga."

6. Appearing nearly four decades after the appearance of his 1977 article on Wright, Goenawan's 2015 *Catatan Pinggir* essay on Wright alludes specifically to Mochtar's claim that Wright wore colored glasses as well as to Asrul's claim that Wright did not understand Indonesian preferences regarding toilet paper ("Bandung").

7. See Vuyk's "A Weekend with Richard Wright," also in part III.

8. The quotation is drawn from Wright, *American* 123.

9. The quotation is drawn from Wright, *Black Boy* 228.

10. For the original discussion, see Wright, "I Tried" 114.

11. For this date, Goenawan seems to be drawing on *American Hunger*'s concluding account of Wright's departure from a May Day procession of 1936 (130–35). See also Wright, "I Tried," 142–46. On Wright's gradual withdrawal from the Party, see Rowley 264 and 291.

12. Wright's English quotation appears in *American Hunger*, 123.

13. For Wright on the plight of becak drivers, see *Color* 504–5. From the 1950s until the gradual disappearance of the becak in big cities like Jakarta during the later years of Suharto's New Order regime, the becak driver was often seen to epitomize the struggle for survival endured by the urban poor.

18

Seno Joko Suyono's "A Forgotten Hotel" (2005)

In 2005, commemorations of the fiftieth anniversary of the Bandung Conference took several forms. April 22 through April 24 saw the convening of the Asian-African Summit in Jakarta and Bandung, with over one hundred nations participating.[1] Commemorative meetings were also held in Tokyo, Japan; Bamako, Mali; Manila, Philippines; and other locales.[2] In addition to prompting meetings, the fiftieth anniversary found treatment in news articles appearing internationally, with many of these articles drawing on Richard Wright's Bandung report, *The Color Curtain*.[3] Among the media outlets for these commemorative articles was *Tempo*, the Indonesian weekly magazine founded by Goenawan Mohamad, which on 1 May 2005 published an article titled "Sebuah Hotel yang Dilupakan" (A Forgotten Hotel), by Seno Joko Suyono.[4]

Born in the East Java city of Malang in 1970, Seno is clearly of a different generation from the Gelanggang-oriented figures Wright knew in the 1950s, or even the figures affiliated with the 1963 Cultural Manifesto that had Goenawan Mohamad as a signatory. As a creative writer and cultural critic, Seno has published poetry and a novel and has examined the writings of French critic Michel Foucault vis-à-vis the human body's relation to European racism and sexuality.[5] As a journalist and cultural editor for *Tempo*, he has been awarded the Jakarta Arts Institute Award for theater and performance reviews (Dian). He was the team leader for *Tempo*'s October 2012 special report, *Requiem for a Massacre*, which took US filmmaker Joshua Oppenheimer's 2012 documentary *The Act of Killing* as an occasion to look back at the mass killings—directed against Communist Party members and sympathizers as well as Indonesians of Chinese descent—that swept Indonesia at the time of President Soekarno's 1965 overthrow and General Suharto's ascension to power.[6] Suharto's rise brought figures such as Takdir Alisjahbana, Mochtar Lubis, and Goenawan Mohamad back into the Indonesian government's good graces. But it subjected writers aligned with Soekarno and the PKI, like Sitor Situmorang and Pramoedya Ananta Toer, to years of imprisonment under brutal and degrading conditions that in many cases resulted in death or permanent disability.[7]

Certainly, Wright's caution during his 1955 lecture to the PEN Club and BMKN was proving prescient in a politically volatile nation in which two successive Indonesian governments took cultural expression very seriously. Wright had warned,

> Leaders arise with new ideologies, and through the use of violence these leaders construct a new society by force. At such times, the position of the writer becomes terribly important. . . . He is hired by those in power to write in a way that leads the people to follow the will of the new government. . . .
>
> However, . . . suppose, as a writer, you support the man in power in 1950, only to find that in 1955 a new man comes to power. In 1955 you might be shot for having supported the leaders who were in power in 1950. . . . So, young writers, enter the political arena, go in search of glory and money, but don't be surprised if you end up losing . . . your head![8]

Ajip Rosidi, who at seventeen must have been one of the youngest to attend this lecture, fared better than many. During a 2013 interview with Brian Roberts, Ajip suggested that he himself had benefited throughout the decades by focusing strictly on remaining true to his art while refusing to align himself with a political party.[9] However, Ajip did not credit Wright's counsel for helping him assume this apparently apolitical position. Now at seventy-five, Ajip did not remember that Wright had given this counsel during his May 1955 lecture at the Cultural Center in Jakarta.

If it is unsurprising that the seventy-five-year-old Ajip Rosidi did not remember the content of a lecture he attended at age seventeen, Ajip's lack of memory regarding the lecture's content might also be taken as emblematic of Wright's treatment in Indonesia during the 1960s through the 2000s. Around the time Goenawan Mohamad published "Politicians," Ajip's brother, Ayatrohaedi, published Indonesian translations of twenty poems drawn from the 1963 anthology *American Negro Poetry*, edited by the African American writer Arna Bontemps. Introducing these translations in the cultural journal *Budaja Djaja*, Ayatrohaedi explained, "Probably the only name we have seen or read with any frequency is that of the poet Richard Wright, mainly because of his works *Black Boy* (1945) and *Native Son* (1940). Nonetheless, it is clear that apart from this poet, there are a considerable number of other Black American poets who are worth knowing" ("Puisi" 756). In his selection of poems, Ayatrohaedi included "Puisi Hokku" (Haiku Poetry) by Wright, among poems by Paul Laurence Dunbar, Gwendolyn Bennett, Mari Evans, Langston Hughes, Angelina Grimké, and others. Yet it would seem that Ajip did not impress upon his brother any particular significance of Wright's 1955 visit, for Ayatrohaedi makes no mention of Wright's Indonesian travels in either the translations' introduction or the accompanying biographical sketch.[10] Neither does the introduction reference Wright's *Konfrontasi* lecture on African American poetry (Wright, "American"), despite that lecture's relevance to Ayatrohaedi's project.

By the 1980s, Wright's 1955 interactions with Indonesian writers continued to seem far removed from cultural memory. In 1984 the Indonesian literary magazine *Horison* published a translation of Wright's 1937 essay "The Ethics of Living Jim Crow." In the biographical sketch accompanying the translation, there is no mention of *The Color Curtain*, Wright's attendance at the Bandung Conference, or the controversies of the 1950s and 1960s regarding his travel writings (Wright, "Etika" 103). And by 1988, even Mochtar himself— once so indignant over Wright's representations of Indonesian conditions and personalities—seems to have determined to leave firsthand memories of Wright unmentioned. Whereas Mochtar earlier criticized Wright in the pages of the CCF magazine *Encounter*, in 1988 the Indonesian journalist and writer compared the social activism of his own CCF-published novel, *Twilight in Djakarta*, to the social activism of Wright's books.[11] Discussing Soekarno's openly stated ambition that "the Indonesian press must become the tool of his [ongoing] revolution," Mochtar positioned *Twilight in Djakarta* as an attempt "to show how the process of erosion of values . . . eventually swallowed individuals and whole groups of people." "All my books," he explained,

> were banned during the Soekarno regime. Why do dictators, or at
> least many of them, reach the point when they find it necessary to

burn books? . . . I believe book-burning is the best proof that books (when loaded with ideas, honesty and truth) can move people to think and make their own conclusions, and in time even to act. . . . There have been enough inspiring books around for a long time already. *Uncle Tom's Cabin* I think played a role in shaking the conscience of many Americans about the abominable slavery in the South of the United States. There are other books written by black writers about their own human and social conditions which have inspired the blacks in America to stand up and fight for their rights. Richard Wright's books must have exercised a great influence on generations of Blacks' minds, as the later Black writers have also done. ("Literature" 78–79)

Although Mochtar's implicit comparison between Wright's books and Stowe's *Uncle Tom's Cabin* bears the distant trace of the mid-twentieth-century moment when *Gelanggang* and *Indonesia Raya* referenced James Baldwin's essay "Everybody's Protest Novel,"[12] the trend in the 1970s and 1980s moved toward silence on Wright's Indonesian travels, such that even Mochtar Lubis, Wright's former host, and Ayatrohaedi, the brother of one of the attendees at Wright's PEN Club lecture, made no mention of Wright's visit to Indonesia when they referred to him during this period. Indonesian cultural memory regarding Wright's visit had converged with the international world's memory regarding his Indonesian travels, leaving *The Color Curtain* as an uncontested account of the Bandung Conference and Wright's interactions with Indonesian cultural figures of the 1950s. Unsurprisingly, then, Seno Joko Suyono's 2005 article "A Forgotten Hotel" does not draw on the accounts of Beb Vuyk, Mochtar Lubis, Asrul Sani, or Frits Kandou but quotes from *The Color Curtain* without any trace of the skepticism displayed by the generation who had actually witnessed the events Wright recounted there. As a result, readers hear of Wright's *Color Curtain* account of witnessing an Indonesian official's antiwhite racism but remain unaware of the alternative version of events recounted in Vuyk's "A Weekend with Richard Wright."[13]

Yet if "A Forgotten Hotel" conforms to international trends in quoting from *The Color Curtain* as an authoritative account of the Bandung Conference, the *Tempo* article's status as emerging from the very city, street, and architectural traces of the Bandung Conference positions it to draw on exceptionally local sources. One such source is Bandung Heritage Society director Frances Affandi, who offers information on 1950s hotel architecture in Indonesia. Another source is an employee at the Museum of the Asian-African Conference, who apparently offers an account that documents a 1990s visit to Bandung by a daughter of Richard Wright, seemingly "follow[ing] in her father's footsteps."

According to the narrative, this daughter gave the museum "a bundle of clippings her father had collected of reports on the conference by American and European journalists" and later sent the museum a copy of *The Color Curtain*. In the article, the reader is informed that the daughter, a "black woman from America," introduced herself as "Margaretha Julia Wright." Readers familiar with Wright's family will be confused by this moment in "A Forgotten Hotel," recognizing that Julia is indeed the name of Wright's elder daughter but wondering about the inclusion of the name Margaretha and doubting the account of Wright's daughter hailing from America. Julia Wright, who was eighteen when her father passed away in Paris in 1960 (Rowley 524), has continued to be based in France until the present day. Indeed, we are informed that Julia Wright did not visit Indonesia in the 1990s.[14]

And yet the packet of clippings that is now held in the museum's collection functions as material evidence suggesting that some type of visit, by an indeterminate person, was made to Bandung. Making his own trip to the Museum of the Asian-African Conference in May 2013, Brian Roberts requested the opportunity to inspect this packet, which was at the time displayed in one of the museum's glass cases among its collection of many other artifacts and mementos from the Bandung Conference. With the help of museum staff, Roberts inspected the four-inch-thick comb-bound packet, titled "Bandung 1955," which is a scrapbook containing newspaper clippings, political speeches, magazine issues, and correspondence regarding the Bandung Conference attendance of Marguerite Cartwright (1910–1986), who was one of the few other African American reporters who traveled to Bandung in April 1955.[15] We have not been able to trace the provenance of the scrapbook and the circumstances that led to its accession by the museum. However, the narrative of a visitor's donation of the scrapbook, in conjunction with a possible confusion between the similar names Cartwright and Wright, has led to a situation where "Margaretha Julia Wright" has been reported as presenting the museum with a scrapbook that originates not from Wright, as stated in "A Forgotten Hotel," but from another African American journalist who attended the 1955 conference.[16]

The precise backstory of the mysterious visitor is less significant than the fact that the character "Margaretha Julia Wright" is a spliced representation of more than one person. In this way the narrative of her appearance at the museum in Bandung is reminiscent of Wright's own narratives of his Indonesian travels.[17] Indeed there is even a certain reciprocity between Takdir Alisjahbana's counterfactual appearance in Europe in the pages of *The Color Curtain* and the counterfactual appearance of Wright's daughter in Bandung in the pages of *Tempo*. Just as Wright must not have created such narratives maliciously but rather (if his Dutch translator Margrit de Sablonière is to be taken as an authority) out of a sense that he was in his right as an author to "kind [of] create figures,"[18] so too there is no suggestion of malicious intent in the *Tempo* article's account of the appearance of Wright's daughter in Bandung's Museum of the Asian-African Conference. Language and cultural differences permeate both of these counterfactual events—whether those differences hinge on the writerly obligations entailed by the term "report" in the subtitle of Wright's *The Color Curtain*, or on the syllable of difference between the names Wright and Cartwright. On paper or in conversation the differences in spelling and emphasis may be small, but when spoken and written across cultures—whether individually between Wright and Mochtar or internationally among the twenty-nine Asian and African entities represented at the Bandung Conference—their ramifications may be very large, and mercurial, depending on the stakes of the individuals or groups involved.

A Forgotten Hotel
by Seno Joko Suyono
SOURCE LANGUAGE: INDONESIAN

It was once a base for hundreds of foreign journalists. From here coverage of the Asian-African Conference spread all over the world. And despite its pitiful condition, it is currently being used for a poster exhibition.

The rooms look like a rubbish dump. The walls are moldy and the window panes are caked in grime. The wooden frames around the windows and doors are black with dust. The curtains dangle across the floor like torn pieces of black tarpaulin. A thick mildew decorates the floorboards, and puddles of water lie in the corners like revolting bits of swampland.

The place has been abandoned for more than twenty years. In all, there are four floors. On each floor there are twin rows of empty rooms without doors. The corridors are deserted. Every floor has an open space, each of different dimensions. All lying empty without a trace of furnishings, apart from piles of rusty corrugated iron and scattered bits of discarded wood. Shafts of light coming in through the ventilators create a strange effect of light and shade.

Looking about on our own that afternoon, *Tempo* opened a padlocked door and went upstairs. The atmosphere was chilling. From one flight of stairs to the next, anxiety levels rose, lest the stairs give way or the roof fall in. Yet fifty years ago, at the time of the Asian-African Conference, this was a chic little hotel that accommodated more than a hundred local and overseas journalists. On top of the roof, the name of the hotel is still legible: Swarha. It is located on Jalan Asia Afrika [Asia Africa Street], formerly the Groote Postweg.[19]

FIGURE 18.1. Hotel Swarha, Bandung. Photograph by Brian Russell Roberts (May 2013).

"The Hotel Swarha is an example of the 'Jengki' style," says Frances Affandi, executive director of Bandung Heritage Society, a foundation that takes an interest in old buildings in Bandung. During the 1950s, after independence, there was a trend toward modern buildings, the work of indigenous architects who had learned their profession working under the Dutch. At the same time, there was a craze among young people for ankle-length pants in the "Yankee" style. In Indonesian, "yankee" became "jengki," and new-style buildings were named accordingly.[20]

From the front, the Hotel Swarha is half oval-shaped, with large square windows. The design of the windows, according to Frances, is influenced by the style of A. F. Aalbers, the Dutch architect who renovated the Hotel Savoy Homann. Looking out these windows from inside, you see a section of Jalan Asia Afrika. The clock on the bank opposite the hotel is clearly visible. In former times you could see the city square, because the hotel stands on a corner directly in front of the square. Now the square is obscured by the extensions to the Great Mosque.

Gedung Merdeka, Hotel Preanger, Hotel Savoy Homann, Gedung Dwi Warna—all of them buildings used by the Asian-African Conference in 1955—are still functional today. Even the Villa Merah on Jalan Taman Sari [Taman Sari Street], the work of Kemal C. Schoemacher, where the former Chinese Prime Minister Zhou Enlai stayed during the conference, is still well-

FIGURE 18.2. Hotel Savoy Homann, one of the hotels where Asian-African Conference delegates were housed. Photograph by Brian Russell Roberts (May 2013).

maintained. But Swarha has suffered a different fate. It hasn't been as "everlasting" as the reports filed by the journalists who once stayed there.

THE 1955 CONFERENCE would not have had the impact it did without the enthusiasm of the foreign reporters who attended it. The telegraph machines provided for use by the press recorded an output of 100,000 to 200,000 words a day.

One afternoon in the 1990s, Dedie Sutardi, an employee of the Asian-African Museum in the Gedung Merdeka, received a visit from a black woman from America. She introduced herself as Margaretha Julia Wright. "She said she was in Bandung to follow in her father's footsteps," said Dedie.

It turned out she was the daughter of Richard Wright, a famous American writer who attended the Asian-African Conference and later wrote the book *The Color Curtain: A Report on the Bandung Conference*. She handed the museum a bundle of clippings her father had collected of reports on the conference by American and European journalists. "Later she also sent us his book, *Color Curtain*," Dedie added.

Wright, who was born in Mississippi, was already well-known for his books *Black Boy* and *Native Son*, which revealed the discrimination suffered by people of color in America. Wright arrived in Jakarta on 12 April. "The heat of

Jakarta was like being in a Turkish bath . . . ," he wrote.[21] Mochtar Lubis, the chief editor of *Indonesia Raya*, was there to meet him.

In Jakarta, he had a startling experience. When he was organizing his press pass in the Ministry of Information, he saw a white American journalist who was also heading for Bandung being given the run-around by an official. However, when it was Wright's turn, everything went smoothly, and his press pass was issued on the spot. It made him think of his birthplace in the southern part of the United States, where instead it was black people who had to stand around waiting for long periods.

On arriving in Bandung, Wright was immediately struck that this was a gathering of people of different races. Delegates of former colonial countries had come from all directions, dressed in their traditional costumes. "This was a meeting," he wrote, "that previously had only been part of the wild imaginings of Western writers like H. G. Wells and Lothrop Stoddard . . ."[22] At first he sensed a reluctance among the delegates to interact with each other, but then the awkwardness melted away, the distrust evaporated.

In Bandung, a white-skinned member of the conference, Adam Clayton Powell, made a confession to Wright.[23] He was thrilled to hear Soekarno say in his opening address in English, "Brothers and sisters . . . this is the first international conference of colored peoples in the history of humankind . . ." Then he told Wright that in fact, his grandfather had been a slave.[24]

A Chinese journalist named Zhang Yan, who in 1955 was also covering the events in Bandung, reacted in the same way as Powell. At the time, he didn't know that Richard Wright was there. Decades later, he wrote an article: "I Wish I had Met Richard Wright at Bandung in 1955." He confessed that those words spoken by Soekarno had sent shivers down his spine. "The whole building seemed to erupt, everyone stood up and clapped, including the Chinese delegation and myself," he wrote.[25]

We can get an idea of the busy pace of journalistic activity during the conference from a twenty-seven-minute documentary film made by the Indonesian State Film Company or PFN. There is a glimpse of Richard Wright and Adam Clayton Powell in discussion.[26] Cameras, typewriters, and telex machines, formerly part of the conference facilities provided for journalists in 1955, are now on display at the Asian-African Museum. There are also books produced by journalists, such as *Bandoung, tournant de l'histoire* by Arthur Conte, or *Histoire de l'Afro-Asiatisme jusqu'à Bandoung* by Pierre Queuille, both of them French journalists. Or *The Afro-Asian Movement* by David Kimche, an Israeli diplomat.

There are also photos. Interestingly, there are many close-up shots of heads of state taken by journalists, suggesting that at that time journalists were free

FIGURE 18.3. When asked by a reporter for his views on "the real impact of this conference upon . . . international politics," Powell responded, "Well, in the first place, I think after this week, Bandung, no nation can continue its policy of colonialism without the full knowledge that Asia and Africa, united, are against them. I think that will be the most tremendous impact on international diplomacy." Film still and quotation excerpted from the ten-minute news film, "Konperensi Asia Afrika" (1955), produced by Indonesia's government-owned film company, Perusahaan Film Negara. Konperensi Asia Afrika, reel 1, cassette 354. Courtesy of Arsip Nasional Republik Indonesia.

FIGURE 18.4. Ethel Payne (left) and Richard Wright (right) during the Bandung Conference. Film still excerpted from "Konperensi Asia Afrika" (1955), produced by Indonesia's government-owned film company, Perusahaan Negara. Konperensi Asia Afrika, reel 1, cassette 354. Courtesy of Arsip Nasional Republik Indonesia.

to come and go without being bound by too much protocol. "At that time it's true that soldiers were not used excessively for security reasons, as is the case today," says Retired Lieutenant-General Mashudi, who at the time was Head of Staff of Military Officers in West Java. "Just imagine, when heads of state walked from the Hotel Savoy Homann to the Gedung Merdeka, they were accompanied by nothing more than a single policeman and an angklung ensemble."[27]

Paul Tedja Surya, 75, a senior photographer, might be seen as a living witness to those events. In 1955 he was working as a photographer in the Preanger studio, a private studio in Bandung. With his Leica 3F, and batteries on his hip to power his flash, he produced a lot of photos: Gamal Abdel Nasser, U Nu, Nehru, Norodom Sihanouk. "At the Husein Sastranegara Airport, a foreign photographer used my shoulders as a tripod," he laughs. He was twenty-five years old at the time. "I remember a lot of foreign journalists were staying at the Hotel Swarha and filing reports from the media center in the Gedung Merdeka," he says.

NOT MANY BANDUNG residents know why the Hotel Swarha wasn't maintained properly, even those active in architecture circles. "I know that it was built as part of the preparations for the Asian-African Conference in 1955, but as for why it was allowed to fall into disrepair, well, there are rumors of conflict over an inheritance," says Yuswadi Saliya, a senior architect at the Bandung Institute of Technology. Suwardjo, a reporter of long standing with *Pikiran Rakyat*, concurs. "People say it's to do with a long-running dispute, but I don't know the details."

The current owner of the Hotel Swarha is a family who operates the Indra textile and shoe stores on the ground floor of the building. Since the construction of the Swarha building in 1950, the ground floor has always been a shopping complex, with the second to fifth floors functioning as a hotel.

The Indra textile store is quite interesting. Its advertising slogan, "Find a cheaper price and we'll return your money," can still be seen on the wall, just as it was when the building first opened its doors in 1950. The current owners, the Bharwani family, are of Indian origin, but in those days the building was owned by a different family. Trouble broke out in 1980 among the heirs to the property, and from that time the hotel ceased to operate. In the end they decided to auction it off.

"Our family decided to buy it," says Merry Bharwani, 56, the proprietor of the Indra stores. She says that the family had plans to get the hotel up and running once more. For her, it was a place of historical significance. Even though at the time of the conference she was still a little girl, she remembers how busy it all was. "All the Indians in Bandung came together to meet Nehru," she says.

Strangely, after Merry bought the hotel from the Office of State Auctions, the West Java regional government refused to permit any type of activity at all in the hotel. That sounded the death knell of the Hotel Swarha, and it was left neglected, becoming a home for bats. It wasn't even used as a storehouse. Merry took the case to court, claiming financial loss, but she didn't get anywhere, even with an appeal to the Supreme Court. However, she intends to put the case up again for review.

For more than twenty years the doors of the hotel have been locked and sealed. All she uses is the landings on the staircase leading up to the second floor, where boxes of shoes destined for the store are piled up for storage. "It was a public auction, after all. If the regional government wanted to use the hotel, why didn't they buy it themselves?" she says in bewilderment.

AND THERE IN THAT silent building, suddenly that day there was a spark of life. On the fourth floor of the Hotel Swarha, amid the dampness and the musty smells, there suddenly appeared posters of Richard Wright, U Nu, Zhou Enlai, and other figures from the 1955 Asian-African Conference. Created in pop art graphic design style, these frameless posters were stuck to cement pillars, curtains, and walls.

The posters are the work of Dipo Andy, a graduate of the Indonesian Art Institute in Yogyakarta. They were placed there as part of an exhibition in the Gedung Indonesia Menggugat in Bandung, the site of Soekarno's famous defense speech. "I made a hundred posters in all. They were also exhibited in the INI Gallery in Jalan Veteran [Veteran Street] in Jakarta," says Dipo. He did his research from old books in the secondhand stores of Senin in Jakarta, to find out who had been at the conference. Among the Indonesians who attended, there were people like Pramoedya and Sutan Takdir Alisjahbana, for example.[28]

Dipo has been nominated several times for the Philip Morris award.[29] Most of his posters are bright, colorful, and make use of the effects of photographic manipulation to produce repeating frames containing facial images. Apart from the pictures of important people who were in Bandung in 1955, he also includes posters of thinkers who were influenced by the conference, such as Frantz Fanon. Fanon is known to have frequently corresponded with Richard Wright over issues of human rights and colonialism.

Dipo's plans to reproduce the posters in large format and position them in public spaces failed through lack of funds. It was a really interesting idea, because it seems that in celebration of the fifty-year anniversary of the conference,

FIGURE 18.5. Photograph of Dipo Andy's April 2005 poster exhibition in the Hotel Swarha. Bearing the caption "TO MAKE THE WORLD ANEW," the poster attached to the first visible column on the left appears to use Richard Wright's face. Used with permission of Usman Iskandar.

Bandung was only decorated with a few formal-looking street banners and billboards that lacked any real spark. "The posters were installed in the Hotel Swarha to mark the fact that the spirit of Asia-Africa was transmitted to the world from here," says Taufik Rahzen, the man behind the exhibition.[30]

The "exhibition" in the Swarha was deliberately staged as though it was just thrown together, without any proper layout or cleaning up of the space. Simple, but full of paradox. "We are also planning to make posters of the heads of state who have come for the 2005 Asian-African Summit that's happening right now," adds Dipo. This is the story of a hotel that has been wiped from memory, a souvenir poster of the sad fate of Asia-Africa.

Notes

Seno Joko Suyono. "Sebuah Hotel yang Dilupakan." 2005. Translated and published as "A Forgotten Hotel" with the permission of Seno Joko Suyono.

1. For a report on this event, see "Asian-African."

2. See "Africa"; Paupp 23; "Final"; and Mushakoji 145.

3. For articles referencing Wright's *The Color Curtain*, see for instance Varadarajan; "Spirit"; and "China."

4. Seno's article was previously translated and published in *Tempo*'s English edition, as "A Forgotten Hotel," on 2 May 2005 (pp. 30–32). The translation here is our own.

5. On these biographical details, see Nur; Tulus; and Seno, "Puisi."

6. See Seno, *Requiem*. In April 2015, Seno was also the team leader, with Philipus Parera, for the production of a special issue of *Tempo* commemorating the Bandung Conference's sixtieth anniversary. Put together by a team of over ninety writers, editors, and contributors, this special issue is titled *Bandung 1955* in the Indonesian edition and *The Spirit of Bandung: Asia-Africa Conference 1955–2015* in the English edition. See this issue's lead article, "Panggilan"; and "Resonating."

7. For a brief account of political imprisonment after 1965, see Samuels. For Pramoedya's own account, see especially *Mute*'s 3–96. Hersri describes the response of writers and other arts practitioners to life under political imprisonment.

8. See Wright's "The Artist and His Problems," in part II.

9. In his semiautobiographical novel based on the life of a young artist in Jakarta in the 1950s and 1960s, Ajip recorded the difficulty of retaining an apolitical stance in the face of the gradual encroachment of politics on Indonesian cultural activity at this time (*Anak* 234–54, 298–301).

10. In 1976 Ayatrohaedi published a book of translations titled *Puisi Negro: Sejemput Sajak para Penyair Afrika dan Amerika Hitam* (Negro Poetry: A Selection of Poems by African and Black American Writers), which includes Wright's haiku poetry and his poem "Between the World and Me" (78–81). This book also makes no reference to Wright's Indonesian travels.

11. Mochtar's 1963 novel, *Twilight in Djakarta*, was an English translation, by the ethnographer and art historian Claire Holt, of a manuscript titled *Sendja di Djakarta*, which political conditions prevented Mochtar from publishing in Indonesia itself. The novel was published as the first book in the CCF's New Voices in Translation series and did not appear in its original Indonesian until 1970, after further translations into a number of European and Asian languages (Hill, *Journalism* 76–77).

12. See *Gelanggang*'s "A Conversation with Richard Wright," in part II, and Vuyk's "H. Creekmore and Protest Novels," also in part III.

13. In the sixtieth anniversary issue of *Tempo*, Wright's story of the Indonesian official's antiwhite racism is repeated ("Dari" 100; "Outsiders" 66)

14. William Reiss to Brian Russell Roberts, 7 July 2014, e-mail.

15. On Wright and Cartwright at the conference, see Fabre, *Unfinished* 420.

16. Archivists at the Amistad Research Center, which is housed at Tulane University and holds Cartwright's papers, have been unable to identify any of Marguerite Cartwright's

heirs (Christopher Harter to Brian Russell Roberts, 2 Aug. 2013, e-mail). Thus we are unaware of who might plausibly be the figure referred to here as "Margaretha Julia Wright."

17. See this book's introduction; and Vuyk's "A Weekend with Richard Wright," also in part III.

18. De Sablonière to Webb, 26 Dec. 1966 (CWP, box 5, folder 10).

19. During the conference, Wright stayed at the nearby Hotel Van Hengel in Bandung (Rowley 467).

20. The spelling of consonants, according to pre-1972 Indonesian orthography, followed Dutch practice, so in the 1950s the English *y* was represented in Indonesian by the letter *j*. As such, *jengki* was Indonesian phonetic spelling for the English *Yankee*.

21. Differing from Seno's rendition, Wright's English quotation appears in *Color Curtain* 503.

22. Differing from Seno's rendition, Wright's English quotation appears in *Color Curtain* 537.

23. Wright described Powell as "a Negro Congressman from New York. . . . Though classed by American standards as a Negro, Congressman Powell is actually a white man, much whiter in terms of skin color than many whites I've known" (*Color* 573).

24. For Wright's narrative of Powell, see *Color* 573–74.

25. Differing from Seno's rendition, the original English version of this quotation appears on p. 279 of Yan's essay.

26. The source text seems to suggest that Wright and Powell appear in the same scene, engaged in discussion together. Rather, what Brian Roberts found at Indonesia's Arsip Nasional was a thirty-second segment of film in which Wright and Powell are each engaged in discussion but not with each other. Figures 18.3 and 18.4 are drawn from these separate scenes.

27. Originating in West Java, the angklung is an instrument composed of two bamboo tubes connected to a bamboo frame. Angklung music was a prominent representative of the Indonesian cultural heritage during the Bandung Conference, with President Soekarno and Vice-President Hatta holding a reception that included angklung orchestras (Jack 6).

28. During the conference, Pramoedya made contact with members of the Chinese delegation (Liu 124–25). As recalled by Takdir's daughter Mirta Kartohadiprodjo, Takdir went to Bandung during the conference in an official capacity (Mirta).

29. The US tobacco company Philip Morris sponsors the annual ASEAN Art Awards, sometimes referred to as "Southeast Asia's most prestigious art competition" (Wu 178).

30. In 2014, Dipo Andy informed Brian Roberts that the physical and electronic copies of these posters were lost in the May 2006 Central Java earthquake (Dipo to Roberts, 9 Aug. 2014, Facebook).

Big History, Little History, Interstitial History:
On the Tightrope between Polyvocality and Lingua Franca

In May 1965, Beb Vuyk published a *Vrij Nederland* article titled "Het Negerprobleem Bemoeide Zich met Baldwin" (The Negro Problem Concerns Itself with Baldwin). Reflecting on the significance of the work of the famous
expatriate African American novelist James Baldwin, Vuyk relied on her familiarity with Wright as a means of contextualizing Baldwin's place in the
African American literary tradition.[1] Implicitly agreeing with Wright's 1955
contention that color was a lens through which the decolonizing world might
appropriately be viewed, she explained,

> The Second World War and the years following it, in particular the
> aftereffects of German propaganda and the decolonization of colored
> peoples, confronted America with the problem of race within its own
> borders. There arose a demand for books about the Negro question, and
> Negro authors became popular. A stream of novels of extremely varied
> quality appeared, with Richard Wright's *Native Son* and *Black Boy* as high
> points, but also very many of a mediocre level, flooding America and
> finding their way to Europe.

Vuyk continued: "Baldwin and [Richard] Gibson, another Negro author, warned
against this phenomenon" of the popularity of Wright and his many imitators:

> In the Winter 1953 issue of *Perspectives*, . . . articles by these two authors
> were reprinted under the title "Two Protests Against Protest." Gibson

advises the young Negro not to become another new Negro writer but "that he become instead a writer who happens to be a Negro."[2] Baldwin's article caused the biggest stir, because it contained sharp criticism of Richard Wright's *Native Son*, identifying and rejecting the generalizing tendency of protest novels.

As readers of this book will recognize, Vuyk in 1965 was drawing on the reading she had done before writing her *Indonesia Raya* article "H. Creekmore and Protest Novels" in the immediate aftermath of Wright's visit to Indonesia.

But when Wright's Dutch translator Margrit de Sablonière read Vuyk's article in the mid-1960s, she did not have access to the Indonesian-language archive on Wright. Rather, she drew on her suspicion regarding Vuyk, a carryover from her reading of Vuyk's 1960 article "A Weekend with Richard Wright" during the final, embattled days of Wright's life. A half decade later, de Sablonière now seized on Vuyk's reference to Gibson, whose enmity with Wright was well known,[3] and began hypothesizing that Wright's Indonesian hosts "had been influenced by Gibson." She felt she "must find out if G[ibson] had been in Indonesia himself."[4] A short time later, de Sablonière wrote in a letter to Wright's first biographer, Constance Webb, that Vuyk "knew the name of Gibson," and "since I know that G[ibson] has been in Indonesia many years ago I . . . am convinced that he paved the way towards hostility towards Richard with those Congress of Cult[ural] Freedom people there."[5] But Gibson reports that he has never traveled to Indonesia,[6] so it appears that we are dealing here with that same mysterious airplane that, at other moments, also conveyed Kwame Nkrumah and "Margaretha Julia Wright" to Jakarta and then on to Bandung.

We draw attention to de Sablonière's discussion of Vuyk and her concomitant false sighting of Gibson as a provocateur in Indonesia to alert readers to the fact that de Sablonière's description of Vuyk, which was later mediated by Constance Webb's 1968 biography on Wright, has played a significant role in marginalizing modern Indonesia's counter-narrative regarding Wright and his account of the Bandung Conference. To be clear, we are not interested in casting judgment on Webb's pathbreaking efforts in narrating Wright's life. As we well know after having spent several years piecing together a narrative regarding the mere three weeks of Wright's Indonesians travels, the project of narrating Wright's entire life reflects an undeniably admirable ambition and commitment on the part of Webb or any biographer. Rather, we mention the prominence of the de Sablonière-Webb narrative of Vuyk as a means of emphasizing scholarly writing's tendency to give priority to English (resulting in Webb's reliance on de Sablonière for an English account of Vuyk's Dutch) and more broadly to European languages (permitting the Dutch-speaking de Sablonière to provide Webb with seemingly authoritative information on Wright's Indonesian contacts and particularly on Vuyk, without a knowledge of the Indonesian-language archive). Indeed, as a result of the epistemic privileging of European languages in general and English in particular, those interested in pursuing the Bandung Conference via Wright's Indonesian travels have been left to rely largely on *The Color Curtain*, while those interested in pursuing Wright's travels via the perspectives of his Indonesian interlocutors have been left to rely largely on Webb's description of Vuyk. Webb's vexed description is based on her missummarizations of de Sablonière's missummarizations of Wright's misunderstandings, as well as on de Sablonière's missummarizations and mistranslations of Vuyk's article. Webb's description stands as follows:

> The fat woman with a yellow complexion and narrow eyes behind round colorless plastic-rimmed glasses impressed Richard as being somewhat opportunistic. . . . Indonesian intellectuals distrusted her because she was always in and out of the American Embassy and they wondered what she might be reporting to the United States government. Beb Vuyk was eventually expelled from Indonesia and began to write a series . . . for *Vrij Nederland*. Two of the articles were about Richard and Miss Vuyk claimed in them that Richard had stayed at the American Embassy in Indonesia; that he had told her that the American Ambassador was a "slave driver"; . . . [and] that [Wright] was a short, fat, little man whose primary interest in life seemed to be eating good food. When [Wright] did some quiet investigating in Paris he was informed that Miss Vuyk, indeed, had worked for the Congress for Cultural Freedom. (381)[7]

Published in 1968, in the wake of revelations that the CCF was covertly funded by the CIA,[8] Webb's account conveyed a version of Vuyk and her article "A Weekend with Richard Wright" that was not only highly distorting but also highly discrediting. Hence it was unlikely that subsequent scholars would take the trouble to treat this essay seriously, despite its importance as the most detailed description of Wright's interactions with some of modern Indonesia's most prominent writers and intellectuals.[9] Indeed, Michel Fabre, in his 1973 biography of Wright, relies in significant ways on descriptions from "A Weekend with Richard Wright" but, perhaps not wishing to discredit himself by openly citing the source Webb had discredited during the previous decade, does not acknowledge his debt to Vuyk.[10] By the time of Hazel Rowley's landmark 2008 biography of Wright, Vuyk's discredited article surfaces only as "a ferocious newspaper attack on [Wright] in the Dutch papers by a Dutch-

Indonesian woman he had met at Bandung" (520), with no name mentioned in the text itself and no indication that Rowley read Vuyk's Dutch-language article in preparing the relevant portions of Wright's biography.[11]

Vuyk's stifled reception in biographical and scholarly writings on Wright constitutes a concrete instance of the way privileging English-language sources tends to impoverish scholarly and general engagement with world-historical events. And beyond the specific case of Vuyk, the privileging of English-language sources has severely distorted and virtually erased any access to an Indonesian view of Wright's travels in Indonesia for the Bandung Conference.[12] Given that such short shrift has been afforded to Vuyk's essay (written as it is in a European language, if not in English), it is unsurprising that prior to this book, virtually none of the many Indonesian-language sources related to Wright's Bandung Conference travels has been cited or mentioned by Wright scholars or, more broadly, by the extensive array of scholars and writers who have relied on Wright to historicize and mythologize the Bandung Conference and its place in postcolonial history. Indeed, the primacy of Wright's English-language account of the Bandung Conference has been so complete that Indonesians themselves have approached Wright's Indonesian sojourn via his English-language work *The Color Curtain* and the English-language scholarship that surrounds it, leaving the Indonesian-language archive virtually untouched.[13]

This situation is perhaps to be expected, given what Ngũgĩ wa Thiong'o, Gloria Anzaldúa, and Robert Phillipson have taught us regarding the place of English vis-à-vis indigenous and non-English European languages.[14] And indeed, we are aware that in translating these Indonesian and Dutch sources into English, we ourselves are to a certain extent reinscribing the centrality of English to discourses of scholarship and general history. We have considered, of course, the dangers involved in the "domesticating" translation practices that have emerged as standard in the production and publication of "fluent" English translations, with upshots including the flattening of source texts and power-motivated reconstructions of source cultures (Venuti 13–15). Nonetheless, even as we suggest that those familiar with Indonesian and Dutch will find their richest avenue in direct study of the source texts, we also acknowledge that many of the stakeholders in this book's narratives and sources are unacquainted with either Indonesian or Dutch, and that virtually no engagement with these sources has taken place during the five or six decades since most of them were written.

Hence, we have offered *Indonesian Notebook* in English, in the medium of a historically contingent lingua franca.[15] And we suggest that English's status as a lingua franca makes it especially apropos as a medium for narrating a story that derives from a collection of primary source documents written mainly in the Indonesian language. Both English and Malay, the language from which modern Indonesian originated, are indigenous languages within specific spheres: English to the portion of the island of Britain that has become modern-day England, and Malay/Indonesian to the Malay Peninsula and parts of island Southeast Asia. Yet each has emerged as a very widely employed lingua franca. While English has come to serve as a linguistic bridge among speakers of the world's several thousand languages, Indonesian has become the means of permitting 250 million people—hailing from some six thousand inhabited islands and over seven hundred linguistic traditions—to communicate with each other.[16] In these ways, then, the Indonesian language attains a structural relationship to the English language that makes it an especially likely candidate for translation into English, as one lingua franca to another. Indeed, our translating of Indonesian into English—specifically as a means of providing this narrative not merely to native English-speakers but to native speakers of diverse languages throughout the globe—is consistent with Wright's own vision of the future of English, as he expressed it in *The Color Curtain*:

> I felt while at Bandung that the English language was about to undergo one of the most severe tests in its long and glorious history. Not only was English becoming the common, dominant tongue of the globe, but it was evident that soon there would be more people speaking English than there were people whose native tongue was English. . . . What will happen when millions upon millions of new people in the tropics begin to speak English? Alien pressures and structures of thought and feeling will be brought to bear upon this our mother tongue and we shall be hearing some strange and twisted expressions. . . . But this is all to the good; a language is useless unless it can be used for the vital purposes of life, and to use a language in new situations is, inevitably, to change it. (592)

It is into this language—an English in flux—that we have advanced our translations and contextualizations of these Indonesian and Dutch sources. They are the products of what Susan Stanford Friedman describes as "the act of digging," the act of seeking "an archeology of new archives—other modernities outside the familiar Western ones," a project whose "avant-garde" are "multilingual scholars . . . locating buried and forgotten texts in the global archive of languages," where "scholars working in translation are . . . essential to bring[ing] knowledge of these modernisms into the *lingua franca* of the field" (492). Ours is a project that resists English as hegemonic even while relying on English as a lingua franca in flux. This resistance and reliance permits a broad spectrum of readers to access a mid-twentieth-century Asian-African modernity via the interchanges and overlaps between African American modernity and Indonesian modernity. These networked modernities gave rise to modernisms interlinked from Jakarta to Paris, from the Gold Coast to India, and from the US South to the global South, operating according to a logic articulated by Beb Vuyk decades before the transnational turn in the humanities and social sciences: "There is now constant exchange and mutual influence across national borders in the field of art and literature."[17] As illustrated by the case of this book, these exchanges often result in misunderstandings and misrecognitions, whether pivoting on the difference between the names Wright and Cartwright, on Asrul Sani's confusion over whether Wright took literary or religious inspiration from the Bible, or on Wright's claim to have interviewed Takdir Alisjahbana in Europe before the Bandung Conference rather than in Indonesia after it. In many contexts, such details may seem small, but as we see so vividly in the Indonesian archive's erasure from the historical record on Wright at the Bandung Conference, small details can reverberate in highly significant ways.

Indeed, small details and differences call out for what Derek McDougall and Antonia Finnane, in the title of their 2010 edited collection on the Bandung Conference, have described as *little histories*. McDougall and Finnane place value on historicizing the conference through "different country settings and casts of characters" (4), and they emphasize that even if "the Western press showed little interest" in its fiftieth anniversary (2), the "Bandung Conference is not among the forgotten events. . . . Yet its history is underdeveloped" (8). This book was conceived as a contribution to Bandung's unpredictable history. It is on one level a sourcebook containing primary texts that are in and of themselves examples of the *little histories* McDougall and Finnane have described. Yet in its development through the course of our research, *Indonesian Notebook* has emerged as generically unstable among academic and educational volumes. Our introductory materials and notes have added an equal or sometimes greater portion of secondary history to the primary texts, to the point where our secondary historical narratives are frequently more extensive than the translated documents they introduce. These introductions constitute secondary history, to be sure, but this material also constitutes *little history*—smaller still than the primary histories to the degree that it is interstitial, needing to fit between and among the cracks, and to make this book's primary little histories contingently legible.

These little and interstitial histories may often appear incidental to Bandung's main narrative: Pramoedya's admiration for the tradition of Negro spirituals, Takdir's villa in Tugu as a literary salon and venue for Wright's lecture, Mochtar's handwritten note regarding Wright's influence on Pramoedya, Vuyk's commentary on Wright's relation to Kwame Nkrumah and Hubert Creekmore, Goenawan's reflections on Wright's stance on the place of the human heart in the "game" of politics, and Seno's recounting of Dipo Andy's depiction of Wright's face on commemorative posters in 2005. Taken together, however, these little and interstitial histories complement, contest, and insist on a reimagining of what has unquestionably emerged as one of the conference's big histories and "fundamental books," Richard Wright's *The Color Curtain: A Report on the Bandung Conference*.[18] And because the Bandung Conference and its attendant notion of Asian-African solidarity "are most often cited as the very foundation of postcolonial politics in a global frame" (Burton, *Brown* 2), reading Wright's big history of the conference in conjunction with *Indonesian Notebook*'s little and interstitial histories of the Bandung moment becomes critical to reevaluating and redefining the larger contours of studies in postcolonialism, black internationalism, Southeast Asian cultural traffic, American transnational exchange, Asian-African solidarities, Cold War–era nonalignment, and the global South. Though the relevance of this book's histories is by no means exhausted by its relation to the Asian-African Conference, these histories are nonetheless vivid reminders that scholarship on Bandung's legacy (its "era" and its "spirit," according to the terms frequently used) requires, as its precondition, foundational scholarship on the multiplicity of interests and differences that surrounded the event itself. Scholarship in this ambit, engaging with planetary history via the planet's own polyvocality of linguistic traditions, stands in perhaps the strongest position to impact our understanding of the event's undeniable and still-ramifying legacies.

Commenting on Bandung's legacies in a May 2015 *Tempo* article published in commemoration of the Asian-African Conference's sixtieth anniversary, Goenawan Mohamad observed that Wright could see that "the real meaning of the Asia-Africa antithesis was oppression everywhere," even as readers of *The Color Curtain* will also see him "here and there drawing wrong conclusions" ("Bandung"). Looking forward from the sixtieth anniversary commemorations toward a reenvisioning of Bandung historiography in future assessments and commemorations of the Asian-African Conference, *Indonesian Notebook* takes its place among a new generation of fundamental books on Bandung, as an invitation and challenge to bring Wright's English-language understandings, conclusions, and basic narratives into constructive dialogue and tension with the Dutch- and Indonesian-language understandings, conclusions, and correctives offered by his Indonesian hosts. Wright ranked his hosts among those postcolonial intellectuals who were lonely outsiders existing precariously and misunderstood at the margins of many cultures (*White* vii). However, the Indonesians with whom he interacted in April-May 1955 saw themselves as citizens of a new nation who were engaging confidently with voices from all parts of the world, speaking back in their own language and their own forms (Asrul, "Surat" 3). Here we see a disjuncture between the outsider perspectives of *The Color Curtain*'s author and the self-perceptions of a group of Indonesians who were dedicated to writing in languages other than English. This is a specific tension, but it nonetheless has wide historiographical relevance for the myriad and planet-spanning fields of knowledge that recognize some of their own origins in the stakes, implications, and spirit of Bandung.

Notes

1. Vuyk's article is a review of Baldwin's 1964 play *Blues for Mister Charlie*.

2. For Gibson's English, see Gibson, "No" 92.

3. On the Wright-Gibson conflict, see Ward and Butler 148–49; and Gibson, "Richard."

4. Margrit de Sablonière to Constance Webb, 3 Nov. 1966 (CWP, box 5, folder 10). In this letter, de Sablonière references Vuyk's 1965 *Vrij Nederland* essay as "an article by Beb Vuyk, a recent one, in which she says that Gibson and Baldwin were the first to attack Richard."

5. De Sablonière to Webb, 26 Dec. 1966 (CWP, box 5, folder 10).

6. Richard Thomas Gibson to Brian Roberts, 24 Sept. 2014, e-mail.

7. For the development of Webb's distorting commentary on Vuyk's ties with the US Embassy, her purported CCF affiliation, and her position among Indonesian intellectuals, see Wright to de Sablonière, 23 Nov. 1960 (MFP, Richard Wright Letters Project, boxes 30–31, folders 23 and 1–3); Wright to de Sablonière, 24 Nov. 1960 (MFP, Richard Wright Letters Project, boxes 30–31, folders 23 and 1–3); and de Sablonière to Webb, 3 Nov. 1966 (CWP, box 5, folder 10, first 3 Nov. 1966 letter). Webb's summary of Vuyk's 1960 article is based on de Sablonière's English-language missummarizations, six years after the fact. See de Sablonière to Webb, 3 Nov. 1966 (CWP, box 5, folder 10, first 3 Nov. 1966 letter).

8. On the CCF and CIA, see Coleman 219–34.

9. Perhaps Wright's, de Sablonière's, and Webb's undocumented suspicions and claims regarding Vuyk's CCF affiliation have played a role in Vuyk's general dismissal from the narrative of Wright's Indonesian travels. Yet to dismiss Vuyk based on these undocumented claims would be more rash than dismissing *The Color Curtain* based on the book's well-documented status as funded (in terms of Wright's travel money) and promoted (via excerpts in international magazines) by the CCF. Neither Wright nor Vuyk may be dismissed as CIA dupes; rather, they were participating in a form of Cold War cultural diplomacy that was nearly ubiquitous among the non-Communist left of this era.

10. For Fabre's unacknowledged reliance on Vuyk, see *Unfinished* 418–19.

11. Rowley's note on this point mentions Vuyk by name: "Beb Vuyk attacked Wright in the weekly *Vrij Nederland*" (590, n45).

12. Some might suggest that an account by a writer of mixed Dutch and Indonesian ancestry is not properly "an Indonesian view." However, Vuyk at this time self-identified as an Indonesian. She was an Indonesian citizen and an insider in the group of Indonesian intellectuals who hosted Wright. When political developments forced her to leave Indonesia, she departed with the unreserved goodwill of her Indonesian friends and associates (Scova Righini 328–29).

13. While finishing his bachelor's degree in English, the Bandung-based Indonesian writer Atep Kurnia completed a 2012 undergraduate thesis on *The Color Curtain*, adeptly drawing on the English-language writings of Edward Said, Mary Louise Pratt, and W. E. B. Du Bois (Atep, "Representation"). Atep has also drawn on the English-language writings of Wright scholar Virginia Whatley Smith (Atep, "Seruan"). In 2015, as this book was in production, Goenawan Mohamad published an article briefly mentioning Asrul Sani's criticism in *Siasat* of Wright's commentary on the place of toilet paper in Indonesia (Goenawan, "Bandung"). Asrul's article appears in this book as "Richard Wright: The Artist Turned Intellectual," in part II.

14. See particularly Ngũgĩ 1–3; Anzaldúa 53–64; and Phillipson 1–16.

15. In describing English as historically contingent, we draw on Ngũgĩ's writings against colonial languages as inevitable replacements for African languages (24–25).

16. Just as privileging English-language sources has obscured the Indonesian archive from the historical record of Wright's visit, our own focus on the lingua franca of Indonesia may have obscured accounts of Wright's visit that were written and published in Indonesia's regional languages. Thanks to Atep Kurnia, who alerted us to the possibility that there may be Indonesian sources on Wright that were published in Sundanese, the regional language of West Java.

17. See Vuyk's "Stories in the Modern Manner," in part I.

18. In his presentation during the 2015 conference Bandung at 60: Toward a Genealogy of the Global Present (organized by the International Institute for Asian Studies in Leiden, the Netherlands), Darwis Khudori ranked *The Color Curtain* as one of the "fundamental books" on the Bandung Conference; Darwis Khudori to Brian Russell Roberts, 2 June 2015, e-mail.

WORKS CITED

Abdulgani, Roeslan. See Roeslan.

Achdiat Karta Mihardja. "Pertemuan Kebudajaan di Tugu." *Pudjangga Baru* Feb. 1951: 241–44. Print.

"Africa Day Symposium on Digital Partnership: Hopes and Inspirations from Bandung." 18 May 2005. *Tokyo Development Learning Center.* Web. 5 Sept. 2014.

Ahmad, Dohra. *Landscapes of Hope: Anti-colonial Utopianism in America.* New York: Oxford University Press, 2009. Print.

Ajip Rosidi. *Anak Tanahair: Secercah Kisah.* Jakarta: Gramedia, 1985. Print.

Ajip Rosidi. Interview with Brian Russell Roberts. H. B. Jassin Literary Documentation Center, Jakarta. 15 May 2013.

Ajip Rosidi. *Mengenang Hidup Orang Lain: Sejumlah Obituari.* Jakarta: Gramedia, 2010. Print.

Akustia, Klara [A. S. Dharta]. "Kepada Seniman 'Universil.'" *Beberapa Paham Angkatan '45.* Ed. Aoh Kartahadimadja. Jakarta: Tintamas, 1952. 82–91. Print.

Aleida, Martin. "Pram, Dukun, Negro Spiritual, dan Impian Nobel." 2006. *1000 Wajah Pram dalam Kata dan Sketsa.* Jakarta: Lentera Dipantara, 2009. 87–92. Print.

Alisjahbana, Sutan Takdir. See Takdir.

Ampiah, Kweku. *The Political and Moral Imperatives of the Bandung Conference of 1955: The Reactions of the US, UK and Japan.* Kent, UK: Global, 2007. Print.

Anzaldúa, Gloria. *Borderlands/La Frontera: The New Mestiza.* San Francisco: Aunt Lute, 1987. Print.

Ashcroft, Bill, Gareth Griffiths, and Helen Tiffin, eds. *Postcolonial Studies: The Key Concepts.* 3rd ed. London: Routledge, 2013. Print.

"Asian-African Summit 2005 and the Anniversary of the Golden Jubilee of the Asian-African Conference." 22–24 Apr. 2005. MKAA: *Museum Konperensi Asia-Afrika.* Web. 8 Aug. 2014.

Asrul Sani. "De Indonesische Letterkunde als Spiegel van de Maatschappij." *Cultureel Nieuws* 30 (1953): 817–25. Print.

Asrul Sani. "Museum." *Konfrontasi* July–Aug. 1956: 15–27. Print.

Asrul Sani. "Sebuah Pembelaan." 1951. *Surat-Surat Kepercayaan*. Compiled by Ajip Rosidi. Jakarta: Pustaka Jaya, 1997. 68–77. Print.

Asrul Sani. "Surat Kepercayaan Gelanggang." 1950. *Surat-surat Kepercayaan*. Compiled by Ajip Rosidi. Jakarta: Pustaka Jaya, 1997. 3–4. Print.

Atep Kurnia. "The Representation of Double Consciousness in Richard Wright's *The Color Curtain*." Undergraduate thesis. Universitas Islam Negeri Sunan Gunung Djati. Bandung, Indonesia. 2012. Print.

Atep Kurnia. "Seruan dari Bandung." *Warabuku* Apr.–May 2013: 1 and 7. Print.

Ayatrohaedi. "Puisi Amerika Hitam." *Budaja Djaja* Dec. 1974: 755–72. Print.

Ayatrohaedi, trans. and ed. *Puisi Negro: Sejemput Sajak para Penyair Afrika dan Amerika Hitam*. Jakarta: Budaya Jaya, 1976. Print.

Bakish, David. *Richard Wright*. New York: Ungar, 1973.

Baldwin, James. "Everybody's Protest Novel." 1949. *Perspectives USA* 2 (1953): 93–100. Print.

Baldwin, James. "Princes and Powers." 1957. *Nobody Knows My Name: More Notes of a Native Son*. 1961. New York: Dell, 1963. 24–54. Print.

Barker, Joshua. "Beyond Bandung: Developmental Nationalism and (Multi)cultural Nationalism in Indonesia." *Third World Quarterly* 29 (2008): 521–40. *Google Scholar*. Web. 12 May 2014.

Barnett, Peter. *Foreign Correspondence: A Journalist's Biography*. South Yarra, Aus.: MacMillan, 2001. Print.

Barnhisel, Greg. "*Perspectives USA* and the Cultural Cold War: Modernism in Service of the State." *Modernism/modernity* 14 (2007): 729–54. *Project Muse*. Web. 7 July 2014.

Barthes, Roland. *Mythologies*. 1957. Trans. Annette Lavers. New York: Hill, 1972. Print.

Beekman, E. M. *Troubled Pleasures: Dutch Colonial Literature from the East Indies, 1600–1950*. Oxford: Clarendon, 1996. Print.

Benda, Harry J. "Democracy in Indonesia." Rev. of *The Decline of Constitutional Democracy in Indonesia*, by Herbert Feith. *Journal of Asian Studies* 23 (1964): 449–56. *Cambridge Journals*. Web. 13 Sept. 2014.

Benjamin, Bret. *Invested Interests: Capital, Culture, and the World Bank*. Minneapolis: University of Minnesota Press, 2007. Print.

Blackburn, Susan. *Women and the State in Modern Indonesia*. Cambridge: Cambridge University Press, 2004. Print.

Bourchier, David, and Vedi R. Hadiz, eds. *Indonesian Politics and Society: A Reader*. London: RoutledgeCurzon, 2003. Print.

Burton, Antoinette. *Brown over Black: Race and the Politics of Postcolonial Citation*. New Delhi: Three Essays Collective, 2012. Print.

Burton, Antoinette. "The Sodalities of Bandung: Toward a Critical 21st-Century History." Lee 351–61. Print.

Camus, Albert. *Caligula*. Adapted into Indonesian by Asrul Sani. *Indonesia: Madjalah Kebudajaan* Sept.–Oct. 1956: 388–469. Print.

Chakrabarty, Dipesh. "The Legacies of Bandung: Decolonization and the Politics of Culture." Lee 45–68. Print.

Chakrabarty, Dipesh. *Provincializing Europe: Postcolonial Thought and Historical Difference.* 2000. Reissue. Princeton, NJ: Princeton University Press, 2008. Print.

"China to Mark Emergence as Leader of Third World." *New York Times* 9 Apr. 2005. Web. 8 Aug. 2014.

Choirotun Chisaan. "In Search of an Indonesian Islamic Cultural Identity, 1956–1965." Lindsay and Liem 283–314. Print.

Coleman, Peter. *The Liberal Conspiracy: The Congress for Cultural Freedom and the Struggle for the Mind of Postwar Europe.* New York: Free Press, 1989. Print.

Collits, Terry. *Postcolonial Conrad: Paradoxes of Empire.* New York: Routledge, 2005. Print.

Conboy, Kenneth J. *Intel: Inside Indonesia's Intelligence Service.* Jakarta: Equinox, 2004. Print.

Congress for Cultural Freedom (CCF). "Manifesto of Congress for Cultural Freedom (Berlin, 1950)." *The Liberal Conspiracy: The Congress for Cultural Freedom and the Struggle for the Mind of Postwar Europe.* By Peter Coleman. New York: Free Press, 1989. 249–51. Print.

Cowen, Tyler. *Good and Plenty: The Creative Successes of American Arts Funding.* Princeton, NJ: Princeton University Press, 2006. Print.

Cribb, Robert, and Colin Brown. *Modern Indonesia: A History since 1945.* London: Longman, 1995. Print.

Curaming, Rommel A. "Beyond Orientalism? Another Look at Orientalism in Indonesian and Philippine Studies." *Kyoto Review of Southeast Asia* 11 (2009): 1–10. kyotoreview.org. Web. 13 Sept. 2014.

"Dari Wright Sampai Kahin." *Tempo* 26 April 2015: 100–101. Print.

Darwis Khudori. "Bandung Conference and Its Constellation: The Fundamental Books." Bandung at 60: Toward a Genealogy of the Global Present. Conference organized by the International Institute for Asian Studies (IIAS), Leiden, Neth. 18 June 2015.

Davis, Charles T., and Michel Fabre. *Richard Wright: A Primary Bibliography.* Boston: Hall, 1982. Print.

Day, Tony. "Still Stuck in the Mud: Imagining World Literature during the Cold War in Indonesia and Vietnam." *Cultures at War: The Cold War and Cultural Expression in Southeast Asia.* Ed. Tony Day and Maya H. T. Liem. Ithaca, NY: Cornell University Press, 2010. 129–69. Print.

de Vaal, Hans. "An Interview with Richard Wright." July–Aug. 1953. Trans. Edward Lemon. *Conversations with Richard Wright.* Ed. Keneth Kinnamon and Michel Fabre. Jackson: University of Mississippi Press, 1993. 154–59. Print.

Dian Yuliastuti. "Tempo Journalist Wins 2014 IKJ Award." *Tempo* 31 May 2014. *Tempo.co.* Web. 13 Aug. 2014.

Dolk, Liesbeth. "An Entangled Affair: STICUSA and Indonesia, 1948–1956." Lindsay and Liem 57–74. Print.

Dubois, Pierre H. "Buah-tangan Albert Camus." *Zenith* May 1953: 301–7. Print.

Elson, R. E. *The Idea of Indonesia: A History.* Cambridge: Cambridge University Press, 2008. Print.

Eneste, Pamusuk. See Pamusuk.

Espiritu, Augusto. "'To Carry Water on Both Shoulders': Carlos P. Romulo, American Empire, and the Meanings of Bandung." *Radical History Review* 95 (2006): 173–90. *Dukejournals.* Web. 16 Jan. 2015.

Fabre, Michel, trans. "Interview with Richard Wright." 18 Aug. 1960. *Conversations with Richard Wright.* Jackson: University Press of Mississippi, 1993. 201–7. Print.

Fabre, Michel. *Richard Wright: Books and Writers.* Jackson: University Press of Mississippi, 1990. Print.

Fabre, Michel. *The Unfinished Quest of Richard Wright.* Trans. Isabel Barzun. New York: Morrow, 1973. Print.

Farouque, Farah. "Laughter 'Not Always about Humour.'" *The Age* 15 Nov. 2002. *theage .com.au.* Web. 3 July 2014.

Feith, Herbert. *The Decline of Constitutional Democracy in Indonesia.* Ithaca, NY: Cornell University Press, 1962. Print.

Feith, Herbert. "History, Theory, and Indonesian Politics: A Reply to Harry J. Benda." *The Journal of Asian Studies* 24 (1965): 305–12. *Cambridge Journals.* Web. 13 Sept. 2014.

"Final Communique: Communique of the International Meeting on the Bandung Spirit—Genesis and Revitalization for the 21st Century." 28–29 Nov. 2005. *Afro-Asian Peoples' Solidarity Organization.* Web. 12 Aug. 2014.

Foulcher, Keith. "Bringing the World Back Home: Cultural Traffic in *Konfrontasi*, 1954–1960." Lindsay and Liem 31–56. Print.

Foulcher, Keith. "Literature, Cultural Politics and the Indonesian Revolution." *Text/Politics in Island Southeast Asia: Essays in Interpretation.* Ed. D. M. Roskies. Athens: Ohio University Monographs in International Studies/Southeast Asia Series, No. 91, 1993. 221–56. Print.

Foulcher, Keith. "On a Roll: Pramoedya and the Postcolonial Transition." *Indonesian Studies Working Papers* 4 (2008): 1–22. *University of Sydney Department of Indonesian Studies.* Web. 17 Sept. 2014.

Foulcher, Keith. *Social Commitment in Literature and the Arts: The Indonesian "Institute of People's Culture," 1950–1965.* Clayton, Aus.: Centre of Southeast Asian Studies, Monash University, 1986. Print.

Friedman, Susan Stanford. "Planetarity: Musing Modernist Studies." *Modernism/modernity* 17 (2010): 471–99. *ProjectMuse.* Web. 29 May 2011.

Gayle, Addison. *Richard Wright: Ordeal of a Native Son.* New York: Doubleday, 1980. Print.

Gibson, Richard. "A No to Nothing." 1951. *Perspectives USA* 2 (1953): 89–92. Print.

Gibson, Richard. "Richard Wright's 'Island of Hallucination' and the 'Gibson Affair.'" *MFS: Modern Fiction Studies* 51.4 (2005): 896–920. *Project Muse.* Web. 17 Sept. 2014.

Gilbert, Elizabeth. *Eat, Pray, Love: One Woman's Search for Everything across Italy, India and Indonesia.* New York: Penguin. 2006. Print.

De Goede Boeken Club. Advertisement. *De Preangerbode* 1 Oct. 1955: 4. *Delpher.* Web. 17 Sept. 2014.

Goenawan Mohamad. "Bandung." *Tempo* 3 May 2015: 130. Print.

Goenawan Mohamad. "Bandung." *Tempo: English* 10 May 2015: 66. Print.

Goenawan Mohamad. "The 'Cultural Manifesto' Affair Revisited: Literature and Politics in Indonesia in the 1960s, a Signatory's View." Ed. and trans. Harry Aveling. *Monash University Centre of Southeast Asian Studies Working Papers* 134 (2011): 1–40. *Monash Asia Institute.* Web. 31 July 2014.

Goenawan Mohamad. "Politikus." *Catatan Pinggir.* Vol. 1. Jakarta: Grafiti, 1982. 389–90. Print.

Goenawan Mohamad. "Politikus Juga." Posted 19 June 2009. *Goenawan Mohamad.* Web. 1 June 2014.

Gonzalez, Eduardo T., ed. "Southeast Asia, Real or Imagined: The Making of Community, Nation, and Region. A Conversation with Benedict Anderson." *Asian Politics & Policy* 5 (2013): 655–66. *Wiley Online Library.* Web. 13 Sept. 2014.

Gordon, Eugene. "Seven Years since Bandung." *Freedomways: A Quarterly Review of the Negro Freedom Movement* 2.3 (1962): 298–306. Print.

Grant, Bruce. "Foreword." *Sidelines: Writings from "Tempo," Indonesia's Banned Magazine,* by Goenawan Mohamad. Trans. Jennifer Lindsay. South Melbourne, Aus.: Hyland, 1994. v–viii. Print.

Greene, Graham. "Henry James: The Private Universe." *The Lost Childhood and Other Essays.* New York: Viking, 1952. 21–30. Print.

"Guide to the International Association for Cultural Freedom Records, 1941–1978." 2014. University of Chicago Library Special Collections. Web. 29 July 2014.

Hakim, L. E. [Pen name of Abu Hanifah (also El-Hakim)], trans. *Kegagalan "Tuhan"-Komunis.* Bandung: "Front Anti Komunis" Indonesia, [Feb.] 1955. Print.

Hakutani, Yoshinobu. "*The Color Curtain*: Richard Wright's Journey into Asia." *Richard Wright's Travel Writings: New Reflections.* Ed. Virginia Whatley Smith. Jackson: University Press of Mississippi, 2001. 63–77. Print.

Hargreaves, Alec. "A Neglected Precursor: Roland Barthes and the Origins of Postcolonialism." *Postcolonial Theory and Francophone Literary Studies.* Ed. Anne Donadey and Adlai Murdoch. Gainesville: University Press of Florida, 2005. 55–64. Print.

Hatley, Barbara. "Creating Culture for the New Nation: South Sulawesi, 1950–1965." Lindsay and Liem 343–69. Print.

Hatley, Barbara. "Cultural Expression." *Indonesia's New Order: The Dynamics of Socio-Economic Transformation.* Ed. Hal Hill. St. Leonards, Aus.: Allen, 1994. 216–66. Print.

Hatley, Barbara. "Postcoloniality and the Feminine in Modern Indonesian Literature." *Clearing a Space: Postcolonial Readings of Modern Indonesian Literature.* Ed. Keith Foulcher and Tony Day. Leiden: KITLV, 2002. 145–82. Print.

Heehs, Peter. *Writing the Self: Diaries, Memoirs and the History of the Self.* New York: Bloomsbury, 2013. Print.

Heider, Karl G. *Indonesian Cinema: National Culture on Screen.* Honolulu: University of Hawai'i Press, 1991. Print.

Heinschke, Martina. "Between Gelanggang and Lekra: Pramoedya's Developing Literary Concepts." *Indonesia* (Cornell University) 61 (1996): 145–69. Print.

Hersri. "Art and Entertainment in the New Order's Jails." Trans. and intro. by Keith Foulcher. *Indonesia* (Cornell University) 59 (1995): 1–20. Print.

Hill, David T. *Journalism and Politics in Indonesia: A Critical Biography of Mochtar Lubis (1922–2004) as Editor and Author*. London: Routledge, 2010. Print.

Hill, David T. "'The Two Leading Institutions': Taman Ismail Marzuki and *Horison*." *Culture and Society in New Order Indonesia*. Ed. Virginia Matheson Hooker. Kuala Lumpur, Malaysia: Oxford University Press, 1993. 245–62. Print.

Holmes, James S. "A Quarter Century of Indonesian Literature." *Books Abroad* 29.1 (1955): 31–35. Print.

Holt, Claire. *Art in Indonesia: Continuities and Change*. Ithaca, NY: Cornell University Press, 1967. Print.

Hughes, Langston, and Arna Bontemps. Preface. *The Poetry of the Negro: 1746–1949*. Ed. Langston Hughes and Arna Bontemps. Garden City, NY: Doubleday, 1949. vii–ix. Print.

Jack, Homer A. *Bandung: An On-the-Spot Description of the Asian-African Conference, Bandung, Indonesia, April 1955*. Chicago: Forward Freedom, 1955. *Hathi Trust Digital Library*. Web. 15 Aug. 2014.

Jackson, Kennell. "Introduction: Traveling while Black." *Black Cultural Traffic: Crossroads in Global Performance and Popular Culture*. Ed. Harry J. Elam and Kennell Jackson. Ann Arbor: University of Michigan Press, 2005. 1–39. Print.

James, C. L. R. *At the Rendezvous: Selected Writings*. London: Allison, 1984. Print.

Jansen, Ena. "The Discourse of Difference in *Reisbrieven uit Afrika en Azië* (1913) by Dr Aletta Jacobs: A Dutch Feminist's Perspective on South Africa and the Dutch East Indies." *Journal of Literary Studies* 14.1/2 (1998): 102–15. Print.

Jansen, G. H. *Nonalignment and the Afro-Asian States*. New York: Praeger, 1966. Print.

Jassin, H. B. *Kesusastraan Indonesia Modern dalam Kritik dan Esei*. 4 vols. Jakarta: Gramedia, 1985. Print.

Jassin, H. B., Asrul Sani, and Siti Nuraini. "Omong-omong Kesusastraan." *Zenith* Feb. 1953: 111–20. Print.

Jedamski, Doris. "Balai Pustaka: A Colonial Wolf in Sheep's Clothing." *Archipel* 44 (1992): 23–46. Print.

Johns, A. H., trans. "Gelanggang: Heirs of the Culture of the Whole World (1950)." *Indonesian Political Thinking, 1945–1965*. Ed. Herbert Feith and Lance Castles. Ithaca, NY: Cornell University Press, 1970. 237–38. Print.

Kahin, George McTurnan. *The Asian-African Conference: Bandung, Indonesia, April 1955*. Ithaca, NY: Cornell University Press, 1956. Print.

Kahin, George McTurnan, and Milton L. Barnett. "In Memoriam: Soedjatmoko, 1922–1989." *Indonesia* (Cornell University) 49 (1990): 133–40. *Indonesia*. Web. 30 May 2014.

Kandou, Frits. "André Malraux: Pemudja Perbuatan." *Siasat* 15 May 1955: 26–27. Print.

Kandou, Frits. "Henri Matisse, Kursi Malas untuk Orang jang Tjapek." *Siasat* 1 May 1955: 22–23. Print.

Khudori, Darwis. See Darwis.

Kinnamon, Kenneth. *A Richard Wright Bibliography: Fifty Years of Criticism and Commentary, 1933–1982*. New York: Greenwood, 1988. Print.

Kiuchi, Toru. "Indonesia." *The Richard Wright Encyclopedia*. Ed. Jerry W. Ward and Robert J. Butler. Westport, CT: Greenwood, 2008. 195–96. Print.

Kiuchi, Toru, and Yoshinobu Hakutani. *Richard Wright: A Documented Chronology, 1908–1960*. Jefferson, NC: McFarland, 2014. Print.

Kloek, Els. *1001 Vrouwen uit de Nederlandse Geschiedenis*. Nijmegen, Neth.: Van Tilt, 2013. Print.

Koesalah Soebagyo Toer. "Pengantar." *Menggelinding I*. By Pramoedya Ananta Toer. Ed. Astuti Ananta Toer. Jakarta: Lentera Dipantara, 2004. xiii–xxvii. Print.

Kratz, E. U. "Islamic Attitudes toward Modern Indonesian Literature." *Cultural Contact and Textual Interpretation*. Ed. C. D. Grijns and S. O. Robson. Dordrecht, Neth.: Foris, 1986. 60–93. Print.

Kurnia, Atep. See Atep.

Lasky, Melvin J. "Report on 3rd Editorial Meeting." Berlin, 2 June 1955. IACFR, series 2, box 241, folder 6. Print.

Lee, Christopher. "Between a Moment and an Era: The Origins and Afterlives of Bandung." Lee 1–42. Print.

Lee, Christopher, ed. *Making a World after Empire: The Bandung Moment and Its Political Afterlives*. Athens: Ohio University Press, 2010. Print.

Lee Kam Hing. "The Taman Siswa in Postwar Indonesia." *Indonesia* (Cornell University) 25 (1978): 41–60. *Indonesia*. Web. 12 June 2014.

Lemaire, Jan, Jr. "Jang Absur." *Zenith* Apr. 1954: 117–24. Print.

Lewis, Norman. *An Empire of the East: Travels in Indonesia*. New York: Holt, 1993. Print.

Lindsay, Jennifer. "Goenawan Mohamad: Man on the Margins." *Australian Book Review* Oct. 2012: 29–41. Print.

Lindsay, Jennifer. "Heirs to World Culture 1950–1965: An Introduction." Lindsay and Liem 1–27. Print.

Lindsay, Jennifer. "Introduction." *Sidelines: Writings from "Tempo," Indonesia's Banned Magazine*. By Goenawan Mohamad. Trans. Jennifer Lindsay. South Melbourne, Aus.: Hyland, 1994. xi–xv. Print.

Lindsay, Jennifer. "Translator's Introduction." *Conversations with Difference: Essays from Tempo Magazine*. By Goenawan Mohamad. Trans. Jennifer Lindsay. Jakarta: Tempo, 2002. xi–xvi. Print.

Lindsay, Jennifer, and Maya H. T. Liem, eds. *Heirs to World Culture: Being Indonesian, 1950–1965*. Leiden: KITLV, 2012. Print.

Liu, Hong. "Pramoedya Ananta Toer and China: The Transformation of a Cultural Intellectual." *Indonesia* (Cornell University) 61 (1996): 119–43. Print.

Lubis, Mochtar. See Mochtar.

Lucas, Christopher. *Indonesia Is a Happening*. New York: Walker/Weatherhill, 1970. Print.

Lüthi, Lorenz. "The Rise and Fall of the Afro-Asian Solidarity." Chapter from book-in-progress, *A History of the Cold War without Superpowers: Asia, the Middle East, and Europe*.

Mackie, Jamie. *Bandung 1955: Non-alignment and Afro-Asian Solidarity*. Singapore: Millet, 2005. Print.

Manik, L. "Lagu-lagu Negro Spiritual." *Zenith: Dari Bumi Sastera, Seni dan Filsafat* Feb. 1953: 121–25. Print.

McCullers, Carson. "Fragmen." Trans. Siti Nuraini. *Konfrontasi* Mar.–Apr. 1955: 36–48. Print.

McDougall, Derek, and Antonia Finnane. "Introduction: Bandung as History." *Bandung 1955: Little Histories*. Ed. Derek McDougall and Antonia Finnane. Caulfield, Aus.: Monash University Press, 2010. 1–8. Print.

McDougall, Derek, and Antonia Finnane, eds. *Bandung 1955: Little Histories*. Caulfield, Aus.: Monash University Press, 2010. Print.

McGlynn, John H., ed. *Indonesian Heritage: Language and Literature*. Singapore: Archipelago, 1998. Print.

Menon, Dilip M. "Bandung Is Back: Afro-Asian Affinities." *Radical History Review* 119 (2014): 241–44. *Dukejournals*. Web. 16 Jan. 2015.

Mihardja, Achdiat Karta. See Achdiat.

Miller, Eugene E. *Voice of a Native Son: The Poetics of Richard Wright*. Jackson: University Press of Mississippi, 1990. Print.

Ministry of Foreign Affairs of the Republic of Indonesia. *Asia-Africa Speaks from Bandung*. [Jakarta]: Ministry of Foreign Affairs, 1955. Print.

Mirta Kartohadiprodjo. Interview with Brian Russell Roberts. Pejompongan neighborhood, Jakarta. 1 May 2013.

Mochtar Lubis. "Literature and Liberation: An Awareness of Self and Society." *Literature and Liberation: Five Essays from Southeast Asia*. Ed. Edwin Thumboo. Manila: Solidaridad, 1988. 71–104. Print.

Mochtar Lubis. "Through Coloured Glasses?" *Encounter* Mar. 1956: 73. Print.

Mochtar Lubis. *Twilight in Djakarta*. Trans. Claire Holt. New York: Vanguard, 1963. Print.

Mochtar Lubis. *Twilight in Djakarta*. Trans. Claire Holt. Singapore: Millet, 2011. Print.

Mohamad, Goenawan. See Goenawan.

Mrázek, Rudolf. *Sjahrir: Politics and Exile in Indonesia*. Ithaca, NY: Southeast Asia Program, Cornell University, 1994. Print.

Mullen, Bill V. *Afro-Orientalism*. Minneapolis: University of Minnesota Press, 2004. Print.

Murphy, Michael. "'One Hundred Per Cent Bohemia': Pop Decadence and the Aestheticization of Commodity in the Rise of Slicks." *Marketing Modernisms: Self-Promotion, Canonization, Rereading*. Ed. Kevin J. H. Dettmar and Stephen Watts. Ann Arbor: University of Michigan Press, 1996. 61–89. Print.

Mushakoji, Kinhide. "Towards a New Bandung: The Global Civil Society and the UN Multilateral System." *The Center Holds: UN Reform for 21st-Century Challenges*. Ed. Kevin P. Clements and Nadia Mizner. New Brunswick, NJ: Transaction, 2008. 145–64. Print.

Naipaul, V. S. *Among the Believers: An Islamic Journey*. New York: Knopf, 1981. Print.

"Negro Author Disappointed." *Times of Indonesia* 25 Apr. 1955: 3. Print.

Newsom, David D. *The Imperial Mantle: The United States, Decolonization, and the Third World*. Bloomington: Indiana University Press, 2001. Print.

Ngũgĩ wa Thiong'o. *Decolonising the Mind: The Politics of Language in African Literature*. London: Currey, 1986. Print.

Nur Mursidi. "Body Reflects Racist Exclusivity." *Jakarta Post* 14 July 2002. Web. 13 Aug. 2014.

Nuraini, Siti. Interview with Brian Russell Roberts. Kemang neighborhood, Jakarta. 4 May 2013.

"The Outsiders." *Tempo: English* 26 Apr. 2015: 66–67. Print.

Owusu-Ansah, David. *Historical Dictionary of Ghana*. 4th ed. Lanham, MD: Rowman, 2014. Print.

Pamusuk Eneste. *Leksikon Kesusastraan Indonesia Modern*. Jakarta: Djambatan, 1990. Print.

"Panggilan Bandung Kembali Menggema." *Tempo* 26 April 2015: 48–52. Print.

"Panitya Indonesia untuk Congress for Cultural Freedom Adakan Rapat." *Budaya* Apr.–May 1956: 205. Print.

Parker, Jason C. "Small Victory, Missed Chance: The Eisenhower Administration, the Bandung Conference, and the Turning of the Cold War." *The Eisenhower Administration, the Third World, and the Globalization of the Cold War*. Ed. Kathryn C. Statler and Andrew L. Johns. Lanham, MD: Rowman, 2006. 153–74. Print.

Passin, Herbert, ed. *Cultural Freedom in Asia: The Proceedings of a Conference Held at Rangoon, Burma on February 17, 18, 19, and 20, 1955, and Convened by the Congress for Cultural Freedom and the Society for the Extension of Democratic Ideals*. Rutland, VT: Tuttle, 1956. Print.

Paupp, Terrence Edward. *Beyond Global Crisis: Remedies and Road Maps by Daisaku Ikeda and His Contemporaries*. New Brunswick, NJ: Transaction, 2012. Print.

Payne, Ethel. *Interviews with Ethel Payne: Recorded by Kathleen Currie for the Washington Press Club Foundation as Part of Its Oral History Project*. Washington, DC: Washington Press Club, 1990. Print.

Phillips, William, and Philip Rahv. "In Retrospect: Ten Years of *Partisan Review*." *The Partisan Reader: Ten Years of* Partisan Review, *1934–1944: An Anthology*. Ed. William Phillips and Philip Rahv. New York: Dial, 1946. 679–88. Print.

Phillipson, Robert. *Linguistic Imperialism*. Oxford: Oxford University Press, 1992. Print.

Pisani, Elizabeth. *Indonesia Etc.: Exploring the Improbable Nation*. London: Granta, 2014. Print.

Plomp, Marije. "The Capital of Pulp Fiction and Other Capitals: Cultural Life in Medan, 1950–1958." Lindsay and Liem 371–95. Print.

Pramoedya Ananta Toer. "Balai Pustaka Dialam Kemerdekaan." *Star Weekly* 16 Feb. 1957: 12–13. Print.

Pramoedya Ananta Toer. "Balai Pustaka Harum Namanja Didunia Internasional—Dahulu." *Star Weekly* 9 Feb. 1957: 10–11. Print.

Pramoedya Ananta Toer. *Bukan Pasar Malam*. Jakarta: Balai Pustaka, 1951. Print.

Pramoedya Ananta Toer. "Dia Yang Menyerah." *Cerita dari Blora*. Kuala Lumpur, Malaysia: Wira Karya, 1989. 171–228. Print.

Pramoedya Ananta Toer. *The Mute's Soliloquy: A Memoir.* Trans. Willem Samuels. New York: Hyperion East, 1999. Print.

Prashad, Vijay. *The Darker Nations: A People's History of the Third World.* New York: New Press, 2007. Print.

Prashad, Vijay. "Foreword: 'Bandung Is Done'—Passages in AfroAsian Epistemology." *AfroAsian Encounters: Culture, History, Politics.* Ed. Heike Raphael-Hernandez and Shannon Steen. New York: New York University Press, 2006. xi–xxiii. Print.

Program Balai Budaja. Advertisement. *Siasat* 24 Apr. 1955: 25. Print.

Record, Wilson. "Role of the Negro Intellectual." *Crisis* June–July 1953: 329–35. Print.

Redaksi. "Dari Redaksi." *Konfrontasi* Mar.–Apr. 1955: 1. Print.

Redaksi. "Dari Redaksi." *Konfrontasi* May–June 1955: 1. Print.

Reilly, John M. "Richard Wright and the Art of Non-Fiction: Stepping Out on the Stage of the World." *Callaloo* 28 (1986): 507–20. JSTOR. Web. 23 Apr. 2012.

"Resonating the Bandung Call." *Tempo: English* 26 Apr. 2015: 20–24. Print.

Ricklefs, M. C. *A History of Modern Indonesia since c. 1200.* Basingstoke, UK: Palgrave, 2001. Print.

Rickles, Milton, and Patricia Rickles. *Richard Wright.* Austin, TX: Steck-Vaugh, 1970. Print.

Roberts, Brian Russell. *Artistic Ambassadors: Literary and International Representation of the New Negro Era.* Charlottesville: University of Virginia Press, 2013. Print.

Roberts, Brian Russell, and Keith Foulcher. "Richard Wright on Bandung, Beb Vuyk on Richard Wright." Introduction. "A Weekend with Richard Wright." By Beb Vuyk. Trans. Keith Foulcher. Ed. Brian Russell Roberts and Keith Foulcher. PMLA 126 (2011): 798–803. Print.

Roeslan Abdulgani. *The Bandung Connection: Konperensi Asia-Afrika di Bandung Tahun 1955.* Jakarta: Gunung Agung, 1980. Print.

Romulo, Carlos P. *The Meaning of Bandung.* Chapel Hill: University of North Carolina Press, 1956. Print.

Rosidi, Ajip. See Ajip.

Rowan, Carl T. *The Pitiful and the Proud.* New York: Random, 1956. Print.

Rowley, Hazel. *Richard Wright: The Life and Times.* New York: Holt, 2001. Print.

Rustapa, Anita K., Agus Sri Danardana, and Bambang Trisman. *Antologi Biografi Pengarang Sastra Indonesia, 1920–1950.* Jakarta: Departemen Pendidikan dan Kebudayaan, 1997. Print.

Said, Edward. *Orientalism.* 25th anniversary ed. New York: Vintage, 1994. Print.

Salim HS, Hairus. "Indonesian Muslims and Cultural Networks." Lindsay and Liem 75–118. Print.

Samuels, Willem. Introduction. *The Mute's Soliloquy: A Memoir.* By Pramoedya Ananta Toer. Trans. Willem Samuels. New York: Hyperion East, 1999. xiii–xxii. Print.

Sandoval, Chéla. "Theorizing White Consciousness for a Post-empire World: Barthes, Fanon, and the Rhetoric of Love." *Displacing Whiteness: Essays in Social and Cultural Criticism.* Ed. Ruth Frankenberg. Durham, NC: Duke University Press, 1997. 86–106. Print.

Sani, Asrul. See Asrul.

Sartre, Jean-Paul. "The Responsibility of the Writer." Trans. Betty Askwith. *The Creative Vision: Modern European Writers on Their Art*. Ed. Haskell M. Block and Herman Salinger. Gloucester, MA: Smith, 1968. 165–86. Print.

Sartre, Jean-Paul. "Tanggungdjawab Pengarang." Trans. H. B. Jassin. *Zenith* May 1954: 130–45. Print.

Saunders, Frances Stonor. *The Cultural Cold War: The CIA and the World of Arts and Letters*. New York: New Press, 1999. Print.

Schuyler, George S. "The Negro-Art Hokum." 1926. *African American Literary Theory: A Reader*. Ed. Winston Napier. New York: New York University Press, 2000. 24–26. Print.

Scova Righini, Bert. *Een Leven in Twee Vaderlanden: Een Biografie van Beb Vuijk*. Leiden: KITLV, 2005. Print.

Sears, Laurie J. *Situated Testimonies: Dread and Enchantment in an Indonesian Literary Archive*. Honolulu: University of Hawai'i Press, 2013. Print.

Sen, Krishna. *Indonesian Cinema: Framing the New Order*. London: Zed, 1994. Print.

Seno Joko Suyono. "Puisi Seno Joko Suyono." *Puisi Kompas* 16 Mar. 2014. Web. 13 Aug. 2014.

Seno Joko Suyono, ed. *Requiem for a Massacre, Special Report: Tempo English*. 1–7 Oct. 2012. *The Act of Killing*. Web. 8 Aug. 2014.

Singh, Amritjit. Afterword. *The Color Curtain: A Report on the Bandung Conference*. By Richard Wright. In *Black Power: Three Books from Exile*. New York: HarperPerennial, 2008. 612–29. Print.

Sizer, Lyde Cullen. *The Political Work of Northern Women Writers and the Civil War, 1850–1872*. Chapel Hill: University of North Carolina Press, 2000. *EBSCOhost eBook Collection*. Web. 4 June 2014.

"Slamet Iman Santoso." *Belajarpsikologi.com* 16 June 2010. Web. 2 June 2014.

Smith, Virginia Whatley. "Richard Wright's Passage to Indonesia: The Travel Writer/Narrator as Participant/Observer of Anti-Colonial Imperatives in *The Color Curtain*." *Richard Wright's Travel Writings: New Reflections*. Ed. Virginia Whatley Smith. Jackson: University Press of Mississippi, 2001. 78–115. Print.

Soedjatmoko. "Mengapa 'Konfrontasi'?" *Konfrontasi* July–Aug. 1954: 3–12. Print.

"The Spirit of Bandung." *Jakarta Post* 6 Apr. 2005. Web. 8 Aug. 2014.

Stecopoulos, Harilaos. *Reconstructing the World: Southern Fictions and U.S. Imperialisms, 1898–1976*. Ithaca, NY: Cornell University Press, 2008. Print.

Stein, Gertrude. "Composition as Explanation." 1926. *Selected Writings of Gertrude Stein*. Ed. Carl Van Vechten. New York: Random, 1946. 451–61. Print.

Stein, Gertrude. *Geography and Plays*. Boston: Four Seas, 1922. Print.

Stryker, Charlotte. *Time for Tapioca*. New York: Crowell, 1951. Print.

Sukarno. "The Forceful Echo of the Indonesian Revolution: Independence Day Message." 1963. *Indonesia's Political Manifesto, 1959–1964*. Jakarta: Prapantja, [1964]. 231–68. Print.

"Surabaya Post, Observer Close over Financial Problems." *Pacific Media Watch* 23 July 2002. Web. 2 June 2014.

Sutan Takdir Alisjahbana. See Takdir.

Suyono, Seno Joko. See Seno.

Takdir Alisjahbana, S. *Indonesia in the Modern World*. Trans. Benedict R. Anderson. New Delhi: CCF Office for Asian Affairs, 1961. Print.

Tan, See Seng, and Amitav Acharya, eds. *Bandung Revisited: The Legacy of the 1955 Asian-African Conference for International Order*. Singapore: NUS Press, 2008. Print.

Teeuw, A. *Modern Indonesian Literature*. The Hague: Nijhoff, 1967. Print.

Teeuw, A. *Pramoedya Ananta Toer: De Verbeelding van Indonesië*. Breda, Neth.: De Geus, 1993. Print.

Thomas, Winburn T. "The Reformed Church in Indonesia." Manuscript. CSCA, call no. A183.12. Print.

Thomas, Winburn T. "Reminiscences." *Richard Wright: Impressions and Perspectives*. Ed. David Ray and Robert M. Farnsworth. Ann Arbor: University of Michigan Press, 1973. 151–53. Print.

"Tiga Madjalah jang Memimpin." Advertisement. Back cover of *Sedjarah Bahasa Indonesia*, by S. Takdir Alisjahbana. Jakarta: Pustaka Rakyat, 1956. Print.

Toer, Pramoedya Ananta. See Pramoedya.

Tulus Wijanarko. "Elegi Sang Guru Klaninet." Rev. of *Tak Ada Santo dari Sirkus*, by Seno Joko Suyono. *Pendapa* 15 June 2012. Web. 13 Aug. 2014.

van der Molen, S. *Bahasa Indonesia: A Textbook of Elementary Indonesian Malay*. Adapted by Harry P. Cemach. Bandung: Van Hoeve, 1949. Print.

Van Sant, John, Peter Mauch, and Yoneyuki Sugita. *Historical Dictionary of United States–Japan Relations*. Lanham, MD: Scarecrow, 2007. Print.

Varadarajan, Siddharth. "Stage Set for New Asian-African Strategic Ties." *The Hindu: Online Edition of India's National Newspaper* 23 Apr. 2005. *The Hindu*. Web. 17 Sept. 2014.

Venuti, Lawrence. *The Translator's Invisibility: A History of Translation*. 1995. 2nd ed. London: Routledge, 2008. Print.

Vickers, Adrian. *Bali: A Paradise Created*. Ringwood, Aus.: Penguin, 1989. Print.

Vitalis, Robert. "The Midnight Ride of Kwame Nkrumah and Other Fables of Bandung (Ban-doong)." *Humanity* 4 (2013): 262–88.

Vreede-De Stuers, Cora. "Augustine Magdalena Wawo Runtu." *Archipel* 38 (1989): 9–12. *Persee*. Web. 13 July 2014.

Vuyk, Beb. "Het Negerprobleem Bemoeide Zich met Baldwin." *Vrij Nederland* 15 May 1965: 13. Print.

Vuyk, Beb. "A Weekend with Richard Wright." 1960. Trans. Keith Foulcher. Ed. Brian Russell Roberts and Keith Foulcher. *PMLA* 126 (2011): 803–12. Print.

Walker, Margaret. *Richard Wright: Daemonic Genius*. New York: Warner/Amistad, 1988. Print.

Wallach, Jennifer Jensen. *Richard Wright: From Black Boy to World Citizen*. Chicago: Dee, 2010. Print.

Ward, Jerry W., Jr., and Robert J. Butler, eds. *The Richard Wright Encyclopedia*. Westport, CT: Greenwood, 2008. Print.

Webb, Constance. *Richard Wright: A Biography*. New York: Putnam, 1968. Print

Wells, Louis T., and Rafiq Ahmed. *Making Foreign Investment Safe: Property Rights and National Sovereignty*. Oxford: Oxford University Press, 2007. Print.

Williams, John A. *The Most Native of Sons: A Biography of Richard Wright.* Garden City, NY: Doubleday, 1970. Print.

Williams, Maslyn. *Five Journeys from Jakarta.* Sydney: Collins, 1966. Print.

Wright, Richard. *12 Million Black Voices: A Folk History of the Negro in the United States.* New York: Viking, 1941. Print.

Wright, Richard. *American Hunger.* New York: Harper, 1977. Print.

Wright, Richard. "American Negro Writing." *Konfrontasi* May–June 1955: 2–25. Print.

Wright, Richard. *Bandoeng, 1.500.000.000 d'hommes.* Trans. Hélène Claireau. Paris: Calmann-Lévy, 1955. Print.

Wright, Richard. *Black Boy: A Record of Childhood and Youth.* New York: Harper, 1945. Print.

Wright, Richard. *Black Power: A Record of Reactions in a Land of Pathos.* 1954. In *Three Books from Exile.* New York: HarperPerennial, 2008. 1–427. Print.

Wright, Richard. *The Color Curtain: A Report on the Bandung Conference.* 1956. In *Black Power: Three Books from Exile.* New York: HarperPerennial, 2008. 429–609. Print.

Wright, Richard. "The Color Curtain." Developmental draft, typescript, corrected. [1955]. RWP, box 29, folder 420. Print.

Wright, Richard. *The Colour Curtain: A Report on the Bandung Conference.* British ed. London: Dobson, 1956. Print.

Wright, Richard. "Etika Hidup ala Jim Crow." Trans. Syahril Latif. *Horison: Majalah Sastra* Feb. 1984: 101–03. Print.

Wright, Richard. "How Bigger Was Born." *Native Son.* Abridged ed., "The Original 1940 Text." New York: Harper, 2003. vii–xxxiv. Print.

Wright, Richard. "I Choose Exile." RWP, box 6, folder 110. Print.

Wright, Richard. "I Tried to Be a Communist." *The God That Failed.* 1950. New York: Bantam, 1959. 103–46. Print.

Wright, Richard. "Indonesian Notebook." *Encounter* Aug. 1955: 24–31. Print.

Wright, Richard. "Indonesisches Tagebuch." *Der Monat* Aug. 1955: 387–98; Sept. 1955: 495–505. Print.

Wright, Richard. "Inner Landscape." *New Republic* 5 Aug. 1940: 195. Print.

Wright, Richard. "Island of Hallucination." Draft, typescript, corrected. RWP, box 34, folder 472–472d. Print.

Wright, Richard. "Jakarta—Asian and African Conference." Journal, 3 Feb. through early May 1955. RWP, box 29, folder 418. Print.

Wright, Richard. "The Literature of the Negro in the United States." *White Man, Listen!* Garden City, NY: Doubleday, 1957. 105–50. Print.

Wright, Richard. "Littérature Noire Américaine." Trans. René Guyonnet. *Les Temps Modernes* Aug. 1948: 193–221. Print.

Wright, Richard. "Mr. Wright Replies." *Encounter* Mar. 1956: 73. Print.

Wright, Richard. *The Outsider.* 1953. Intro. Maryemma Graham. New York: Perennial, 1993. Print.

Wright, Richard. *Pagan Spain.* 1957. Intro. Faith Berry. Jackson: University Press of Mississippi, 2002. Print.

Wright, Richard. "Questionnaire for Jakarta Afro-Asian Conference." RWP, box 31, folder 434. Print.

Wright, Richard. "Retreat from Paradise." RWP, box 31, folder 433. Print.

Wright, Richard. *White Man, Listen!* Garden City, NY: Doubleday, 1957. Print.

Wu, Chin Tao. *Privatising Culture: Corporate Art Intervention since the 1980s.* London: Verso, 2002. Print.

Yan, Zhang. "I Wish I Had Met Richard Wright at Bandung in 1955 (Reflections on a Conference Attended by Both Wright and the Author)." *Mississippi Quarterly* 50 (1997): 277–87. Print.

Young, Robert J. C. "Postcolonialism: From Bandung to the Tricontinental." *Historien* 5 (2005): 11–21.

INDEX

Photographs and illustrations are indicated by italicized page numbers.

Mochtar Lubis (*continued*)
Suharto regime, 215; Vuyk on, 186–87, 197, 203; as Wright's host, 15, 17, 18, 57, 68, 125, 222; on Wright's influence on Indonesian writers, 235; on Wright's lecture to Konfrontasi Study Club, 107, 128; on Wright's social activism, 216–17

modernism, 19, 20, 57, 59–63, 101, 186, 233–34; modern Indonesian culture and literature, 13–14, 16, 20–25, 26, 27, 35–42, 60–61, 90, 93, 95, 112, 127, 136n5, 140, 170n7, 230, 231; modernists, 13, 14, 18, 29n26, 37–38, 59

modernity, 57, 99, 100, 131, 139, 150, 153, 166, 175, 194, 196, 220; modern conditions, 13–14, 16, 20–27, 35–42, 60–61, 90, 93, 95, 112, 127, 136n5, 140, 170n7, 230–31; modernization, 14, 19, 27, 129, 155, 188, 233–34

Mohamad, Goenawan. *See* Goenawan Mohamad

Mohammed Ali, Chaudhry, 81, 83

Mohammed Fadhil El Jamali, 79

Molotov, Vyacheslav, 105n8

Der Monat magazine, 17, 145, 146, 185, 202

"Le monde occidental à Bandoeng" (Wright), 160

Moravia, Alberto, 63

Mullen, Bill V., 6

Museum of the Asian-African Conference, 27, 217–19, 221, 222

Mythologies (Barthes), 3, 6

Nasser, Gamal Abdel, 79, 83, 84, 128, 155, 224

Nasution, A. H., 71, 183

nationalism, 36, 37, 125, 146, 151n12, 196

Native Son (Wright), 44, 97, 112, 156, 157, 161, 165, 169, 216, 221

Natsir, Mohammed, 85, 88n22, 160, 174, 178

naturalism, 47, 105n9, 170n7

Nehru, Jawaharlal, 79, 83, 128, 155, 224

Nenni. *See* Siti Nuraini

New Negro, 140, 141, 230

Newton, Isaac, 132

Ngũgĩ wa Thiong'o, 232

Nietzsche, Friedrich, 103, 167

Het Nieuwsblad voor Sumatra newspaper, 68, 70, 77–78, 81–84, 86n3

De Nieuwsgier newspaper, 69, 70, 72–73, 77, 86n3

Nkrumah, Kwame, 4, 128, 149, 155, 188, 196, 206n30, 210, 230, 235

Nonaligned Movement, 2, 3, 4, 27, 36, 186, 235

Norodom Sihanouk, 224

"A No to Nothing" (Gibson), 153, 154, 156, 229–30

Nuraini, Siti: in Europe on scholarship, 162, *163*, 213n2; in Konfrontasi Study Club, 14, *15*, 109, 200–201; on race and African Americans, 110; on racial discrimination, 204n7; Vuyk on, 186, 194; and Wright's "American Negro Writing" lecture, 107

Of Mice and Men (Steinbeck), 39, 54

Oppenheimer, Joshua, 215

Orientalism, 8, 9, 28–29n17

The Outsider (Wright), 21, 56–58, 98, 101, 115, 125, 130, 159, 162

Owen, Wilfred, 49n5

Pakistan, 67, 84

Palmer, William, 205n29

Partai Komunis Indonesia. *See* Indonesian Communist Party

Partai Sosialis Indonesia. *See* Indonesian Socialist Party

Partisan Review, 21, 60–63

Payne, Ethel, 26, 223

Pedoman newspaper, 68, 73, 86n3, 96

PEN Club: Achdiat Karta Mihardja as leader and representative of, 14, 30n30, 106; Mochtar Lubis as member of, 9, 17; in Wright's notes, 22; Wright's lecture for, 69, 85, 97, 122, 124–25, 139, 140, 153, 215

Penguin New Writing magazine, 63

Perburuan [The Fugitive] (Pramoedya), 54

Perspectives magazine, 153, 156

Pertjikan Revolusi [Sparks of Revolution] (Pramoedya), 54

www.ingramcontent.com/pod-product-compliance
Lightning Source LLC
Chambersburg PA
CBHW071734270326
41928CB00013B/2668